CONTENTS

CHAPTER ONE

STONEHENGE

We were on the A303 driving through rain and wind, and drivers had on their sidelights. Massive clouds sailed overhead in voluminous shades of grey on this late autumn afternoon. A lorry ahead of us sent up a fine rose-spray of mud which covered the windscreen. The Druids revered water and propitiated the gods with prayers and ceremonies to assure good crops and avert natural disasters such as floods. They also worshipped the Earth goddess - water and earth equalled mud, but as far as I knew there was no god or goddess of mud.

"I must get past this monster," Harry said, and put his foot down. He had enough visibility through the fan-shape of windscreen-wiped glass to see his way past. I shut my eyes. My faith in Harry's driving was never great as his attention tended to stray to the open fields rather than stay on the road; he did, however, drive at his best when speeding with other cars and passing articulated lorries. I opened my eyes, involuntarily said 'Oh, my God!' as I saw the massive wheels spinning alongside on a level with my head, and closed them immediately.

My expletive, considering my tendency not to believe in God, was quite odd. It was inbuilt, a part of everyday life. The vicar, when I asked him one day to explain God to me, said that I had only to look at the flowers and the trees and the birds and all of nature, and there God was. I didn't think that was a proof of God at all, only of nature, but was too polite to say so.

It was unfortunate that the day was stormy as it was the one day that English Heritage had given us permission to go in amongst the massive prehistoric stones of Stonehenge on Salisbury Plain. We were allowed one hour along with twenty-three other ticket holders, and would be admitted at seven-thirty p.m.

I'd passed Stonehenge on numerous occasions driving to and from London, but had never felt drawn to the site. Had there been the elegant columns of a Greek temple standing against the skyline, I'd have stopped and paid my respects, but there was nothing beautiful about a group of upright monoliths, some of them with lintels. They didn't excite in me anything more than the question 'why?' Rather like a boorish dullard could never be ignored but, just by being there, drew attention to his existence, so I was aware of these as a landmark whenever I passed by.

There was, I supposed, a sort of simplistic grandeur about Stonehenge - the product of minds which had never been influenced by any earlier architectural achievement because there hadn't been any. Today people only gasp with admiration at the sheer superhuman effort of getting the stones there and lifting them upright. It suggests there must have been some momentous and worthwhile reason for men to have gone to all that bother. I'd read that they'd been brought to that particular site on Salisbury Plain because astronomers could see the sky to the horizon all around.

But there were other reasons also which I'd learned several weeks ago when I'd been part of a group walking the Stonehenge landscape - in contrast to today's stormy weather that day had been a cloudless warm one. The gently undulating open landscape with its swellings and shallow depressions had been looking at its best with the fields stretching to the horizons all around, enlivened by the occasional coppiced woods with their autumnal tints. Walking the landscape on that fine windless autumn day I'd learned that there were burial mounds all around Stonehenge. These were easy to overlook unless you were told about them. To be taken to the right location and have the outline of ditches and embankments, and the variously shaped barrows pointed out had been an amazing and informative experience - bell barrows, bowl barrows, disc barrows, saucer ones and pond ones. They were the burial mounds of Bronze Age luminaries who'd been either buried or cremated together with a few personal possessions to accompany them to the afterlife, such as weapons, tools, articles of gold, amber or jet, and pottery bowls. As far back as the Neolithic Age (the New Stone Age) there had been barrows, but they had been long barrows for mass burials. The interesting thing about these Bronze Age ones was that each had an outer ditch and embankment surrounding it and, with the soil being chalk, when it was first dug it would have stood out against the open landscape as a glaring white memorial to the deceased.

Before the stones for Stonehenge were erected it is believed there had been timber uprights. The stones began to be brought around 2,500 B.C. but Stonehenge was not completed till five hundred years later in 2000 B.C. They represented an attempt to appease the powers that be; they were the aspirations of human beings who had, no doubt, the same basic hopes and fears regarding survival that we have today. Little is known about those people except what has been discovered from rudimentary finds such as stone tools, antler picks, flint axe heads, and crude pots suggesting a settled community. It is believed that by that time they were no longer wandering hunters and gatherers, but tilled the land and grew crops and tended animals, depending very much on the seasons and the sun for light and warmth. The occasional eclipse of the sun must have filled them with dread. If the power of the sun were to suddenly fail, then what?

The hauling of the stones to Salisbury Plain had been a supreme and momentous trial of strength. It is thought there must have been a command structure, a chieftain or else many tribes led by men with enough authority to get the task done. Hundreds of people had been involved in order to haul the bluestones on rollers from where they were strewn on the Preseli mountains in Pembrokeshire; then to lever them onto rafts and sail with them down the Bristol Channel; next transfer them onto boats for their trip upriver, before a final overland haul on rollers to their new home on Salisbury Plain.

"What was the point of it?" I'd asked Harry when I'd informed him of the gargantuan labour which had gone into it. "What prompted them to ever think of doing it?"

"Their gods?" Harry suggested.

"I suppose the Egyptians had their walloping temples at Luxor at that time," I agreed. "But then we know why. We know which Pharaoh did what."

"And the study of the heavenly bodies?" Harry went on.

"But why haul all those stones from Wales? There were perfectly good sarsen stones from the Marlborough hills twenty miles away."

I wasn't likely to find an answer as all the scholars down the centuries had remained baffled. The only certainty was that the main entrance into the stone circle was aligned with the midsummer sunrise when facing outwards from the centre, and with the midwinter sunset when facing the opposite direction.

Harry had become smitten by a booklet on Stonehenge which gave a comprehensive account of its astronomical purpose. From it he'd learned that Stonehenge had been built originally as a solar temple. The Druids had begun to use it when they'd emerged as priests, but that hadn't occurred till centuries later, about 300 B.C. The theory was that the stones had been arranged with precision in order to track the daily, monthly, and annual movement of the sun - not only the sun, but the moon and the five wandering stars also. The latter were the planets Venus, Mars, Jupiter, Mercury and Saturn, which passed across the night sky, varying their movements though never straying beyond their set boundaries.

I found celestial wonders totally mystifying, and wished I could imagine the spinning and the circling of planets so I could comprehend their precise movements in relation to each other. But I could only understand observable facts such as the sun rising in the east and setting in the west (when it was visible), and the moon waxing and waning, making it sometimes a slither of an old moon, and then a crescent new moon. That is the limit of my understanding regarding things astronomical. Galaxies and constellations are just features in the night sky which to me are a wonder and a mystery.

I am, however, interested in the fact that the moon after waning is not to be seen for two days and seems to have died before it miraculously resurrects itself on the third day. I have often wondered whether it is why Jesus was said in the Gospels to have risen on the third day. After all, he could equally well have risen on the second, fourth or any other day. But no, he rose on the third day which just happens to be when the new moon is seen again.

"Where are these wretched stones?" Harry demanded. We'd been driving for about an hour and a half and had been expecting to see Stonehenge over the crest of every slope. In the grey and dismal light I could see huge black dollops on our left. But the dollops turned out to be black plastic-wrapped bales of straw dotted about a prairie-like field. We'd passed a number of corn fields, most of them harvested but several with the corn still to be cut and far from golden, more a dull grey and somewhat flattened.

Fifteen minutes later when the rain was miraculously easing, though the wind was gale force buffeting the car and causing the branches of trees to dance about, we at last saw through the drizzle the gloomy group of upright stones clustered together like a chorus in a Greek tragedy. A herd of Hereford bullocks stood disconsolately in a nearby field.

We turned left and followed the signs till we reached the car park. The stones were no longer visible. It was odd how the landscape deceived. The English Heritage woman whom I'd spoken to on the phone when I'd made my enquiries regarding access to the stones, had assured me that the weather, even if atrocious during the day, usually cleared towards dusk. Surprisingly, when we finally pulled up in the car park, although it was still gloomily overcast, it was no longer raining. A tall, gaunt young man with thick matted hair drawn back in a ponytail, and wearing torn jeans, sodden trainers and a leather jacket, strolled past with his girlfriend with horns on her head. I wondered if they were modern Druids.

There was nothing distinctive about anyone waiting to be shepherded through to the stones. All looked bedraggled, windswept and cold. One had on a Viking helmet. The only thing that varied was the energy level of those waiting. Some looked eager, while others appeared only as despondent, tagging-along companions. There were several security guards responsible for keeping us under control. The whole of Britain would be up in arms if the stones were to vanish.

While we waited, I told Harry how legend had it that the wizard Merlin (of the King Arthur stories) had magically brought the stones from Ireland where it was said giants had erected them on Mount Killaraus.

"Geoffrey of Monmouth wrote it all down in his History of the Kings of Britain, and he was a bishop so you wouldn't expect him to lie," I said, trying to keep sarcasm out of my voice.

"He was Welsh," said Harry, as though it explained everything.

"He also wrote that Uther Pendragon, King Arthur's father, was buried in the heart of Stonehenge."

We were beginning to move forward with the others. Our tickets were taken, and a security guard now led the way down steps, through an underground tunnel and up within the perimeter fence surrounding the stones. We had arrived. The assurance given that the weather would clear at dusk was correct. Overhead was a canopy of light rainless cloud while all around on the horizon was clear colourless sky.

The strong persistent wind left me feeling bemused but Harry took charge. He took out his compass and trudged me off over the wet turf. "We must start with the Heel Stone at the perimeter," he declared. "It marks the ceremonial entrance to the stones at the northeast of the outer circle, and is aligned with the midsummer sunrise." That as a start I found baffling; I thought the sun rose in the east and now I was being told it could vary.

"It always keeps within a certain band," said Harry. "Where it rises depends on the time of year. Those are Aubrey Holes, look! There and there and there! They go around the stones and there are fifty-six in all. If you move a marker one Aubrey Hole every six and a half days, daybreak to daybreak is one day, and daybreak to nightfall or vice versa being half a day, then 6½ multiplied by 56 = 364 days to complete the circle. The one and a quarter days' error in the year is corrected at midsummer and midwinter."

Would it? Could it? I was mentally out of my depth.

But Harry was well away. "You need to look at the stars from the same point every night, and you'll find a constellation will move by degrees and be back where it started after one year. Great stuff! And they had moon markers too. Move the moon marker one Aubrey Hole in the morning and one in the evening and it will make a circuit in twenty-eight days."

Harry and his compass marched around the outer circle noting the Aubrey Holes and making announcements such as: "Slaughter Stone! Station Stone!"

I followed in his wake but could only think of stars in relation to Greek myths which appealed to my imagination such as the story of Atlas, the Titan, who, for his offence in taking part in the battle against the Olympian gods had, according to legend, been condemned to hold the heavens on his shoulders for eternity. He was the father of the Pleiades, the group of stars named after his seven daughters by Pleione.

As I followed Harry with his compass trudging across the turf towards the monster stones grouped together in the centre, my mind remained with the Pleiades who, according to another story, had been pursued by the hunter Orion for which misdemeanour Orion had also been turned into a constellation. Yet another story was that Orion, out of jealousy, had been killed by Artemis, goddess of the hunt, because he was loved by Eos, goddess of the Dawn. Artemis had been identified with the moon, just as Apollo (her twin brother) had been with the sun. Apollo remained Apollo under the Romans, but Artemis became Diana.

Enough of the stars! Now I was among the stones I must apply my mind to them. I remembered what I'd learned from the guide on that walking-the-landscape day: that Stonehenge and its surrounding barrows had been for the dead in the Neolithic and Bronze Age, and the land to the east of it had been for the living. An archaeological dig had uncovered a Neolithic village near to the river Avon known as Durrington Walls.

A huge henge bank inside which was a great ditch twenty feet deep and forty-three feet wide surrounded Durrington Walls, and inside that were two circles of timber the largest of which was seventy-five feet in diameter. Recently a gravelled pathway aligned to the rising sun on midsummer's day had been found. Within the henge bank were found the remains of a number of houses dating from 2,500 B.C., each rectangular, about seventeen feet long, with a central hearth. Large quantities of animal bones had been found, mostly of young pigs which suggested ceremonial feastings both at midwinter and midsummer.

On that day we had viewed the location of Durrington Walls from a distance, having just visited Woodhenge. There there had also been a round bank and internal ditch within which were six concentric circles with pits containing upright timbers. Its entrance was also aligned with the midsummer solstice. The Avenue leading to Stonehenge began a few kilometers south of Durrington Walls close to the river Avon, and it was thought that ceremonial burials had gone in procession along this Avenue starting at sunrise from the wooden henges (wood being associated with the living). The belief was that the mourners had gone down the river Avon to disembark close to where the Avenue began, timing their arrival at Stonehenge at sunset (stone being associated with the dead).

On that sunny walking-the-landscape day with not a cloud in the sky we had picnicked seated on the ground at one end of a long grassy stretch known as the Cursus. This was an unusual extended earthwork enclosure with a ditch and bank over a mile and a half long and three hundred and thirty feet wide aligned east to west (sunrise to sunset).

The date for such a feature (and there was another much shorter one, the Lesser Cursus, north-west of Stonehenge) was 3,500 B.C. when the long barrows were constructed.

Now at the heart of Stonehenge Harry was doing calculations. "The largest stone," he read from his booklet, "is twenty-four feet, and the heaviest fifty tons. It must be this one, what do you think?"

But I was away with my own thoughts regarding the Druids at Stonehenge. In Julius Caesar's account of the Gallic War he'd commented favourably on the Druids he'd come across: '...They are chiefly anxious to have men believe the following: that souls do not suffer death, but after death pass from one body to another; and they regard this as the strongest incentive to valour, since the fear of death is disregarded. They have also much knowledge of the stars and their motion, of the size of the world and of the earth, of natural philosophy, and of the powers and spheres of action of the immortal gods, which they discuss and hand down to their young students.' (Gallic War VI. 13-14).

"It must be sarsen from the Marlborough hills," Harry remarked. "Sarsen - blue stones - they all look much the same except for their size."

I was still musing. Julius Caesar had gone on to write: '... The Druids are concerned with the worship of the gods, look after public and private sacrifice, and expound religious matters. A large number of young men flock to them for training and hold them in high honour. For they have the right to decide nearly all public and private disputes and they also pass judgment and decide rewards and penalties in criminal and murder cases and in disputes concerning legacies and boundaries...'

Druids had been the philosophers and the educated ones in society though, being illiterate, they'd left no records. To compensate they had formidable memories. It was the Romans who'd brought writing to Britain.

I had recently discovered that writing had begun six thousand years B.C. Before that there had only been pictorial symbols or hieroglyphs, or a mere notch marked on wood or stone to denote a number. I found it amazing that no one could read or write; they could only commit to memory and recite. It took twelve to twenty years training for a would-be Druid to qualify.

Harry was pacing around a Trilithon (two uprights with a lintel).

"How in God's name did they get that lintel up and get it on the holding notches! The penalty for misjudging would be twenty-five tons of stone on your head! Hell!"

But I wasn't really listening as I was still musing over the Druids. I'd read that in Druid times baldness had been regarded as a sign of wisdom, and the Druid priests had adopted a form of tonsure, to be copied later by Christian monks to promote the idea that they too had learning and wisdom. The Druid tonsure had been triangular with the point towards the forehead, and in order to distance themselves from any pagan ideas the Catholic monks adopted a round-the-head one.

The Druid priests had been highly venerated and had had the ability to read signs and omens. They divined the future from observation of birds on the wing, observed nature, and saw in unusual phenomena portents and omens. They were regarded as intermediaries between men and the gods. I supposed they were somewhat similar to the ancient priests at Delphi who'd interpreted the ambiguous answers given by the Pythia, Apollo's priestess.

There was a belief held by some scholars that Stonehenge had, in fact, been a sacred enclosure dedicated to Apollo as a sun god. Apparently, a contemporary of Julius Caesar, a Sicilian historian named Diodorus Siculus, had written about such a thing quoting from an account (now lost) which had been circulating three centuries earlier describing the 'magnificent precinct sacred to Apollo and a notable spherical temple' on a large island in the far north. Julius Caesar must have been aware of this great solar temple. My guide of two weeks earlier had said that there must have been a certain amount of Roman activity around Stonehenge because many Roman coins had been found in the area as well as pottery.

The custom for Druid priests who were dressed in white robes, was to cut mistletoe from an oak tree with a golden sickle on the sixth night of the moon, and to sacrifice two white bulls. Whoever received the mistletoe was expected to prosper. Mistletoe was said to be the soul of the oak and was gathered at the midsummer solstice and the midwinter one. The golden sickle used to cut it was symbolic of the new moon. The goddess Demeter's daughter, Persephone, had used mistletoe to open the gates of the underworld when returning to her mother in the spring.

In Nordic mythology mistletoe was the sacred plant of Freya, goddess of love, whose son was called Balder and was god of the summer sun. But he dreamed of death which alarmed Freya as all life would end if Balder died. So she appealed to fire, water, earth, plants and animals and got them to swear that no harm would come to Balder. But one enemy remained and that was Loki, a sometimes malicious, sometimes mischievous god. Loki was aware that Freya had overlooked the mistletoe. He made an arrow of it which accidentally killed Balder. Immediately the sky grew pallid and all wept for Balder, the sun god. For three days they tried to restore him to life, and were finally successful on the third day (like the moon reappearing on the third, and Christ's resurrection on the third). The story goes that Freya's tears turned into the pearly white berries of the mistletoe and, with the triumph of the resurrection of her son, she kissed everyone who passed beneath it which is why today it is used over the Christmas period, the time of year when the sun's light is on the increase.

I told the story of the mistletoe to Harry. But Harry was into the stones rather than gods. "These inner stones must be the bluestones," he announced. "These inner ones must be the horseshoe lot, and these outer ones the ring. And these outer outer ones have to be the sarsen stones."

I hauled my mind back to the monoliths towering over me and, for the first time noticed they weren't haphazard blocks of upright stones, some with lintels, but were arranged in a circle. I'd read that the outer sarsen stones were supposed to be 'dressed', in other words hammered and chiselled, and that the bluestones were blue. Well, maybe they were. To my untutored eye they all looked much the same. I had, though, been shown small samples of sarsen and bluestone by the guide on our walk, who had told us that when first erected and pristine, the sarsen stones at Stonehenge would have been a cream colour, and the interior of the bluestones were indeed a rich deep blue.

I noticed a young woman standing between two fallen monoliths, her eyes closed and both arms outstretched, her fingertips in contact with the two recumbent stones either side of her. She must have been communing with nature or trying to absorb energy from them.

Bluestones were known to have healing qualities. They were brought from the Preseli mountains in Wales where water running over them was said to have miraculous healing powers. Many human skeletons excavated around Stonehenge had been found to have wounds or else some deformity, and it is thought that people may have come as invalids in the hope of a cure. Stonehenge may well have been the Lourdes of the ancient world.

"Somewhere there are some carvings," announced Harry, the authority on Stonehenge. "There should be a dagger and a mother goddess symbol." I remembered that I'd read about it, and was particularly keen to see the latter. We began to examine the stones, but there was a lot of surface to these monoliths and we couldn't find anything.

A man nearby was holding forth to three depressed looking individuals in waterproofs. As he looked confident and knowledgeable about the stones, I asked him if he knew where the carved symbol of the mother goddess was. He looked at me haughtily, and said: "I'm instructing my group, if you don't mind."

I hastily apologized and Harry hauled me away. I asked one of the security guards who was waiting patiently for the hour to elapse before being released from keeping an eye out for possible vandals and stone robbers.

The security guard led us directly to the carving of the dagger. It was, I'd read, similar to the sort found at Mycenae, the royal palace of King Agamemnon near Argos in Greece. It was Agamemnon who'd led the Greeks to war against the Trojans, in order to retrieve the beautiful Helen of Troy (his sister-in-law) who'd run off with the King of Troy's son, Paris.

"And can you point out the mother goddess symbol?" I asked the security guard. He pointed to something scratched close to the dagger, and for a moment I took it for the mother goddess symbol and studied it with interest, till my wits returned and I saw it was some vandal's initials, by which time the security guard had had his joke and had gone grinning back to his sentry duties.

The woman with her eyes shut and her arms outstretched turned about to face the opposite direction. Her hour of communicating with the stones would soon be over. I'd come across a book on stones and crystals, which said the colour blue helped people regain a state of peaceful awareness, so they became more receptive to information. What information and from where it didn't say, but I supposed it must be with the spiritual world. She was a woman in her mid-thirties with chestnut coloured hair loosely fastened back with a butterfly clip; her anorak and trousers and shoes were of good quality.

"What's that woman think she's doing?" Harry demanded. "Is

she in a Druid trance or something?" His voice was quite audible, especially with the wind blowing his words in her direction. I told him to keep his voice down, and drew him out of earshot. Stones, I told him had energies and magical properites and she was, no doubt, drawing on their power and strength to find peace.

"Nuts!" said Harry.

"Shhhhh!"

I expected her to open one eye to see who was speaking, but she remained profoundly connected to whatever it was, just as I had been connected with the landscape those two weeks ago. That particular and memorable walking-the-landscape day had ended tramping along a rutted hard-packed chalk track; we were heading for a barrow with a large single tree on it silhouetted against the skyline known as Bush Barrow. Looking back the way we'd come Stonehenge had been clearly visible, with long shadows cast from one great monolith to another by the sun which by then had been low in the sky. The track we'd been on had been on a gentle downhill gradient, so that gradually the upright stones had disappeared from view with only the lintels visible, before they too had dropped from sight. We'd eventually come to a prominent barrow known as Prophet Barrow from which preachers had once held forth about weighty biblical matters - the end of the world and the need for repentance, and suchlike. We'd been told there were bible thumpers who calculated that God had created the world in 4000 (some said 5000 or 6000 B.C.) and proclaimed that Stonehenge had survived the great Flood of Noah's time. That walking-the-landscape day had ended as cloudless and windless as it had begun and the sun, that all important celestial orb without which there would be no life as we know it, had all but set leaving a magical gold-pink glow in the sky.

A woman in our group that day had told me how she'd driven past one night in a terrific thunder storm, and how demonic it had seemed when she'd seen forked lightning zipping down from the sky, momentarily illuminating the stones. J.M.W. Turner had painted Stonehenge in a storm in which forked lightning had struck dead a flock of sheep together with the shepherd. The only creature left alive was the sheepdog who had his head up to the sky howling. In contrast John Constable had painted Stonehenge with a rainbow in the sky. With so many different moods experienced under the vast heavens, it was little wonder that our ancient ancestors had done all in their power to tame the forces of nature.

From the various books I'd read on the Druids, I'd discovered that their rituals were not only tied in with the solar cycle and the annual death and rebirth of the Sun god and his Earth goddess, but were aimed to promoting peace. Each ceremony was thought to have started with a salutation of 'Peace to the Quarters', the idea being that peace would radiate to all parts of the earth from where the ritual was taking place. Today's Druids also have an affinity with Nature and all living things. They emphasize the centrality of Nature and the Seasons, and the sanctity of the landscape, and the worship of Earth as Mother-goddess and the Sun as Father-god. They have adopted the Druid slogan: 'Do what thou wilt but harm none'.

A few days back I'd told Harry that I thought that at heart I could be a Druid and that I could join the International Grand Lodge of Druidism. I'd been reading from the list of the various modern Druid Lodges. There'd been the Ancient Order of Druids, and the Order of Abards, Ovates and Druids with a PO Box number in East Sussex. "And before you tell me not to be a blithering idiot," I said, "you might like to know that here it says that Churchill was actually inducted into the Albion Lodge of the Ancient Order of Druids at Blenheim in 1908, so how about that!" Harry had merely shrugged and said something about me not being Churchill and not to make an exhibition of myself and upsetting the vicar.

Deep down I knew I would never join one of the Druid Lodges; I really wouldn't want to be tied in to people all feeling earnest about Nature. I could be earnest alone if I wanted.

The Druids had recognized the source of all life as water, and worshipped a fertility goddess. Rivers and streams were living expressions of the Earth Mother. The moon was greatly revered for its power over the tides and its influence on women's monthly menstrual cycle. The sun received due honour also. Ritual prayer averted the threat of evil demons and natural disasters, and also gave comfort and hope to those who suffered as it does today.

It was interesting to speculate on the fact that throughout all those millennia B.C. the sun had never ceased to rise and bring its light, or set bringing darkness, and the moon also never ceased to wax and wane and follow its monthly cycle and annual orbit. The sun and moon had been constants whereas gods and goddesses had come and gone as they lost popularity.

As for men, they were transitory. While alive they worshipped the gods of their day, leaving behind when they died memories of themselves in the minds of their contemporaries. The memory was an amazing phenomenon in the human mind.

I suddenly noticed that the light canopy of cloud overhead had quite astonishingly gone, leaving a wide dome of clear sky. But all around on the horizon there was now a ring of cloud like whipped cream lit up by the setting sun. And there in the heavens was a half moon also.

"Look!" I said. "The moon! And look at that ring of cloud!"

Twilight at Stonehenge was curiously mystical. At one with Nature. It appeared that all the old pagan gods had their place down the generations of men, whether they were true or not, and whether they were truly believed in or not. And maybe Christianity was another expression of God being central to Nature as the vicar had said to me - the great Spirit (something which I certainly related to and could accept). It was anyway a thought worth pondering.

CHAPTER TWO

GLASTONBURY

"What exactly is a shaman?" I asked politely.

We were seated at a long table having breakfast in a B&B with one other woman. It was hard work making polite conversation to a stranger at that time of morning. The woman was middle-aged, plump, and had short spiky mauve hair with blonde highlights. I tried not to stare at it.

"Shamans? They were powerful pagan priests who could get into a state of ecstasy to make contact between the human and the spiritual world," she replied. "They sometimes wore antlers on their heads and took on the guise of animals to get closer to nature."

Harry clearly had serious misgivings about the woman and gave her swift assessing glances between mouthfuls of porridge. He never spoke to foreigners when abroad if he could avoid it, and I doubted in this country he'd want to speak to somebody so alien to what he considered normal.

Our landlady came in bearing a platter of fried eggs and bacon which she placed on a hot plate on the sideboard. She was a rather attractive landlady with long fair hair in a ponytail, and a certain agile nimbleness as though she practised yoga or some other daily exercise.

"Excuse me, I've been wanting to ask you, is that a carnelian around your neck?" It was the mauve-haired woman speaking.

"This? Oh, yes. I always wear it."

"For fertility?" enquired the woman.

"Yes, as a matter of fact."

"Have you ever tried moonstones? If you have emotional stress in the sacral chakra, you want to lie down with a moonstone on either side of your pelvis, and one on your head, and you'll find your stress levels rapidly subsiding. It was moonstones that got me pregnant," she said with conviction, wiping organic yoghurt from the corner of her mouth.

Harry stared into his porridge bowl, he was quite out of his depth with moonstones and chakras.

"They're excellent for relieving menstrual pain," went on the mauve-haired woman. "You'll excuse us talking women's talk," she said to Harry, "but when women are infertile they need to know about these remedies. They help with impotency too," she added with a jolly laugh and an eye on Harry who pretended he hadn't heard.

I felt I needed to say something for politeness sake. "How interesting!" I remarked. I wished I could think of something cleverer, but it was too early in the morning. I settled for a much easier topic. "Can I get you eggs and bacon?" I enquired.

"No, thanks. I don't eat fried chicken foetus."

Harry shot her a sideways look, then glanced at me and continued eating in silence.

Fearing he might say something we'd all regret, I said brightly: "Did you remember your blood pressure pill?"

"Blood pressure pill! God!" And he picked up his porridge bowl and left the room with it.

"Sorry about that," I said to the woman.

"Oh. For a moment I thought it was something I'd said!" She scraped back her chair and stood up. "Well, my crystals call." And she also departed.

I finished my breakfast alone. We'd driven to Glastonbury the day before, coming across the Somerset Levels which by its very name implies a dull, flat and featureless landscape. In fact, much of the time our road had been flanked by picturesque willows and alders, and we'd driven alongside a series of old ditched watercourses, and over bridges spanning several rivers. There were distant rolling hills with billowing white clouds rising over them into the blue sky. The terrain definitely had a charm all its own.

Glastonbury was said to be where the earth met the sky. Celtic belief was that its highest point, the Tor, which rose five hundred and eighteen feet above sea level, was the gateway between things celestial and the dark forces of the underworld.

Glastonbury was also known as the Isle of Avalon because it had once consisted of several small islands rising from a shallow inland sea.

With the coming of Christianity, a monastery had been built on the Tor though all that remains of it today is one solitary tower.

I quickly finished my breakfast and went upstairs to find Harry. The Tor was to be our first destination that morning.

"The Celts believed in the soul passing freely from the deceased back to the living again - a rebirth," I told Harry. "They also had a cauldron full of magical potions for rejuvenation." Harry stood like a statue trying to get his breath back after the stiff climb to the top of the Tor. Far below were trees in their autumn tints, and the gentle hill of the Chalice Well which we planned to visit later. From where we stood we were able to see the curious grassy terraces spiralling up around the hillside. They were a mystery, and some said that they marked an ancient processional way which, on reaching the summit, disappeared into the depths of the Tor.

We approached the ruins of the Tower of St. Michael where we were able to sit on a wide polished stone seat inside the tower. The sound of a dove cooing high up on a ledge was soothing.

"The Tor represents the gateway to the underworld," I said, reading from a book I had on the subject. "It was known in Celtic times as Annwn," I added. "It sounds Welsh and I don't expect I'm pronouncing it correctly - Annnnn-wn." I paused and scanned the printed page. "Oh, you'll like this! The entrance to Annwn was guarded by Gwynn, who was the leader of the Wild Hunt, and whose symbol was a red dragon. His spectral horses galloped out from the Tor on the dark night of Samhain accompanied by his red-eyed Hounds of Hell. Are you listening?" Harry sat vacantly swinging his walking-stick backwards and forwards between his knees.

"Hounds of Hell. Yes. Carry on."

"They went on a hunt for the souls of the dead or dying in order to take them to the underworld. They were white hounds with red eyes and ears. In fact - " I closed the book, "you may be interested to know that the Hounds of Hell will soon be emerging because their night of Samhain - the night of the Wild Hunt - is Hallowe'en. And this is what's really interesting!" And I went on to tell Harry how the Church had adopted the annual Celtic Samhain festival. A vigil was held on the night of Hallowe'en in preparation for All Saints' Day (the

1st November), the day following becoming All Souls' Day. "How's that for a Christian take-over?" I asked.

"Hounds of Hell," Harry ruminated. "I think I've heard of Hounds of Hell."

"Can you imagine them all galloping out from the Tor here?"

"Or maybe I'm thinking of the Hound of the Baskervilles," he pondered. He was obviously more interested in hound stories than Christian ones.

There had originally been a monastery up on the summit, possibly as early as 600 A.D. Its church had been rebuilt on a much smaller scale after an earthquake in 1275, and the St. Michael's tower had been added a century later. To me the interesting thing was that St. Michael, who was in fact Michael the Archangel, was regarded as the guardian of the souls of the dead by the Church, so he too had been enlisted to obliterate earlier Celtic thinking.

I left Harry still swinging his walking stick, and went to look at a carving above the arched entrance to the tower which was of an angel weighing a soul in judgement. The weighing of a soul was similar to a newly deceased person having his heart weighed against the feather of the ancient Egyptian goddess Maat, and being rewarded or punished appropriately according to his good or bad deeds.

Another stone carving on the tower was of a truncated St. Michael with a dragon beneath his foot depicting the death of the symbolic red dragon of Gwynn, guardian of the underworld.

I collected Harry and we went to a look-out point where a big round stone had on it an engraved brass disk pointing to such surrounding landmarks as the sea, the hills, towns and villages. He waved his stick towards each one which caught his attention, turning in a clockwise direction. "Weston-super-mare - Bristol - Mendip Hills - Bath - Salisbury - Cheddar Gorge - Ilminster - Polden Hills - " he announced.

The sky overhead was a fine canopy of dull and colourless cloud, while to the east were spectacular storm clouds brilliantly lit by the sun from behind. It was an extraordinary battle of light and darkness. At the Celtic festival of Beltane held on 1st May, it had been believed that the god Gwynn, who represented the dark forces of the underworld, had been locked in battle with his opposite number Gwythyr. Gwynn could not be allowed to win because if he did his Hounds of Hell would run wild, and it would bring about the destruction of the world.

From our vantage point it wasn't difficult to imagine Glastonbury as an island in a vast sheet of water. It was sometimes known as the 'Isle of Glass' which may well have given its name to the town (Glass-town-borough). One of the great Glastonbury legends was that Joseph of Arimathea had come there by boat, some said he had even brought Jesus as a young boy. We would be exploring the Joseph of Arimathea part of Glastonbury later.

It was time to leave the Tor if we were to see the Chalice Well gardens before lunch. We began the descent along the concrete path laid for the convenience of visitors. At the bottom of the hill we noticed two trees some distance away on either side of the pathway. The one to the left had strips of coloured rags tied to its branches, a few of which had words such as 'freedom' and 'peace' written on them. The strips of rag, I was later to discover, were called 'cloughts' or 'cloots'. Those seeking a cure for some ailment, or beseeching the powers-that-be in order to fulfil some wish, would dip the rag in a Cloutie well (the Chalice Well?) before tying it to this tree. The tree on the right was a well-established young oak with Buddhist prayer flags attached to it. A notice declared this to be the 'Mother Peace Tree'.

"Mother Peace Tree!" scoffed Harry. "Just the sort of daft thing that woman at breakfast would get into. I can just see her tying flags and ribbons to a tree expecting them to change the world."

"Every small contribution has to help," I suggested.

"Moonstones to get pregnant!" Harry scoffed and he made for the wicket gate as though the Hounds of Hell were after him.

We entered the Chalice Well gardens. Legend had it that after Christ's death Joseph of Arimathea (who had persuaded the authorities to allow him to take the body of Christ and give it proper burial in his own tomb) had also managed to acquire the Holy Grail or cup used by Jesus at the Last Supper. Joseph of Arimathea, they said, had used the Holy Grail to collect drops of blood from Christ's body at his crucifixion. After his Resurrection it was rumoured that Christ had appeared to Joseph in a vision, and had taught him certain words by which the Grail would help him. Thus it was that by its powers Joseph of Arimathea had been divinely guided by the Holy Grail and was brought to Britain. It was believed that on his arrival at Avalon he'd washed the Holy Grail in what has now become known as the Chalice Well. As a result the water of the spring which rises in the carefully landscaped garden, is said to be red, symbolic of the blood of Christ.

I was full of expectation. Blood-red spring water?

"Is this it?" Harry enquired. We had reached a sculpted lion's head in an old stone wall from whose mouth clear water flowed into a none-too-clean looking tumbler. It was strategically placed on a circular two-tiered stone structure within a shallow semi-circular shaped pool to receive the trickling water. A russet-coloured residue stained the stonework over which the water ran.

"Try some," I suggested. "It might have miraculous results - cure your blood pressure, for instance."

"No fear! I'd rather stick with my pills, thank you."

I cupped my hands under the lion's chin and took a sip; the water tasted metallic. We sat for a while in the tranquil silence of the garden, listening to the trickling water. I'd read that many people came here repeatedly to regain their equilibrium, sort out their mental problems, calm their nerves, get away from the rat-race of life. We were there to see and absorb the atmosphere.

Nature when at peace with itself is always remarkably restful. Its visible, physical reality conceals quite the most intricately miraculous and unexplained mysteries. It is the insanity of the human mind which spins stories and creates webs of fantasy because it is quite unable to comprehend the absolute mystery locked into nature.

"Isn't it odd," I said to Harry, "that all you have to do is plant a potato in the ground, and it grows and produces more potatoes?"

"What else would you expect?"

"Well, it never gets confused. It could, after all, grow into a rose, or absent-mindedly become an onion?"

"Fortunately it doesn't," Harry said practically.

"But that's my point," I said. "Nature is astonishingly consistent within itself. There just have to be unseen energies unceasingly at work, to keep the different species stable as they annually recreate themselves."

A pleasant looking young man strolled into our corner. He drank water from the tumbler at the Lion's Head, nodded at us in greeting, then sat down on a seat and shut his eyes. Was he absorbing the energies from the Chalice Well's blood-of-Christ idea? Or the earlier idea of a cauldron which brought rejuvenation to the soul?

The waters of the Chalice Well were believed to come from some twenty miles away, possibly from the Mendip hills. From there they flowed in subterranean channels beneath the Tor before rising in these gardens. Apparently, the Chalice Well water had an astonishing consistent flow and constant temperature which never varied whatever the rainfall or water-logged conditions above ground. The temperature was always a never-failing 52 degrees Fahrenheit, and the water flowed at one thousand gallons an hour; it seemed a lot of water.

Remarkably, a second spring named the White Spring also flowed through subterranean channels beneath the Tor and rose a couple of hundred feet away in Well House Lane. Its water had a calcium content which left white deposits on the surface of twigs, moss, stones, and anything with which it came in contact. The fanciful religious minds saw the White Spring as the sweat of Christ. The two springs flowing from the Tor were riddled with Christian symbolism.

Regarding the Holy Grail itself the monks of Glastonbury had encouraged the idea of its hidden presence on the Tor, or in the vicinity, in order to eradicate the Celtic pagan belief in the 'greal', a magic potion concocted in a cauldron by the goddess of inspiration and poetry called Ceridwen. There were several magical cauldrons on the Tor. There had been the Mother Goddess' cauldron of rebirth, and the cauldron of Dagda which provided unfailing nourishment and rejuvenation.

Dagda's daughter had been Brighid, the Celtic goddess of the hearth and fire as well as poetry. By subtle means the Christian saint, St. Brigid, had in time absorbed some of the pagan goddess' attributes. St. Brigid had been born in Ireland; she was protector of wells and springs and was, so I'd read, patron saint of Glastonbury. According to Celtic legend she'd been born at sunrise on the 1st February, the day of the Celtic festival of Imbolc. Her mother was said to have been in the service of a Druid. The festival of Imbolc on the 1st February was the Celtic celebration of the renewal of the sun's warmth from its winter's rest, and the promise of a new year of fertility.

We left the Lion's Head and wandered on to The Sanctuary, an oval flagstoned area with flower borders of white Japanese anemones. It was enclosed by a stone wall with niches containing statues. It should have been quite silent, but a woman sat knitting and making irritating busy-with-her-needles clicking sounds. A middle-aged couple sat on another seat looking into the far beyond, either thinking deeply or with their minds quite vacant.

We continued our amble; it would be sacrilegious to move with speed, so we pondered and went slowly in order not to disturb the meditative qualities of this garden with its regenerating energies brought about by the waters of the Chalice Well.

We came to the well itself with its wellhead of black wrought-iron depicting the sacred Vesica Piscis symbol of two interlocking circles, resulting in a central shape like a dover sole on a plate.

There was nobody here and we loitered and peered into the well with its ferns and foliage growing up to the light from the interior brickwork. I wondered why the water never rose above the well-top. One thousand gallons a day? Where did it all go to?

A quiet stroll back again, past the woman knitting, and the solitary young man still seated with his eyes closed.

Eventually we came to the path up to The Meadow where the landscaped garden was left behind. We trudged up the track to a wooden seat. From there we had a direct view to the Tor which rose above the lower woods.

I'd read that water diviners had difficulty with dowsing on the Tor; they experienced so many palpable energies rising from its depths that the forked stick became impossibly active.

By now the storm clouds had gone, and large white and rainless clouds were moving slowly across the sky, casting shadows over the earth. Somewhere in the garden there were two ancient yew trees from which it is thought the Druid priests had begun their processional ascent, spiralling up the labyrinthine terraces to the Tor's summit. Yew trees were associated with death and rebirth. You could die from eating its evergreen leaves, or red berries, but if the tree became hollow and was itself in danger of dying, it sent out new shoots from its hollow interior, thus giving the idea of rebirth. Every churchyard had its yew tree and it was even suggested that the yew sent a root out to the mouth of every corpse to bring about his or her resurrection.

"Have I told you the story of St. Collen?" I asked Harry.

"Never heard of a saint called Collen," came the reply.

"He was Welsh and was Abbot of Glastonbury in the seventh century. His name was actually pronounced CoFlen."

"What about him?"

"After his spell as Abbot, he lived as a hermit at the foot of the Tor. The story goes that one day he heard a couple of peasants discussing Gwynn whose subterranean kingdom was on the Tor - or rather, inside it. The peasants were speaking about how visitors to his castle with its gleaming towers would be taken hostage. When St. Collen heard them he dismissed their fears as superstitious nonsense."

"Which, of course, it was."

I looked at Harry. "Well, if it was, that makes Collen's story nonsense also," I said firmly. "Anyway, his story was that after overhearing these peasants and dismissing their fears, St. Collen received a visitor who was not altogether human and who invited him to visit Gwynn's castle. The saint declined the invitation but, when it was repeated several times, he felt he shouldn't be fearful of going and took with him a phial of holy water. He went up the Tor where he was taken to the great castle of Gwynn. When he saw it, he was overawed by its grandeur and the beauty of its inhabitants. He was shown into a great banqueting hall where Gwynn sat on his golden throne. Wisely the saint declined to eat anything, knowing that if he once tasted Gwynn's food he would immediately become his hostage. Instead, he sprinkled the holy water he'd brought with him, and its power caused Gwynn and his courtiers and the castle itself to vanish into the mists of the Tor. So how's that for a fantasy?" I asked.

"As good a story as any, I suppose," Harry remarked, using his stick to flatten a thistle.

"But unbelievable?" I asked.

"Yes. No. Yes. Well - "

"There you are!" I said. "It served its purpose at the time when the monks wanted to convince people of the power of their Christian faith. It was a typical Christian way of overthrowing ancient beliefs."

We sat on long enough for Harry to flatten a second thistle before we left and found a pub nearby which served bar meals. We needed to fortify ourselves before spending the afternoon at the Abbey.

✢❦✢

We entered the extensive grounds around the ancient Glastonbury Abbey and were struck by the soaring elegance of its ruins rising from its thirty-two acres of parkland. Several sit-upon mowers were doing their job at the furthest ends of the Abbey grounds, sweeping around majestic, well-established trees.

The entire area in which the Abbey stood was yet another place to stroll and find tranquillity, a complete contrast to the small enclosed area of the Chalice Well garden with its flowers and flagstoned corners. Here seats were placed at strategic spots with vistas across the beautifully kept acres of parkland; they were an invitation to sit, survey, contemplate and relax.

We approached the ruins of the Abbey and tried to be intelligent, but felt quite overawed by the sheer dimensions of what remained of the Great Church, rebuilt after a fire in 1184. I would never have believed that ruins could be so toweringly magnificent.

My main interest was the location of its first small church which legend claimed had been founded by Joseph of Arimathea, though more realistic minds are of the opinion that it was in fact built by monks in the second century. Whoever founded the church the dedication had been to the Virgin Mary. It had been a simple construction of interlaced reeds and saplings made watertight with cob. Building it with wattle and daub was in keeping with the Druid idea of staying close to nature. The dedication too was very much in line with the Celtic belief of communion with the natural world: the powers of the Celtic Earth Mother had given way to the powers of the Mother Church and the Virgin Mary. The present Lady Chapel to which we were going had replaced the earlier church dedicated to the Virgin Mary which had been destroyed along with the Great Church in the 1184 fire.

Having got our bearings with the help of a site-plan, we found the Lady Chapel. Its entrance of curved arches receding into the thick stone wall, each arch richly carved with foliage, was impressive. The Chapel itself was down some steps in a flagged area whose original floor, it was said, had been designed with esoteric symbolism.

In the south wall were two dark arched recesses, one of which contained a well. In Celtic times, springs and wells were the domain of gods or goddesses. The wells had healing powers and were regarded as the entrance to the underworld, and to rebirth. Here it had become a sanctified holy well as soon as the first church dedicated to the Virgin Mary had been consecrated.

We approached the altar, a rectangular shape of stone blocks with a slab on top. It was situated under a wide arched recess to the east of the Chapel. Two wooden benches were before it and for a while we sat down.

That Joseph of Arimathea had sailed to the Isle of Avalon with twelve men, said to have been sent by the apostle Philip who was evangelizing Gaul, and that he'd disembarked at Wearyall Hill (one of the hills which at the time was an island), was a heaven-sent story to boost pilgrimage to the Abbey and the area.

Another inspired legend, spun by the monks when their fortunes had been at a low ebb after the 1184 fire, was the discovery of a tomb in the Abbey's ancient cemetery, said by the monks to be the tomb of none other than King Arthur and his wife Guinevere. I noticed from our site plan that the cemetery was about fifty feet south of where we were sitting in the Lady Chapel. They claimed to have dug down and found a large lead cross with a Latin inscription stating that below it 'lay King Arthur, in the Isle of Avalon'. They'd found in the coffin the bones of a man of great physique, and the smaller bones of a woman. Apparently the woman's hair had been golden but had crumbled to dust at the touch.

The imaginative mind had been set alight with the idea of King Arthur being buried there, and pilgrims had at once poured in to pay their respects. Pilgrims meant revenue, which was after all what it was all about, money always being a necessity.

I told Harry about King Arthur's tomb. "Don't you think it's interesting that King Arthur had twelve knights of the Round Table?" I asked.

"Why interesting?"

"The number twelve," I said. "It's a mysterious figure, twelve. Twelve Olympian gods - twelve tribes of Israel - twelve disciples - twelve knights of the Round Table - twelve signs of the zodiac - Joseph of Arimathea sailing here with twelve companions. Don't you find that interesting?"

"Twelve hours on a clock," said Harry unhelpfully. "Twelve months in the year. Hum." He was getting restless. But I was hyped up about King Arthur.

King Arthur had been a Christian king of exceptional courage with a wealth of stories attached to his name. People looked back on his reign as a golden age, where courage and faith, together with a little magic, thanks to Merlin the wizard, had guided him through the more critical times in his life.

We left the peace of the Lady Chapel and made our way to the soaring ruined walls of the Great Church. We found ourselves near a small group of tourists with a guide dressed in Tudor costume. He had on a white-plumed black velvet hat, brown velvet knickerbockers with gold threads running through the cloth, a full-sleeved white ruffed shirt, and on his spindly legs the required hose of Tudor times, and black pointed shoes. He was drawing the attention of his small group to the remaining massive pillared wall of the Great Church, to its width and height, and decorative carvings. He was an elderly rheumy-eyed man and spoke with a Somerset accent. He saw us hesitating within earshot and, with a sweep of his arm and an exaggerated bow, said: "My lord and my lady, feel free to join us!"

We stood with the others and, as we were taken through the historical facts with many pauses, I began to wonder whether the guide had ever accompanied a group before. He frequently faltered in mid-sentence, his watery blue eyes appearing to look frantically inwards as though trying to read the next text written in his brain which had momentarily erased itself. With many hesitations he nevertheless managed to tell us how, despite King Arthur's many victories against the Saxons, the latter had finally conquered 'Zoomerrzet' in the seventh century and King Ine of Wessex had then built a new church of stone at the west end of the nave. This had subsequently been enlarged in the eighth century, before... before... before... ah!... St. Dunstan, the Abbot had made it even larger in the tenth century.

"Then, my lords, ladies and gentlemen - and I call your attention to it too, young maidens - " He cast his rheumy eyes in the direction of two obese ten-year-olds who were looking bored. "Then came the Norman Conquest." And he finally told us how the Abbot... Abbot... Abbot... ah!... the Abbot Herlewin, dissatisfied with the enlargement made by the Saxons, had brought about an even greater building project for the Abbey.

We followed the Tudor figure in his plumed velvet hat across the grassy nave of the Great Church to a small area surrounded by a low black metal chain, and heard how the bones of King Arthur had been moved from the ancient cemetery to this more central position.

"And I expect you young maidens have heard of King Arthur and Queen Guinevere? And Merlin, his guardian wizard? Then there were his knights Lancelot and... and... ah!... Sir Percival and... and... and... Sir Galahad and his Round Table, and his mighty sword they called Excalibur? So this is where they say King Arthur lies. Now, my lords, ladies and gentlemen - and young maidens - will you please follow me." And he led the way to the north transept and to the Choir where he stopped and waited for his small following to gather round.

When he was satisfied we were all paying attention, he said:

"Now you all know the saying 'to have your back to the wall'? Well, look along that wall there. Those who came for Sunday worship, and who got tired standing, they'd seat themselves along the wall, see? So what was they doing?" He sent an enquiring look at the two children who looked blank. "The maidens have no answer?" The burly father felt the need to prompt them: "They 'ad their backs to the wall, stupid!"

We all murmured and smiled at this newly acquired bit of information before following the plumed hat on to the High Altar and to the Edgar Chapel. Eventually, he came to the grand finale of the Abbey's history which came with Henry VIII's dissolution of the monasteries. We were told how 'His Majesty' had taken no more than five years to abolish eight hundred monasteries, convents and friaries throughout the kingdom in order to replenish his depleted coffers, and how 'oh, lackaday!' Glastonbury Abbey had come to its tragic end when 'poor Abbot... Abbot... Abbot... ah!... Abbot Whiting, a frail old man' had been faced with trumped-up charges of wrongdoing and condemned to death. "And, never mind he was an old man," said our guide, "he was dragged from here to the Tor." And the Tudor figure made a sweeping gesture towards the hill with its ruined tower on top. "And there on the Tor Abbot Whiting he was brutally decapitated."

The group muttered its horror. The guide was gaining confidence as he neared the end of his guided tour duties.

"Rrrrrrr!" he shouted, and he seized a dagger from its sheath at his waist and brandished it at the two bored-out-of-their-minds ten year olds. "And they placed his bleeding head here at the Abbey for all to see! And they quartered him nicely and put each part of him on view at Bridgwater, Ilchester, Bath and Wells."

"Why?" I asked. "Why did they do that?"

The guide eyed me uncertainly, and his eyes faltered as he searched his blank mind. "Why?" The answer came to him, and he announced it triumphantly: "So as not to make a martyr of him at Glastonbury, that's why, m'lady. So they carried his quartered body to the four different places!"

"So that's why people were quartered!" I said.

"And on that tragic note, my lords, ladies and gentlemen, not forgetting the maidens," he added, with a wary look at the girls, "we've come to the end of our Glastonbury Abbey tour." His eyes darted around us. He had done his best and was clearly relieved that all was over. The small gathering began to disperse, murmuring their thanks as they departed.

We took ourselves out to the scant remains of the cloisters, and beyond it found a wooden seat with a vista across newly mown grass, to majestic solitary trees, and the Abbots Kitchen, a solid building set apart in a corner of the grounds,

"I hate to say it," I began, "but all the prayers in the world from all the monks and nuns, priests and bishops of the day, failed to save these religious monasteries. Henry VIII was just an over-sexed fanatically minded megalomaniac who committed every possible sin, and got away with it. How do you explain that?" But Harry wasn't prepared to explain anything. He was jangling the keys of the car in his pocket, summoning the energy for our last planned visit of the day.

"If you're looking for Joseph of Arimathea you'll find him round the corner!" A jolly-faced, grey-haired woman looked at us briefly from under the bonnet of her car. We'd slowed down and I'd only called out, 'Excuse me, can you tell us...' when she'd given the answer. Clearly anyone who drew up at her gate asked the same question.

"Thank you very much!" I said to her rear view; she was already bent over tinkering with her car again.

We drove the several hundred yards further and, sure enough, around the corner we found the wicket gate to Wearyall Hill and a parking place for the car. When Joseph of Arimathea arrived with his twelve companions it had been an island and he'd come by boat. The story being that they'd been so tired, having rowed or sailed across the English Channel, around Cornwall, and over the shallow inland sea to Avalon, that they'd dropped anchor and, as they were 'weary all', so it became known as Wearyall Hill.

The first thing Joseph of Arimathea did on arrival, so the pious story went, was to plant his wooden staff in the ground where it immediately rooted itself and grew into a tree. The monks were keen to spread the wonderful fact that it was due to Joseph of Arimathea's associations with Jesus that the tree miraculously flowered every year at Christmas. In fact, although it was a shame to spoil the story, that particular species was one that always bloomed at that time of year; it was a type of hawthorn unlike any native tree to Britain but was similar to a species which grew in the Levant.

We followed the well-trodden muddy track up the gentle slope to the famous Joseph of Arimathea tree which was encircled by a barbed wire fence. Ribbons and prayer flags fluttered from its branches. It wasn't, however, the original hawthorn; that had been cut down by the Puritans in the late sixteenth century. Fortunately, as cuttings had been taken from the first (many given as gifts to visiting dignitaries) so this, its decendant, was there for those coming with petitions and prayers today.

Another wildly imaginative story spread by the monks was that the Virgin Mary's mother, Anne, had been a Cornish queen who had herself (like her daughter to be born) immaculately conceived. As a consequence she'd been cast out by her husband. Apparently, Joseph of Arimathea had been making one of his trips to Britain at that time and, on hearing about the queen's plight, had taken her back with him to Judaea.

"That's why they say Jesus was brought as a boy because he was curious about his grandmother's past," I explained. "Come to think of it," I went on, "he could have brought James, his brother, as he would also have been interested."

"Or maybe he brought the Virgin Mary who'd undoubtedly have wanted to see where her mother had been queen?" said Harry speculatively. He paused as his mind turned over the possibilities. "Or he could have brought Joseph who would have wanted to see where his espoused wife's mother had immaculately conceived? Or John the Baptist or his mother Elizabeth, or Zechariah - " He was becoming inventive with the many figures from Jesus' childhood.

"Have I told you that they say he brought Mary, her sister Martha and Lazarus their brother who was raised from the dead?" I asked.

"No. But it wouldn't surprise me."

All things appeared possible with Joseph of Arimathea once the seed of the idea of his having come had rooted itself (like his staff which had blossomed). He was said to have been a merchant trading in tin so he could have sailed to Britain on numerous occasions.

"There's another hill beyond this called Beckery Hill which is sacred to Mary Magdalene. Would you like to see that?" I asked, hoping for the answer which I immediately got.

"No fear! Another blessed hill would kill me!"

We sat down on a convenient seat for 'wearyall' visitors, and I told Harry the little I knew about the hill we wouldn't be seeing. I was, in fact, slightly confused between what was called Bride's Mound and Beckery Hill, and wasn't too sure whether the former was on the latter or was a separate tinier landmark nearby. A chapel had been built there dedicated to Mary Magdalene, and I knew that the Irish born saint, St. Brigid, had visited it in 488 A.D. There was believed to have been a chapel dedicated to her which had an opening to it through which those who passed were healed of their various complaints. Bride's Mound had also been said to be the gateway to Avalon, where those who arrived spent the night in prayer and vigil before following the processional way to the sacred sites.

"The reason why it's called Beckery Hill," I told Harry, "is because it's where Irish born St. Brigid's relics were kept and, as so many Irish pilgrims came flocking over to pay their respects, so it became known as 'little Ireland' or 'beck Eire' - Beckery." And I followed up this interesting bit of information with two other equally enthralling ones (to me anyway) firstly, that the Celtic pagan goddess Brighid had been goddess of fire and healing waters, as well as poetry and inspiration, and St. Brigid had inherited her attributes; secondly that St. Patrick, who'd evangelized Ireland, had come to Glastonbury and had become its first Abbot.

It was at her chapel on Beckery Hill that another legend was spread by the imaginative monks. King Arthur, they declared, had been converted to Christianity at the celebration of a mass held there during which he'd seen a vision of the Virgin and Child. When the priest had come to the part where the sacraments were offered to the congregation, King Arthur in his vision had seen the Virgin Mary presenting the baby Jesus to the priest for sacrifice. Then, despite the communicants consuming his body and blood, the vision had revealed the mortal body of Jesus as quite untouched. Afterwards Mary had picked up a crystal cross which had been on the altar and had given it to King Arthur who, in his turn, had presented it to the Abbot of Glastonbury who had placed it above the high altar in the Abbey church. The point of the story being that as a result of this vision King Arthur had converted to the faith. From then on he'd abandoned the image on his coat-of-arms of three red lions on a silver background (some say it was a dragon) and, instead, adopted the Christian cross and an image of the Virgin and Child.

"It's strange," I said, as we stared out towards the Somerset Levels, "strange that these hills were islands and all around was water. Do you realize it was here that King Arthur received the gift of Excalibur from the Lady of the Lake? Can you imagine that? Her arm coming up magically from the depths holding the new sword to replace his old one which had been broken in battle?"

"Umm," said Harry dubiously.

"She was believed to have been a water goddess or anyway some supernatural being. Have you heard of Morgan le Fay?"

"No. Who was he?"

"Not he, she."

"She, then."

"Well, some people said the Lady of the Lake was Morgan le Fay, and others that she was Arthur's sister, though how that could be if she was a water goddess, I really don't know." And I told Harry how Morgan le Fay was believed to have been the guardian of the mysteries of Avalon, concerned with death and rebirth. According to that story, she and Arthur had had an incestuous affair resulting in a son called Mordred. Mordred had made an attempt on Arthur's life because he'd wanted the throne, but had only succeeded in wounding him. Morgan le Fay, Arthur's so-called sister, had then taken him to the Tor where she'd cared for him, till something had annoyed her, and she'd let him die.

"I thought everyone who died got dipped in the cauldron of rebirth?" Harry queried.

Sometimes Harry remembered things that I'd forgotten. But I supposed that King Arthur, having become a Christian, wouldn't have been thinking about the cauldron of rebirth, but would have been hoping for resurrection from the dead and life everlasting according to the Church's teaching.

Was there that much difference?

❧✦❧

"Crystals help activate and energize the chakras," said the mauve-haired woman at breakfast the next morning.

"Chakras?" I queried.

"We spoke about them yesterday - they're the energy sensitive points in the body. There are seven of them," she said.

She'd just been telling us how she'd already climbed the Tor that morning to perform her 'salute to the sun' exercises. When I'd asked her what that entailed, she'd got up from the table and given us a brief demonstration, first standing upright, before swinging her arms up and back over her head, then down to her toes. Harry had continued eating his porridge as though she weren't in the room.

"Take your throat as an example," went on the woman sitting down again, and warming to the subject of chakras.

"My throat?"

"It's your means of communication," she said. "Few people are aware of the importance of their throat chakra." She fingered the chakra point at her neck. "If I wake up anxious about possible communication difficulties with a client that day, then I use a blue crystal. I lie down and put it on my throat to renew the energy levels there."

"Oh, yes?"

"And, perhaps, another on my brow," she said.

Harry threw her a sideways glance, then put down his table napkin and got up to help himself to bacon and eggs at the sideboard.

"How very interesting," I said.

"To be able to communicate," went on the woman, "depends entirely on the throat and the energy levels at the chakra. We're so used to talking that we don't notice that we breathe in, and are able to speak only on an outward flow of air."

"Really? Yes, isn't it curious!" I said, breathing out.

"But you can't breathe in and speak at the same time. And you can't swallow and breathe either, nor swallow and speak."

Harry gave her another swift assessing look as he returned to the table with his bacon and eggs.

"Without the throat and the development of speech there'd be no past to talk about, no future to discuss. We'd be living only in the present like animals."

"I suppose so," I said.

I buttered a piece of toast and spread on some marmalade. I thought a change of topic might be less mentally demanding for so early in the day. "So as a life coach people come to you for advice?" I asked, picking up on what she'd told us earlier while eating a grapefruit.

"That's right. You'd be surprised how screwed up some people get, and if I can help - "

Harry's eyebrows raised a fraction as he focused on his bacon and eggs.

"It's all a matter of breaking down individual prejudices,

opening up horizons and helping people to become aware of the choices they have."

Quite unexpectedly she leaned forward and, looking directly at Harry, said: "If you don't mind my saying so, it's stress. I can always tell. You should try the blue crystal." She indicated where it should be placed below the neck. "Alternatively, you could try a rhodonite to identify the area of tension. Stress can lead to - " She silently mouthed the word 'constipation'. "If you do happen to have problems in that department, a pink crystal placed below the abdomen can - "

Harry's intake of breath and energy levels caused him to exhale suddenly with the words: "Good God! I wouldn't have a crystal, I'd take a dose of salts!"

I looked at the mauve-haired woman, then at Harry, then her again, then him. They were locked in eye contact.

"He speaks!" the woman said with a certain satisfaction. "It's a correct balance of energies at the throat chakra which is important, otherwise pressure builds up. Well, I must go. I've a bus to catch!"

"It's been fascinating," I found myself saying, trying to bring things to a peaceful conclusion. "All those chakras, and I never knew I had one!"

She grabbed her shoulder-bag from the floor and slung it round her neck. "Here's my card," she said. "If you want to question me on crystals, I'm always glad to help."

When she was gone Harry eyed me and neither ate, swallowed nor spoke for a full minute. When the words came, they blew out in a snort: "The woman doesn't need a crystal on her chakky whatnots, she needs a rock dropped on her head!"

An hour later we were driving home. A last fleeting look at the Tor which brought pilgrims flocking to it for its mystique, and the Abbey below which brought inquisitive tourists to its ruins. What did it matter what people did or thought providing they did no harm to others? While some lived fraught lives trying to make money, others found peace by placing crystals on their prostrate bodies, or sitting cross-legged in meditative calm. Gods came and went and, as we drove away it seemed to me the only certain constant was the earth's unchanging landscape.

CHAPTER THREE

BATH

"Why on earth do you want a hat?" Harry demanded. "You've no reason to buy a hat."

"Absolutely none, but in Jane Austen's city a small diversion is to be encouraged," I replied, and I removed a hat with antennae and tried on a tall furry affair perched over the brow. It was a bitterly cold winter's day in January and a furry hat might keep me warm.

"How about this one?"

"It's more you, I suppose." Whether that meant I looked good in it or not, I wasn't sure.

I had to admit I was way off course for the real purpose of this visit, which was to discover the ancient Celtic and the Roman gods of Bath –

I was amazed at what a hat could do for the female face, never mind if the passing years had made that face an etched cartoon of its youthful self. A becoming hat did wonders for morale, but was it becoming because of the face, or would it be more becoming if the face wasn't there?

In due course I realized most of the hats looked much better without me, and the price of those that did anything was exorbitant. We left and went up to the Jane Austen Centre for another small diversion on this, our first afternoon in the city. I was hoping there to have 'Tea with Mr. Darcy' as was promised by the tea rooms. But by the time we'd ferreted around its small museum and seen the elegant clothes worn by Jane Austen's 'genteel society', the tea rooms were closed.

We walked back to our hotel, a Georgian building in South

Parade. By now it was dark, though it was only five o'clock. The warmth of the interior of our hotel enveloped us as we entered. We retrieved our key from reception and passed through the empty lounge furnished with pink brocade upholstered Georgian armchairs, past the large dining-room, and climbed the carpeted staircase to the third landing and our ensuite room with its 'January special offer'. The thought of sipping tea propped up on our beds reading or watching television was appealing. Tea with Mr. Darcy? Tea with Harry was more like it. Tea made with tea-bags and no fuss.

Pillows behind my back and my slippered feet up on the bed. While Harry watched television, I opened a book and was soon back on course reading about the goddess Sulis Minerva.

We crossed Pierrepont Street into North Parade Passage, and were soon approaching the looming edifice of the medieval Abbey with its buttresses and pointed arched windows, and its great open space at its west end.

On the way I told Harry the legendary story of King Bladud's discovery of the healing powers of the spring, around which the Roman baths had been built.

"King Bladud? Never heard of him," said Harry.

"Well, Bladud is descended from King Brutus who is said to have founded London," I said. "King Brutus was himself descended from the King of Troy whose son caused the Trojan War when he gallivanted off with the beautiful Helen," I went on. I gave Harry a moment to digest this interesting piece of information. He appeared to be listening, so I continued. "The story goes that as a young man poor Bladud was sent to study in Athens where he contracted leprosy, though how that could be I don't know as he lived centuries before Athens became an academic centre. But, I suppose, it's only a legend. Anyway, having got leprosy, he returned home only to find himself banished by his parents."

"Tough!" commented Harry.

"Very," I agreed. "So instead of completing his studies, he was forced to eke out a living as a humble swineherd, and found himself here with his pigs who, by the way, also caught the disease."

"Do pigs get leprosy?"

"Well, they had some sort of skin disease." I stopped in the middle of the great open area before the Abbey. "You have to imagine this place being a swamp," I said. "One day whilst the pigs were scavenging for whatever pigs scavenge for, they found a nice warm marshy bog where they all decided to have a good wallow. When they lumbered out Bladud discovered that their leprosy had vanished. So Bladud also submerged himself and hey presto! He found he too was cured. He then returned to his family who welcomed him with open arms. When later he inherited the throne, he honoured the hot spring here by turning it into a centre of healing. Much of which, I suppose, is speculation but it makes a nice story."

We came to the entrance to the Roman Baths, bought our tickets and were given audio devices to listen to. It was ten o'clock and as yet few other visitors were there.

We followed the tourist trail to a terrace raised on elegant columns some of which had impressive Roman statues rising from them against the skyline. From there on this chilly winter's morning we were able to look down on the Great Bath below filled with murky green water.

The Gothic Abbey tower and a large portion of the Abbey church building rose spectacularly beyond the nearby roof-tops like an anxious mother watching, fearful that her children were straying beyond her control. Well, as I was there for the Celtic and the Roman period, my concentration certainly was not on her for the moment but on the pagan deities of the ancient past.

We followed the arrows which took us down a stairway to the hot spring itself which bubbled up into a small pool from which steam rose. We paused to look at it through a protective glass window - it was our moment to pay our respects to the goddess of the spring, known to the Celts as Sulis.

When the Romans invaded Britain in 43 A.D. they soon noticed the importance given to this hot spring. They were determined to prove to the stubborn people of this northern outpost of their empire that it wasn't all doom and gloom to have the Romans here. In Rome itself baths had been a central meeting place for its citizens, a place where they could gather, relax, debate, be entertained and, of course, take their baths. Constructing such a centre at this spring the Romans rightly believed would help win over the rebellious Celts who, they hoped, would enjoy a good wallow like King Bladud's pigs.

"No electricity bill either. Lucky them!" Harry said as he watched the steam rise from this natural spring of bubbling hot water. Before our recent electricity bill could get a grip of him, I quickly added: "Another reason too was that the baths gave a great boost to the morale of the Roman soldiers who hated the weather in England with its wind, rain, cloud and fog. Far from seeing England as a green and pleasant land, the Romans found it green but otherwise thoroughly unpleasant," I said.

From the book I'd read, working with the hot water had been remarkably difficult as the archaeologists of the nineteenth century were to discover when they excavated the area and found the broken drains and shattered pipes with the steaming spring water continuously flowing and needing to be pumped away. The Romans, however, had set to work clearing the alders and willows, and using all their technical and engineering skills to channel the water along drains and conduits to the various baths. The considerable surplus of water had been syphoned off to the river Avon along a great arched stone drain, high enough for a man to stand in.

And so they turned the spring of the goddess Sulis to their advantage renaming it Aquae Sulis Minerva, retaining the name of the Celtic goddess and linking it to their Minerva, goddess of wisdom and the arts.

We went on to an area where the water fresh from the spring was channelled through a stone arched area and cascaded into a small pool from which it was piped to the baths. The orange sediment staining the stones revealed the heavy iron content of the water.

Passing on through the various excavated areas we came to the major exhibits. I saw Harry pressing the numbers on his audio device followed by the green button, and raising it to his ear. He was very attentive as though listening to his doctor advising him what pills to take. I punched in the same numbers and heard that we were viewing stone-carved figures of Jupiter and Hercules. These had once supported two of the four corners of the sacrificial altar which had stood before the temple of Sulis Minerva. The third carved figure was of Bacchus (god of wine), and the fourth of an unidentified goddess, believed to be a goddess of fertility pouring a libation from a vessel which she held. As she was unidentified, I liked to think of her as Sulis Minerva pouring her spring water.

"Sacrificial altar," said Harry, nodding towards it. He listened intently for a moment, and then said, "Ooooof!" He'd just heard how the priest or augur would slit the stomach of the sacrificed beast and examine its entrails for good or bad omens. I could only suppose there was something in it or they wouldn't have bothered.

"Just the sort of thing pagans would do," said Harry dismissively.

The temple had to be imagined. I'd already read that when the Romans built it in the first century, it had been a fine classical building set on a platform with a flight of steps leading to it from its colonnaded courtyard. Four Corinthian columns had supported its ornate pediment in the centre of which had been a Gorgon's head on a shield flanked by two winged Victories. The sculpted stone slabs for this centre-piece were on view and required another number to be pressed for an explanation. Harry dutifully did his bit and eyed me as he listened. "Gorgon's head," he mouthed at me.

"You've heard of Medusa?" I asked.

"Medusa? Yes."

"She was a Gorgon - the famous one. She had glaring eyes and snakes for hair, and turned all who set eyes on her to stone." And I told him how in ancient Greece the Gorgon's head had been used on the shields of warriors to terrorize the enemy. Athena herself had been born from the head of Zeus and had emerged fully armed with a shield on which had been the Gorgon's head.

The interesting thing about the ferocious-looking Gorgon's head sculpted on the plaque before us was that it fused the Roman with the Celtic. The pediment with its round disc bearing the head was not the usual female one with snakes for hair, but had a moustache and was depicted as a Celtic warrior. Its flowing hair standing up around the crown was Celtic-warrior like, and the rest of the flowing locks (to those in the know) had similarities to Neptune, Roman god of the sea.

"Neptune was the Roman equivalent to the Greek Poseidon, god of the sea," I said. "And for what it's worth, apparently Poseidon had a fling with Medusa, and got her pregnant - not exactly the most pleasant of experiences if she had snakes for hair and glaring eyes - but maybe he was so in love he didn't notice," I said, giving him the benefit of what seemed very doubtful.

At some stage the Romans made significant changes to the original temple in order to correct subsidence and to further beautify the buildings. A raised portico with a sculpted pediment had been constructed along a wall on the south side of the temple courtyard. Piecing together the evidence from the discoveries recovered by the archaeologists, it was believed that this pediment had for its centre-piece two water nymphs supporting a large circular disc on which was the head of Sol, the sun god.

"And it's thought that if they had an elaborate pediment on the south wall, then there had to be another on the north wall," I told Harry, who was looking increasingly bemused by the quantity of information given by his audio. Because I'd refreshed my memory with the book the day before, I knew roughly what to expect. "The Romans would never have been satisfied with a building that didn't have balance and harmony," I said, and I pointed to several richly sculpted stone pieces which fitted in with the idea of this north wall pediment. There was a stone slab thought to have been the centre-piece which was of Luna, the moon goddess, with a crescent moon behind her and in her hand a riding whip. "So you have to imagine the Sun god on one side facing the Moon goddess on the other with the sacrificial altar between them," I said. "The altar stood before the great temple of Sulis Minerva, and the sacred spring was only a few meters away," I explained.

"Well, whatever you say," said Harry.

We found ourselves staring at a pool of clear water into which coins had been thrown by those who hoped it might bring them luck. All ancient votive offerings had been thrown into the spring itself, from where the flow of water swept them on to whatever destination where they were found by the archaeologists hundreds of years later. Wiped and cleaned they were now on show in the present museum. There were engraved gem stones, pewter and silver handled cups, many coins, items of jewellery and so on. Each Roman artefact represented a human problem, or a fulfilled wish. Who knows what was in the mind of the anonymous donor. All that is certain is that whoever it was had as much faith and trust in Sulis Minerva and her bubbling hot spring, as Christians today when they go down on their knees and beseech or light a candle. The human mind is a weird and wonderful place filled with unseen mysteries born of belief. Or do I mean faith?

There were also in the museum many pewter curses retrieved from the area. These were carefully written messages to the goddess, asking her to punish the petty thief or someone who'd caused offence. It couldn't have been much fun to know the goddess had your name and had been told of your crime, not if you believed she had the power to punish you.

We came to the beautiful gilded bronze head of the goddess Minerva herself, thought to have come from the cult statue which would have stood in the innermost holy place of the great temple. It was not unknown for the early Christians to decapitate statues of pagan deities, hence the head only.

We were told by the audio to keep an eye out for the worn lower stone steps. Dutifully we cast our eyes in the right direction. Whether they were steps up to the temple I wasn't sure, and had no inclination now to replay the audio to tell me. They were worn stone steps and that was that. Enough. Several hours underground being instructed by a voice to look here and there was wearying. But persist we must, and we did.

"Good God! King Bloody, or whatever his name is!" Harry announced, pointing to some distant arched recess in a stone wall where the small crowned and robed figure of King Bladud was seated on a throne. The king looked startled and, if it weren't for his crown, bore a resemblance to the Gorgon's head with its flowing locks and thick moustache.

At last we emerged at the open-air Great Bath which we'd seen from the terrace on our arrival, with its columns supporting the terrace above on which were the statues of Roman figures against the skyline. Set back around the stone-flagged walkway were wide arched recesses with stone benches in them where visitors could rest. A vaulted roof had originally been built over the whole, with windows high up to let in daylight, but that was long gone.

I felt the murky green water and found it pleasantly warm. The pool was at the same depth the whole length and had steps all around for bathers to lower themselves into it. It still contained its original triple layer of lead-sheet lining.

We explored further where other baths had been built for the enjoyment of those who would expect nothing but the best, and those others who'd experienced nothing like it before. Each bath was regulated at a different temperature, starting with a warm room to get accustomed to the heat, then a hot steam room where they could sweat it out, and finally a quick plunge into the 'frigidarium' to close the pores and rinse away the scented oils rubbed in by masseurs.

"Not forgetting," I said to Harry, "that invalids and arthritics came from far and wide hoping to be cured."

We were seated in one of the alcoves set back from the water. We had been wandering the complex now for over three hours and I'd been trying to ignore the fact my back was breaking. What I wanted though was not a wallow in the warm waters but food and gentle pampering - well, lunch served in style in the Pump Room was the idea.

We left the stone bench and went on around the bath heading for the exit, passing as we did so an open gulley of water running into the bath. I ignored the warning sign which said 'Do not touch' and put a finger in the water. Interesting. It was considerably hotter than in the main bath and must be flowing from the spring close by. We were very near to the source of the Sulis Minerva spring.

A glance up to the skies and there the great Gothic Abbey tower with its turrets at the four corners was still keeping its parental watch. Next day would be Sunday (the day of the sun) and maybe we'd pacify this anxious parent with a visit. And then the day after would be Monday (the day of the moon) when we would be home again. And so the week would pass.

But today was Saturday, the Jewish Sabbath and their day of rest. Well, I wasn't bothered which day people chose to rest, I only knew for sure it was high time to rest ourselves whatever day it was. So to the Pump Room.

✥❧❦❧✥

A woman in a black trouser-suit and white shirt was the one who allowed those queuing to be admitted or not. She appeared to be endlessly in motion from one end of the long Pump Room hung with chandeliers, to the other, weaving her body like a shuttle in and out between the tables and the seated guests. A continuous medley of piano pieces was being played by a man at a grand piano on stage. It was all very genteel, very Jane Austen and 'polite society'.

We were beckoned in after ten minutes and seated on hard-backed Chippendale chairs. A bowl of soup each, thank you, we told the tall slender waitress dressed (as were all the waitresses) in a long white wrap around apron with a pale green check waistcoat. No, no wine, thank you, but can we try the mineral water please?

From where I sat I could see the Pump Room fountain against

the high Georgian sash window. The large urn with its various outlets spouted water from bronze scallop shells into the open mouths of bronze fish poised on their tails ready to receive it. The urn stood on a tall Bath-stone basin which took the overflow. The window overlooked the Great Bath below where we'd just been.

"Ugh!" Harry proclaimed after the first sip. He put down the glass of water he'd been handed by the waitress. "You have a sip." He passed it across to me and I dutifully drank it. I wondered how hygienic it was, but supposed it must meet with health and safety standards.

The audio had informed me that the water originally fell as rain in the Mendip hills more than six thousand years ago. The voice had also told me that the rain had seeped down to a depth of several thousand metres where it had become heated to something like ninety degrees centigrade before rising and emerging as the spring, and flowed at about two hundred and fifty thousand gallons a day. I wondered if that meant that thousands of years ago there had been two hundred and fifty thousand gallons of rain, but when I'd mentioned it to Harry, he hadn't thought the question worth answering.

Now I came out with a newly acquired bit of information that I'd read somewhere: "Do you know that the earth's crust alone is twenty-five miles thick?" I asked. "Only the crust, mind you, not the whole world."

"Is it? I expect so." Harry was buttering a roll.

"And the centre of the world from the earth's crust is nearly four thousand miles!" I went on.

"Is it?" Harry wasn't going to get over excited about anything until he'd had his soup.

"And rocks such as basalt and granite," I pursued, "were once liquid at the centre of the earth but because of fire and the extreme heat at the earth's centre they were forced in their liquid form to rise through cracks and God knows what till they reached the earth's surface where they became rock. What do you think of that?"

But Harry's eyes were fixed on the great sash window behind me. "There's a man on a high bicycle juggling with flaming torches," he remarked.

I turned and saw the spectacle. The great open area before the Abbey drew buskers and entertainers to it. Turning back again, my attention was drawn to two small boys, one of whom had a paper dart and was clearly considering throwing it to liven up the Pump Room guests, but just in time the waitress brought him a hot chocolate. The paper dart was left on the table as soon as he spied the drink coming.

By now the Pump Room was divided into those who were there for lunch and those for afternoon tea. The manageress was still weaving in and out amongst the tables. The pianist was playing 'Clair de Lune', a composition suitable to the occasion where the goddess Luna had once had her place in the Roman temple complex. I wondered if his ambition had once been to be a concert pianist touring the world, but had had to reconcile himself to playing as background accompaniment to people talking, or as a vague diversion for those who had nothing much to say.

Now we were refreshed we felt it time to leave, to give those queuing at the door their chance to sit. For a while we watched the entertainers outside before deciding to take a walk up the hill, through the residential area of Bath to see the crescents.

We left the shops behind, and were glad to be able to stride out and get going. The road we were on took us high above the main hubbub of Bath where only a few pedestrians, some with dogs, were to be seen. Looking back we saw the hill rising beyond the city to the south. We reached Campden Crescent, a graceful curve of Bath-stone Georgian houses sweeping away to our right. Beyond them to the east rose a distant wooded hill with stately houses revealing themselves through the trees. We continued on up and up heading north. The traffic now looked more purposeful, the cars passing us were heading out of Bath, driving on to Bristol or, perhaps, some nearby village. We saw a tall church and, on examining our street map, found we had walked further than intended, our target being Lansdown Crescent.

We walked back down and soon saw the sweep of Georgian houses gracefully curving to the west, with their wide road frontage, each house with a black wrought-iron arch and hanging lamp before its entrance. Across the road, and dropping away to our left as we walked the length of this crescent, were shrubberies and lawns surrounded by black railings with a central gate. It was after four o'clock and there was no one down there. There was no one up where we were either. We seemed alone in Lansdown Crescent and for that moment it belonged to us only.

On this late January afternoon it was cold and the sky as ever was overcast and gloomy. There was, however, a small treat in store for us because, as we walked along the crescent, the tiers of Georgian sash windows all shone suddenly as though the electric light in each had been switched on. And there to the west we saw that the gloomy cloud which had been hanging over the city all day had parted enough to reveal the brilliance of the setting sun. The light flooded the crescent like the beam from a powerful torch shining from under a coverlet. It was nothing much, and yet the beauty of the crescent Georgian houses, and the bonus of the sudden sunlight, made it memorable. The god Sol was peeping out at us.

Five minutes later it had sunk beneath its coverlet of cloud, and we were left in the dreary rawness of a bitterly cold January evening.

On our way back to our hotel we unexpectedly heard the sound of distant rushing water. When we crossed the road to investigate we found the river Avon in full spate flowing swiftly past, and the rushing-water noise was coming from a weir some twenty yards up river. Beyond it was the flood-lit Pulteney Bridge with the lights of its small shops and restaurants spanning the river. It was enchanting. I realized that somewhere nearby the surplus water from the Roman Baths would be draining into it, water from the sacred spring of Sulis Minerva would be flowing with it.

Like the ever flowing river we were for ever moving towards the future. Where next to look for gods in Britain, I wondered? Well, I had a long list to choose from.

CHAPTER FOUR

LONDON

I examined the faces of the passengers seated opposite. It was late February, and we were on the Central Line heading for Bank underground station. We were a motley lot wearing wet anoraks, raincoats, scarves and carrying dripping umbrellas. Opposite me was a Moslem woman swathed in black with only her eyes visible, mysterious and beautiful. Beside her was a high cheek-boned square-jawed woman of Russian appearance, with fair hair piled up and fastened on top of her head in such a way that the ends curled over in a lighter blonde colour like the crest of a wave. She caught me looking at her and, as always when eyes meet, we each looked away instantly. It is odd how human beings fear to be the focus of a stranger's attention. It must be an innate jungle instinct not to fall prey to a predator's hypnotic stare. I quickly turned my attention to the underground map above the dark windows through which the grimy tunnel walls flashed by. I saw that Bank was two stops away.

We were on our way to the Guildhall, the administrative centre of the City of London. I was interested because it was said to be built on the site of the palace of the first ever King of Britain named Brutus whose forbears had founded Rome. He was believed to be the great grandson of the Trojan prince Aeneas whose mother was Aphrodite, goddess of love, no less. Before his birth, a magician rightly predicted a great future for him. As a young man Brutus travelled to Greece, and there obtained the freedom of a number of Trojan slaves before setting sail with them to an unidentified island, some say Malta, where he offered up a sacrifice to the goddess Diana. That night the goddess appeared to him in a vision and said: 'Brutus, beyond the setting of the sun, past the realms of Gaul there lies an island in the sea, once occupied by giants. Now it is empty and ready for your folk. Down the years this will prove an abode suited to you and to your people; and for your descendants it will be a second Troy. A race of kings will be born there from your stock and the round circle of the whole earth will be subject to them.'

On his journey to the island 'beyond the setting sun', Brutus came across another group of Trojans who joined him. Their leader's name was Corineus; he was both wise and courageous which was just as well because the goddess had been incorrect about the island being 'empty and ready' and 'once occupied by giants'. Sailing up the river Dart they came to Totnes where they were immediately faced by a band of angry hostile giants. Corineus threw himself into the thick of them and there was a bloody battle resulting in the death of many giants, and the fleeing of others into Cornwall.

One giant in particular called Gogmagog stood head and shoulders above the others. Undaunted by this terrifying spectacle Corineus managed to wrestle him to the ground, and finally toppled him over a cliff to his death on the rocks below. Some say it was at Plymouth Hoe.

By Tudor times another version of the story was being told. Gogmagog was now two giants, Gog and Magog, and in this story Brutus captured them and brought them to his palace (site of today's Guildhall) where he chained them to the entrance, and they became the guardians of his newly founded city which he named New Troy, or Troia Nova. These powerful guardians are today represented by two large wooden statues which stand above the entrance to the Great Hall; they are brought out annually to join in the procession at the Lord Mayor's Show.

Our train drew up at Bank and we followed the other passengers to the exit. Emerging up at street level in the heart of the City of London, my first impression was of lofty grandeur: the Greek temple-like Mansion House, the Bank of England and the Royal Exchange were striking. Tucked between less majestic buildings close to the Bank of England was the small Church of St. Margaret Lothbury with its tall Portland stone tower topped by a lead obelisk spire on a bell-shaped dome.

It had stopped raining but the sky was as leaden as the church dome and spire, and there was an icy north-east wind. As it was

Saturday there was little traffic and few pedestrians in the City. We got our bearings from the black City signposts with their gilded lettering pointing the direction to the various City landmarks.

Once inside the main visitor's entrance to the Guildhall, we had to undergo strict security checks before being allowed through a doorway to a quadrangle leading to the Great Hall. It was raining heavily again and we put up our umbrellas. Peering out from under mine I saw the medieval Great Hall ahead of us. Above its impressive doorway was the London coat of arms flanked by ornate turrets.

I remembered I'd meant to ask the security guard the whereabouts of the London Stone which, according to legend, had been brought by King Brutus to his new city of Troia Nova.

I cursed myself aloud from under my umbrella.

"What's up?" The voice came from under Harry's alongside me. I told him about the Stone brought by King Brutus.

"The Gog and Magog King Brutus?" asked the voice from Harry's umbrella.

I was surprised he'd recalled the names and said from under mine that the Stone was thought possibly to have been the altar stone of the Temple of Diana where Brutus had had his vision telling him to come to the 'island beyond the setting sun'.

"Island of no sun at all, is more like it," muttered the voice from his umbrella.

We reached the Great Hall, shook ourselves like wet dogs, and entered. The interior with its lofty high ceiling and rib-shaped ancient oak beams, and its great arched stained-glass window at its far end were imposing. Numerous round tables filled the hall, each with brown leather straight-backed dining chairs set around it; every chair had a gold City of London coat of arms on its back depicting a shield and helmet topped by what I took to be oak leaves; on the shield was the cross of St. George, and either side were rampant dragons, with a ribbon below them on which was the civic motto 'Domine dirige nos' (Lord direct us). For the occasion of the Lord Mayor's Banquet the tables would be spread with white damask cloths, and laid with the best silver and cut-glass. The marble statues of such eminent figures as the Duke of Wellington, Nelson and Churchill looked on sightlessly from their positions around the hall.

The overhead chandeliers were switched on by an attendant. These hung down in tiers of dark bronze with numerous tiny russet coloured lamp shades. Their light revealed what I hadn't previously noticed, the banners of the main City of London Livery Companies hanging either side high up near the rib-shaped beams.

But where were Gog and Magog? I asked the attendant who pointed to a minstrel's gallery above the west entrance. There I saw in the shadows the two carved wooden nine-foot high statues of the giants. They looked benign and somewhat resigned to the chore of guarding London. One had ragged locks and a long flowing beard, the other was marginally tidier with a moustache and small beard. Both had strange foliage-like tall head-dresses, and wore what looked like Roman style tunics. Each grasped what were either long weapons or symbols of authority, and one of them held a shield with a phoenix on it to represent the rising from the ashes of the City after its various devastations such as the 1666 Fire of London, and the London Blitz in World War II. On both occasions the earlier statues of the giants together with the Guildhall had been destroyed.

With our umbrellas up again, we made our way from the Guildhall to the Museum of London along Wood Street. Wood Street! I found the names of the City of London streets comical. Since Bank underground station there'd been one named Poultry, and we'd passed a road on our left called Bread Street; around the Bank of England was Threadneedle Street and Cornhill, and now we'd just turned off Cheapside. These roads represented the market areas of old London where the cheapest products had been sold.

We turned left from Wood Street into London Wall; from there we were able to look down to the remains of medieval walls whose foundations were the old original Roman walls. But I wasn't there for the walls, I was there for the gods, and we were soon in the comfortable warmth of the Museum of London where we spent the rest of the day, Harry in the million years B.C. gallery, and I in the Roman London one.

I found I was just in time to join a small group about to start a guided tour of the Roman galleries. A young man led us to the more interesting exhibits. He told us that the Romans had been easy-going regarding the different religions in the lands they'd conquered, and had often combined the indigenous gods with their own. When they'd come to Britain they'd brought with them several religions from the eastern part of their empire such as Mithras from Persia, the great mother goddess Cybele from Anatolia, and the mother goddess Isis from Egypt - he didn't mention the Son of God, Jesus, who'd been born in Palestine under Roman rule.

He waved an arm, pointing up or down like a railway signal, at various marble heads which had been recovered from the temple of Mithras in London. There was a head of Minerva, goddess of wisdom, another of Mercury, guardian of the souls of the deceased, and small clay figures of Venus and, most important of all, a head of Mithras, a head I'd taken to be of a beautiful young woman. But, no, it was of Mithras the god, the Phrygian cap he wore identified him as he always wore it. From where I stood I thought it looked less like a cap than a cobra draped over the crown of his head.

The arm pointed to a clay tablet with four mother goddesses, suggesting the worship of such deities. I was interested in the fact that the Virgin Mary had replaced these pagan mother goddess figures. In fact, I'd read that there had actually been a fourth century sect in north-east Greece called Collyridians who had worshipped the Virgin Mary as a goddess - something which the early Christian fathers had been quick to stamp out.

We came to a limestone relief from the ruins of the temple of Mithras in the City. Mithras had been symbolic of the ever-rising, unconquered sun. Persians had believed him to be the son of the one great creator God, Ahura Mazda, god of all goodness and light; they regarded Mithras as the mediator between his father and mankind, somewhat similar to Jesus, Son of God, who is mediator in Christianity.

With a lot of arm waving and signalling, the guide indicated the rituals and beliefs of Mithraism. In the centre of the relief was Mithras in the act of killing the sacrificial bull, with his eyes averted. Blood was spurting from the wound - the blood of purification and eternal life. This large circular marble disk also depicted the wheel of the year with the signs of the zodiac. At the top, placed outside the circle, was Sol (the sun) ascending to the heavens, with Luna (the moon) opposite in her chariot. On either side of the bull-sacrifice were two torch bearers, Cautes and Cautopates (the guide had to repeat the names so I could scribble them down as I'd never heard of them). Cautes was symbolic of light and held a torch up towards the sky, while Cautopates, was symbolic of darkness, and held his pointing downwards. Light was central to the Mithras religion - light against darkness, the eternal fight between good and evil.

Mithraism, our guide informed us, had been for men only, and had been very popular with the Roman army as it had been a religion of honour, courage, faith, trust and also believed in resurrection.

When I asked Harry afterwards over a pot of tea in the café why he thought it was - since both Christianity and Mithraism believed in resurrection - people had switched from Mithraism where only a bull was sacrificed, to Christianity where the Son of God had been, he replied he hadn't a clue. If I wanted the answer to that sort of question, then I must ask someone at St. Paul's cathedral the next day, and he immediately began telling me about the million year old auroch skull he'd just seen, and a bison's skull, and neolithic axes dredged up from the Thames. His thoughts were far removed from my Roman ones, though the mention of the Thames reminded me of something our guide had said. Water, he'd told us, had been regarded as the gift of the gods because it came from the heavens as rain, and came up from the depths of the earth as springs. Votive offerings had been thrown into the river to be carried off to the gods, and so had curses which in those days had been taken very seriously.

When Harry had finished his account of skulls and bones and axes, I told him about one of the exhibits our guide had spent time on, an implement which looked like ornamental brass nut-crackers. They were, the guide had informed us, not at all what they appeared to be, large nut-crackers with serrated edges, but castration clamps used for castrating the priests of the mother goddess Cybele. They'd been found in the Thames close to London Bridge, suggesting that this mother goddess had been worshipped in Roman London.

"Well, there you are!" said Harry positively. "That's why Christianity spread - no castration!"

The next day was Sunday, the day of the Sun (and the day was sunny). Since it was the holy day of Mithras, it was appropriate to hunt out his temple which had been dug up from its original site on the east bank of the Walbrook (once a tributary of the river Thames, but now a road), and re-sited in Queen Victoria Street behind St. Paul's cathedral.

Being a weekend there was again little traffic: a few cars, several cyclists, and the occasional red double-decker bus trundling along. The road was flanked by imposing buildings. We tramped along in what I hoped was the right direction, and came to a long stretch of dark green hoarding alongside the pavement.

"Excuse me, but can you tell me where the Temple of Mithras is?" I enquired of an elderly woman with a small dog who looked as though she lived nearby and might know.

The woman appeared mystified, and turned this way and that with an index finger to her lips as she gave the matter some thought. "Is it one of these Hindu temples, dear?"

"No."

"A mosque, then?"

"No, it's an ancient ruin."

"Oh, then I can't tell you. Maybe if you hail a taxi, the driver will know? Sorry, dear." And she and her dog went on their way.

We continued along the hoarding which I reckoned was hiding building work, ignoring Harry's 'you'll never find it!' then came to a gap in the hoarding before it stretched on again. In the gap were dreary looking stones around hard-packed earth, and a small notice stating it was the temple of Mithras.

"All the way to London to see that! Good grief! I could have built you that at home!" was Harry's instant comment.

Whatever it had once been, it was no longer. There were no magnificent marble columns, sculptures or statues, or anything at all to inspire me, let alone Harry. The whole temple area was surprisingly small.

Various finds suggested that other Roman deities had also been honoured there: Bacchus (the Roman god of wine and drama, known as Dionysos to the Greeks) had been a popular god. Hercules was another - he had been a mortal raised to the status of deity at his death. Traces of the Dioscuri had also been found; they, like Hercules, were mortal and raised to god status to become protectors of sailors. They'd all been sons of the supreme god, Zeus, by various mortal beauties.

My thoughts were interrupted by Harry. "Back to St. Paul's, then, before we freeze to death!" he announced, and began walking.

Reluctantly, I turned from the disappointing ruins of the temple of Mithras and followed him.

There were many people from many lands converging on St. Paul's that Sunday morning. I particularly wanted to approach it from Ludgate Circus, because it was how it should be done to appreciate its architectural beauty. It was a major landmark in the history of London and it was important to do it justice. Harry didn't care how I approached it, so long as he didn't have to walk further than strictly necessary, so said he would wait on the steps of the cathedral for me.

I made my way down to Ludgate Circus, that small bull's eye of a circle where four roads converge: New Bridge Street coming from Blackfriars Bridge which meets with Farringdon Street, Fleet Street and Ludgate Hill. Ludgate was the gate of King Ludd, and there was a possibility that he'd been Llud of the Silver Hand, a legendary hero in Welsh mythology. His lineage was thought in some convoluted way to have come from the god Nodens, a river god of the Severn estuary.* Some thought that there'd once been a temple of Ludd where St. Paul's now stands.

But far more interesting to me was the belief that there had been a temple of Diana there. She'd been the goddess who'd come in a vision to Brutus and had instructed him to come to Britain.

I noticed as I walked back up Ludgate Hill that it was not so much a hill as a very gentle slope. The huge domed edifice of St. Paul's, topped by its cupola and gilded cross stood majestically ahead, dwarfing the small figure who stood smiling on the steps as he saw me coming. Maybe the cathedral's immensity and beauty was a deliberate attempt to clobber the egos of mere mortals who paled into insignificance before this stupendous architectural masterpiece. Its grand facade with its Parthenon-like central feature on which stood statues of the apostles standing guard, and flanked by baroque towers, were powerful attractions in themselves, though the eye was continually drawn back to the great central dome and the gold cross against the skyline.

The present St. Paul's cathedral was the inspiration of Sir Christopher Wren after its destruction in the Great Fire of London. It was the third time since its foundation that it had been burned to the ground. The miracle of today's building was that it had survived the London Blitz when buildings all around had been destroyed by bombs. It was tempting to think that it had been the Almighty's intervention that had saved it - an Almighty hand batting away the bombs as they threatened his sacred building.

The first cathedral church had been built there in 604 A.D. by

*See Lydney Park chapter.

a St. Mellitus who had been sent by Pope Gregory I, to hurry up the conversion of the heathen English. As St. Paul had been the key figure in spreading Christianity, so the cathedral was dedicated to him, and he became patron saint of London.

The inside of the cathedral was even more magnificent than its exterior, and full of light. We walked down the nave with its many Corinthian columns and archways, and gazed at its semi-domes with scenes from the life of Christ depicted in glistening mosaics. Nothing was too much or too little, all was a harmonious whole, superbly planned to the minutest detail in order to give aesthetic pleasure. Around the walls were marble statues and tombs and plaques in memory of men of renown who had served their country.

After wandering around the main body of the cathedral we went down to the crypt where there was a shop and café. We'd been told evensong was to be held at three-fifteen so we were glad to sit and rest before the occasion.

We'd just seen Holman Hunt's great masterpiece The Light of the World and I'd been struck by how the halo appeared to be singular to Christian art.

"You know the halo?" I asked Harry.

"The halo halo?"

"What else?"

"What about it?"

"Do you suppose they used halos around the heads of Jesus and his saints in order to lure Mithras worshippers to Christianity?" I asked.

"I haven't the foggiest."

"What's the betting the word comes from the Greek for sun which is 'helios'."

"I'm sure you can make halo into whatever you like," Harry said, finishing his soup with a flourish.

In fact I later discovered that the etymology for 'halo' came from the Greek 'halos', meaning 'disk of the sun or moon, ring of light around the sun or moon', which I thought gave a certain clout to my inspired theory that Christianity had adopted it to win over Mithras worshippers.

At two-thirty the bells of St. Paul's began to peel in multiple thunderous, tumbling tones. We went up to the main body of the cathedral, and found a couple of dignified, silver-haired men in pin-striped trousers, and tail coats, each with a red ribbon around his neck from which hung a gold medallion; they were standing by a cordoned off area, to greet those wanting to attend evensong. I mouthed a hushed thank-you at the one who handed me a service sheet together with a small envelope for a donation. As he wasn't exactly pressed for time and there was nobody else waiting, I said pleasantly and, no doubt, stupidly: "What wonderful bells. Are they switched on electrically like the call to prayer in mosques?"

The silver-haired warden/marshall/usher, or whatever official position he held, drew himself up. "Most certainly they are not! We have a set of twelve bells and twelve bell-ringers!"

"A dozen bells!" I said in amazement. "Like twelve apostles, and twelve tribes of Israel?" I queried. The words had come out spontaneously as twelve seemed to be a mystical number for so many things.

"Indeed!" said the warden/marshall/usher, and he handed an evensong service sheet and small envelope for a donation to Harry. As I had the man's whole attention for this brief moment, I couldn't resist another question.

"Is it true that there was once a temple of the pagan goddess Diana here before St. Paul's was built?" I enquired.

He eyed me steadily. It was a rogue question and one that needed unaccustomed thought.

"Indeed, I understand that might once have been so," he replied, eyeing me cautiously.

As he wasn't aghast I asked another question.

"And that there was once a temple of Apollo where Westminster Abbey now stands?"

Harry took my arm before I ploughed on with the question he himself had suggested, about why Christianity had taken over from Mithraism when both religions believed in resurrection, and the latter only required a bull sacrifice. The warden/marshall/usher also decided it was time to cut short this pagan interest in this Christian establishment.

"I think not," he murmured (our conversation was conducted in low tones). "Down at Westminster there was nothing but bog and marsh. A pagan temple at Westminster would have been impossible." There was a finality to his voice as he looked past me to greet a Japanese tourist and his wife, and to hand out another two evensong service sheets, and two more small envelopes for donations.

We sat near the front as the organist began to play. The fortissimo, and sometimes pianissimo flute-like tones, were a brilliant way of building up the spiritual levels of those who were seated for evensong, and to encourage others within earshot to come, either those below in the crypt, or outside walking up Ludgate Hill.

Before us on the floor was a large red, black and white marble star around which was engraved an epitaph to Sir Christopher Wren. The black and white check floor stretched on to the chancel steps, beyond which were the choir stalls. Nearby on the right was a large impressive and ornately carved and canopied pulpit. I noticed from the service sheet that the Dean of St. Paul's was to preach.

Seated there awaiting evensong I was able to admire the series of gilded and inter-linking domes decorated with glistening mosaic scenes which led onwards to the High Altar. Above the High Altar was a mosaic of Christ the King whose head was ringed with the all important halo.

The difference between Mithraism and Christianity was that in the former there was a baptism with the blood of the bull which was sacrificed for the occasion, and in the latter with holy water which was considerably more pleasant.

It was interesting, though, that after baptism in either the initiate was believed to have been purified and absolved of his sins. Some scholars claim that the eucharist of the Christian faith, a shared sacred meal of bread and wine, originated in Mithraism.

And just as the day for the birth of Mithras was midwinter on the day of the winter solstice (the day which heralded the increase in the light of the sun), so same period was decided on for the birth of Christ in the fourth century. Before then there was no known date for his nativity. Augustine of Hippo advised all Christians who attended the Roman festival of Sol Invictus (the Invincible Sun) which also celebrated the rebirth of the sun's strength, not to worship the sun itself, but the great Almighty God who'd created it.

As for the mysterious number twelve, is it coincidence that Mithras had twelve priests, and Jesus centuries later had twelve disciples?

Maybe religion was just a question of being aware that the mystical, although unseen, existed; after all, there were a lot of things which were invisible though you were aware of them. If you sang a hymn, or a psalm, for example, you couldn't see the music in the air; if you prayed, you didn't see the words spoken; if you pondered something, you couldn't see the thoughts. God may be there - or he may not. The idea of him at least stretches the human mind beyond itself which does no harm.

Evensong began and the choir (men only this afternoon) came in in their white surplices over black, led by a small woman with short straight hair and spectacles wearing a black gown and carrying before her what looked like a silver wand. The choir was followed by a priest and the dean, and the long column ended with a man in black also carrying a silver wand. Throughout the service the priest went nowhere, nor did the dean, without the woman or man with the silver wand leading the way.

A psalm was sung which contained words referring to 'the Lord hath chosen Jacob unto himself: and Israel for his own possession...' which immediately made me wonder why since it had triggered so much misery and human conflict.

The wand led the dean to the steps of the pulpit, and then stood aside for him to mount up to deliver his sermon. We were told that God, when he created the world, deliberately kept back in his jar (I supposed he was making a sort of comparison with Pandora's box) rest and contentment because God knew that otherwise men would never strive after him. I didn't think that was in the bible at all, but it was an interesting concept. I did strive after God, but why I'd no idea.

After the sermon the wand led the dean back to his place, and a hymn was sung while Harry and I hunted for money to put into our envelopes. We were ill prepared and had to decide between parting with twenty pound notes or two fifty pence pieces.

The silver-haired wardens/marshalls/ushers, with their red ribbons and medallions, trod around with their offertory plates. They handed the plate to the first in the line, and it was handed on from person to person. We placed our small envelopes with the others, and I hoped the outline of the coin couldn't be detected, but the man who received back our plate gave me a sharp sideways look as though he knew I'd withheld my twenty pound note. He then went forward with dignity, like a butler with a glass of whisky for m'lord, and delivered it to the dean (maybe it was the priest) who received the offertory plate with its fifty pence pieces, and raised it high above the altar for God's blessing.

The hymn over, we remained standing to receive our own final blessing, before the woman with her silver wand led the procession of choir and clergy back to the vestry, with the second wand taking up the rear.

We finally left to the sound of the organ playing an all-senses-into-the-melting-pot Organ Voluntary. It was yet another day of failed enlightenment. But tomorrow in Westminster Abbey I might get that long awaited certainty that Almighty God existed.

We emerged from Westminster underground into Whitehall where pedestrians thronged the pavement waiting for the traffic lights to turn red, and a little green man to give them the all clear to cross over to the central island. Black taxi-cabs, private cars, red double-decker buses and tour coaches streamed past.

For a moment we stood bewildered and unable to get our bearings. It was a bright sunny day, and the sky was blue with woolly threads of white cloud. It was the sort of cold but crisp early spring day that cheered everybody up, and instilled renewed optimism and an upsurge of energy. We were so close to the Houses of Parliament that we were unable to see them, hence our inability to identify our surroundings. A couple of police officers wearing yellow vests were on duty at one of the gates; they had the phosphorescent word 'police' printed on their chests for idiots who needed to know they weren't firemen or dustmen. They pointed us in the right direction for the Abbey, and we crossed the road at the lights, skirted Parliament Square, passed St. Margaret's Church and came at last to the immense Gothic edifice of Westminster Abbey.

Westminster had once been an island known as Thorney Island. When I'd told Harry we were going to Thorney Island, he had supposed we were to take a boat, till I explained that the Westminster area had been an island at the time of the Romans, caused by the Thames and two tributaries of the river Tyburn. The silver-haired gentleman at St. Paul's Cathedral had been right to say the area had been marshy, though wrong in supposing the Romans couldn't drain and build there, so there could well have been a temple of Apollo there. We were unprepared for a queue at the ticket office before being allowed into the Abbey. The entry fee was now a hefty fifteen pounds a head (twelve pounds concession rates) unless we were there to worship, in which case we could go in free. No small envelopes here in the hope of donations. No. Payment first, then entry.

It didn't stop people coming. While we waited in the queue I tried to imagine myself on Thorney Island all those centuries ago. In the seventh century A.D. when it was still an island, a church had been built here and the same Mellitus who'd founded St. Paul's Cathedral in 604 A.D., dedicated the small church to St. Peter - well, that was his intention. In fact, legend has it that the day before he was due to do it St. Peter himself came flying down from heaven to perform the consecration. For some reason he landed at Lambeth and had to ask a fisherman to ferry him across the Thames to Thorney Island, rewarding him with good salmon fishing for life so long as he never fished on Sundays. On setting foot on Thorney Island St. Peter struck the ground twice which mysteriously produced two springs; he then dedicated the church in his own name and flew back to heaven. When Bishop Mellitus arrived for the dedication ceremony the following day he found he'd been beaten to it by the great apostle himself; what he thought goes unrecorded.

So there had been two early churches in London, one in honour of St. Peter and the other of St. Paul, replacing the two pagan temples, one of Apollo and the other of his twin sister, Diana.

Another few paces forward. Now that we were very near the ticket office, Harry said he thought there was absolutely no point in spending all that money on two tickets, when we could get inside for nothing if we wanted to worship. I said, there were certain things I needed to see, but if he wanted to say his prayers at no expense, I was quite happy to enter alone, and so our ways parted. In fact, when we met up later, he admitted he hadn't liked to ask if he could go in to worship only, so had gone to see the Houses of Parliament and the river Thames from Westminster Bridge instead.

The sombre dark interior of Westminster Abbey with its numerous ribbed columns rising to pointed Gothic arches, its high vaulted and fanned ceilings, chapels, stained-glass windows and memorials, made all who entered feel they were at the very heart of British history.

Thanks to the audio device which came with the ticket, I learned that up some wooden steps was Edward the Confessor's Chapel. A woman in a pale green gown (all officials in the Abbey wore them and looked relaxed and approachable) stood beside the steps and smiled as I drew near. The steps were cordoned off and only those prepared to join in a ten-minute prayer session which was about to begin were allowed up, she told me.

I said I would like to attend and she unhooked the cord to let me pass. The few people waiting to take part in the prayers sat on wooden benches facing Edward the Confessor's large shrine, a three-tiered monument in sombre colours with small gilded colonnades around it. Beyond was an ornately carved marble pulpit in Gothic style, with a sculpted figure wearing a crown which I supposed must be Edward the Confessor. Beyond the chapel were solid pillared columns supporting high pointed ribbed arches.

A priest in suitable vestments for the occasion stood before the altar on which was a white altar cloth, brass candlesticks and a large cross. A heavy black metal tomb was to my left containing the bones of Edward. All was holy and in keeping with the Abbey's historic past.

The priest welcomed his small gathering, then in solemn, measured tones began the prayers at the end of which, instead of saying the usual 'we beseech thee, oh Lord,' or 'Good Lord, deliver us', he said, 'Holy Edward, grant us', or 'we beseech thee, Holy Edward'. When the prayer session was over, I asked him why he'd used 'Holy Edward'. Because, the king was canonized, I was told.

"Oh, really? So is he St. Edward?"

"St. Edward the Confessor," said the priest.

"And the word 'Confessor'?" I asked.

"That's because he confessed the faith. It was he who founded the Abbey at Westminster."

"But there was an early Church of St. Peter here, wasn't there?" I asked.

"Oh, certainly. The Abbey was built around the church," came the reply.

As the priest looked interested, I then asked: "Do you know whether before the early church there was a temple of Apollo?"

"That could well be so," came the ready reply. "The early Christians often built on old pagan sites." No curt dismissal. No hot denial. We shook hands and I thanked him and left.

Moving on I came to the Coronation Chair elevated on a high stand, its back to Edward the Confessor's Chapel.

Of all the unroyal looking seats, this was it. Highly polished, but on the shabby side. I doubted an antique dealer would be keen to have it in his shop with the graffiti scratched over the back where Westminster schoolboys had carved their initials.

The original plan had been for a bronze chair which would have been appropriate for the crowning of a monarch, but it was soon realized it would be too expensive and, as money was short, so this wooden one was commissioned in its place. It was of oak, had a high pointed back, sloping solid sides for the monarch's arms, quatrefoils below the seat, and a lion at each corner for support. Had the chair been of marble it would have been remarkably similar to the one I'd seen on which the mother goddess Cybele was often portrayed.

The Coronation Chair had been constructed in order to take the Stone of Destiny under the seat for the crowning of the monarch, and had been used as such since 1399, some think even earlier. The Stone of Destiny had for years been a point of fierce controversy between England and Scotland. Much to the latter's fury it had been seized from Scotland by Edward I (not Edward the Confessor) after a fierce battle and brought to England. It is now back in Scotland on the understanding it will be allowed back to the Abbey for the coronation of British monarchs.

I'd seen photographs of the Stone, and a boring lump of sandstone it appeared to be. But it wasn't just any old Stone, it was one with a story. It was reputed to be the Stone which had been Jacob's Pillow (Abraham's grandson); the Stone on which Jacob laid his head and dreamed of a ladder reaching to the heavens with angels ascending and descending it. At the time he'd been very aware of the presence of God, and God had spoken to him promising him his protection and his guidance, and to his numerous descendants also, so long as they all worshipped him and kept his commandments. (Genesis 28: 11-17).

I hoped to see the Stone itself one day in Edinburgh, but meanwhile here was the Coronation Chair. In due course it would be placed before the High Altar for the crowning and annointing of the next monarch with the Stone of Destiny beneath it. A quotation from a psalm (Psalm 118:22) has been found to give it greater authenticity: 'The stone which the builders refused is become the head stone of the corner'. It is odd how the human mind can soar with imaginative ideas which become legitimized and sanctified and consequently accepted as truth despite scientifically proven evidence to the contrary.*

I left the Coronation Chair, looked in at Poet's Corner, then at the superb Henry III Chapel nearby with its impressive tombs, stained-glass windows and fanned ceiling as exquisite as the finest lace. I continued on to Henry III's Chapter House. Facing its entrance were the large arched windows in the octagonal walls, each with panels of stained-glass with coats of arms of those who'd contributed historically

*Chapter 8 on Edinburgh goes into more detail on the Stone.

or financially to the Abbey. Below the windows were three tiered-steps on which those assembled for a meeting would sit, and between the top step and the windows were triple-arched recesses with medieval wall paintings. The floor tiles were also magnificent in a dark russet hue, with geometric patterns, and the three lions of England flanked by centaurs (half man, half horse, figures from ancient Greece). Images of salmon also were a reminder of the apostle Peter's gift of good salmon fishing to the ferryman who'd brought him to Thorney Island; or they could equally well have represented the ancient secret symbol used by the early Christians when they'd feared persecution.

I went on to the Abbey cloisters. Few people were there. From it I could see across a stretch of grass to the main outer body of the present great Abbey. Along the cloister walls were carved memorials.

I walked on to another area where I saw a door ajar marked 'Private'. As it was open I peered through to a grassy rectangular patch. Around this area were medieval houses which I took to be grace and favour houses for the dean and others attached to the Abbey. It was a secret corner in the heart of London which few people were aware of.

I stood and stared at this oasis. Could the several column drums I was looking at possibly be the ruined remains of the early temple of Apollo? Or were they there for urns and flower pots in the summer?

I remembered King Bladud who'd discovered the hot healing springs at Bath, and recalled the story that he'd fixed a pair of feathered wings to his shoulders attached with wax (like the ancient tale of Daedalus). Legend had it that King Bladud had flown through the sky all the way to London where the wax had melted and he'd fallen to his death on the temple of Apollo which, if true, would have been where I was now standing.

Strange tales. King Bladud's son had been King Lear, of Shakespearean fame, and when he'd died his daughter had buried him near Leicester in a chamber dedicated to the god Janus - a Roman god who was depicted with two faces looking in opposite directions.

I found myself in the Little Cloister, the most ancient part of the Abbey, looking out at what was said to be the oldest garden in London, the College Garden, created in 1065. There was a rectangle of grass with a central paved area and a fountain. Around the edges of the grass were flowering hellebore, while in the grass were snowdrops and mauve crocus. Was this, I wondered, the earliest part of the Abbey attached to the Church of St. Peter? This Abbey was later to become known as West Minster, while St. Paul's was the East Minster because it too had had a monastery.

I looked at my watch and saw it was time to drag myself away from this oasis in the heart of London, away from where the audio told me the monks had had a pig farm, orchards, vineyards and had grown herbs and vegetables. Beyond the rectangle of this Little Cloister was a high Gothic tower, which I thought might be the Houses of Parliament. High in the blue sky a passenger jet gleamed in the sunshine, its vapour trail a thin silver line behind it.

Yes, it was time to go; time to meet up with Harry at Waterloo station.

Waterloo station. No Harry yet, so I am sitting on one of those ice-cold, clamped-to-the-ground metal seats in the station forecourt eating a sandwich. I have my back to the platforms and am looking towards the entrance and exit of the Jubilee Line underground. I have an uncouth looking fellow on my right, and a reasonably pleasant looking youth on my left. For security I have my handbag hooked around my neck, the opening flap against my ribs.

It's amazing watching people pass by - coming, going, hesitating, some rushing for a train. There is a man waiting anxiously and at last being greeted by his girlfriend, a look of relief and delight on his face. A harrassed mother with a push-chair and a child in it - another with her small four year old daughter in a pink woolly outfit walking as fast as she can beside her mother wearing a denim jacket, and a short flowery skirt over black tights and ankle boots - a Moslem woman with her head covered in a white silk scarf wearing a long black coat - a poverty-sricken, unshaven Asian is standing by the wall near the ticket office being questioned by a patient young policeman; I wonder whether he is an asylum seeker newly arrived in this busy, self-obsessed city. Now a heavily built man is swaggering by with his Rottweiler on a lead, and they disappear down the steps to the Jubilee Line.

And all these people are in motion, driven by some inner force and energy directing them here or there away from home. Now a turbaned Sikh and his beautiful wife in a sari pass me looking up at the notice boards. And there comes Harry behind them, his eyes scanning the departure board. I call his name and he stops and turns towards my voice. "Oh, there you are!" he says with relief. "They haven't put up the number of our platform yet."

The youth beside me whom I think is a lout turns out to be a really nice young man as he gets up and offers Harry his seat. We thank him and he slouches off.

Harry says he had a sandwich on a seat beside the Thames. He says it was surprisingly warm in the sunshine out of the wind, and he enjoyed watching the tugs, motor-launches and barges going up and down the river. He saw a seagull pecking a duck to death, he tells me; a vicious, diabolical act of cruelty undertaken by one living creature on another. He's never had anything against seagulls, he says, but now he can see the evil in their eyes. The poor duck was resigned. Didn't you throw stones at it, I ask? No, because the tide carried them both up river out of reach, and he couldn't find anything to throw except his sandwich and, thanks a lot, he wasn't going to lose that, it cost over two quid.

Peace and tranquillity in certain parts of London, but horror stories too; lots of fear, loathsome ugly goings on you hope never to see or experience. The law of contrasts: good and evil - beauty and ugliness - tranquillity and stress. And so it goes on.

Our platform number comes up, and we hurry off to our train.

⋇⋇⋇

I'm in semi-slumbering mode, vaguely remembering things I wish I'd done and maybe will do one day. The Tower of London, for instance. It is said that the head of the giant, Bendigeidfran, commonly known as Bran, and supposedly once king of Britain, is buried there. He was Welsh and went to war with Ireland. The reason for this war was because Bran had arranged that his sister should marry the king of Ireland. But, as he hadn't consulted his half-brother about these great marital arrangements, his half-brother became annoyed and caused trouble, whereupon the king of Ireland was outraged and everyone was furious. Things only calmed down and peace restored when Bran offered the Irish king his greatest treasure, the Cauldron of Rebirth. But the marriage was not a happy one, and the new bride was treated badly and condemned to the palace kitchen to do the chores. When Bran received word from her about her situation, he set sail with an invading army. Being a giant of great stature no ship could carry him, and so he waded through the Irish Sea alongside his fleet.

During the course of the battle Bran was fatally wounded, and his last request was that he should be decapitated and his head buried on Tower Hill in London with his eyes towards France so that he could keep the British safe from invasion. Bran's head, however, didn't stop the Romans from invading in 43 A.D. Then later, when King Arthur reigned, he had the nerve to declare that a mere dead giant's head was of no use at all, and only he himself, a Christian king, could be relied upon to keep the enemy from British soil. He defied all such superstitious nonsense and had Bran's head dug up, which some may say was why the Saxons invaded and, though at first successfully repulsed by King Arthur, were ultimately victorious.

Today, the safety of Britain is believed to be dependent on the ravens at the Tower of London, not to mention the London Stone and the two giants, Gog and Magog. The Celts regarded ravens as sacred birds; they were thought to be the messengers of war, even the embodiment of dead warriors. Because ravens are carnivorous, they were once connected with death, and also with fertility and new life. Their cry was regarded as the voice of the gods of war (and Bran was considered a god as well as a king). His full name, Bendigeidfran in fact means 'Blessed Raven'.

It is, of course, still believed that if the Tower of London ravens fly off, Britain will be doomed. There is a warden appointed as keeper of these birds who are tagged, named and have their wings clipped. In reality, it is all a lot of superstitious nonsense. During World War II the ravens were either blown to bits in the bombing, or died of fright or of old age, or else they flew away. That suddenly the ravens were gone was kept hushed up in order that public morale wouldn't crack. It is interesting how superstition can instil fear and defeatism.

My somnolent state is interrupted by the refreshment trolley being trundled through our carriage. We buy ourselves snacks and drinks. The sun is setting, and the sky over the Wiltshire downs is spread with a nearly transparent dove grey film of cloud. The sun itself is an opalescent brilliance which I can't look at - a sort of transfiguration.

Where to next, I wonder?

CHAPTER FIVE

LYDNEY PARK

Spring is here! It is the end of April and the day is fine and warm. The hawthorn's out, decorating the hillsides with a haze of white. The woodlands are showing the first signs of leaf, some trees are already shades of green, and here and there we see wild cherry blossom.

I try to look at England as though I were a foreigner and realize how fortunate we are with our multiplicity of deciduous trees. An Arab coming from the Middle East would marvel at the sight of England's countryside if he or she was only used to desert dust and palm trees. How many countries have such subtle colours and variety to their landscape?

Harry is driving and keeps telling me that on this fine spring day he should be home digging his vegetable garden. I ignore this as I am glad the sun is shining on this one day we've arranged to see the temple of the Celtic god Nodens at Lydney Park close to the Forest of Dean.

I am map-reading - well, not looking at the road-map really, but calling out the list of B- or A-roads we should take, as well as the villages we should pass through which Harry's jotted down for me. So far I have successfully brought him to Bathampton. It is east of Bath and here we cross over the river Avon, and have to pay a pound for the privilege of getting to the other side.

Bathampton is a most attractive place with picturesque pubs overlooking the river where there is a weir like the one we saw in Bath itself when we were there. It would be nice to stop but Harry has but one purpose and that is to get me to that temple and back home again. So we drive on.

We cross the river Severn over the suspension bridge, an engineering feat which is one to marvel at as here the river is about a kilometre and a half wide. Soon a notice informs us we are entering Wales, but not long after, another tells us we are back in England. Why do I feel absurdly proud to be back in my own country? There seems to be in all of us an innate sense of where our roots belong which we call home.

In due course, and with extraordinary luck as I happen to be looking in the right direction at that moment, I see a signpost pointing to our left with the words Lydney Park on it.

We turn into a long driveway lined with daffodils. Parkland stretches either side in which are stately trees, a herd of cows, and on our left a deer park where numerous fallow-deer are grazing.

We drive up to the house, a grey stone building with a French castle-like pointed slated tower at one end, and a square one at the other. It is a mix of different architectural features, of after-thought additions. Before its entrance a magnolia is in full bloom.

We follow notices and head for the car park, stopping first where we have to buy our entry tickets. We pay our dues, pay extra for a booklet to tell us what is where, and drive down a slope to park the car amongst the few others in a wide valley.

A signpost points us to the Roman Camp and temple up a hillside path. Numerous trees stand loftily, each one exhibiting its height and width to advantage as we climb the track. There are oak trees just in leaf; many others that we can't identify, and one close to the path with a massive girth, its bark etched and rugged with vertical strata, making us curious as to what species it can be; it is misshapen with a scar of a round hole which looks like an eye, and an odd branch like a protruding horn which, together with the eye, we think resembles a rhinoceros; we do not recognize its newly-from-the-bud foliage, but learn later it is a sweet chestnut.

A whiff of deer reaches us as it wafts our way on a gentle breeze. On the stony hillside by the path we glimpse miniature violets and wild strawberry flowers. Harry is impressed. In fact, he is enjoying his day, and is glad to be out and walking on this fine spring morning where nature is renewing itself after its winter sleep.

The Celtic god Nodens was associated with water and with healing. If the ruins of the temple complex on the four and a half acre summit of the hill were not exactly attention-grabbing, the choice for their location was. The entrance to the temple's inner sanctum (the cella) was aligned south-east, as opposed to the usual rising-sun direction to the east. Normally the cult statue kept within a cella would face the rising sun, but here if there had been a cult statue at all, it would have looked towards something quite unusual and amazing, a bow-shaped stretch of the river Severn, its over-a-mile-wide sheen of water about two miles distant appearing to curve gently with the contour of the hill we stood on. It was glimpsed through distant trees, a wide glint of water in the spring sunshine.

As we stared out towards the Severn in the distance, I told Harry how the god Nodens was said to be the father of the Irish Nuada or Nudd, alias Lludd in Welsh myth, or Lud of Ludgate Hill and London fame - Lud of the Silver Hand, some think.

"You remember Gwynn ap Nudd, leader of the Wild Hunt, who lived in his kingdom on the Tor at Glastonbury?" I asked.

"Didn't he gallop out on Hallowe'en on his spectral horses with his Hounds of Hell?" Harry queried.

"That's the one. Well, ap Nudd means 'son of Nudd' and as Nudd is a variant of Nodens, so Nodens must be Gwynn's father."

"Well, whatever," said Harry, raising his binoculars to his eyes.

A couple of women appeared up the track. They had the distinctive air of English upper class, the older one with wild grey hair, and wearing a tweed skirt, sensible shoes and ribbed stockings, the younger dressed casually in trousers, with longish dark hair, clear complexion and rather beautiful features.

"Well, I'm jolly well sitting down having got here," said the older woman who turned out to be the younger one's mother. "I don't know where your father's got to, still talking trees with the head gardner, I suppose."

The daughter, holding the Lydney Park booklet open, called out to her mother: "It says here that the main activity of the Romans on this site was centred around iron-mining and Nodens was Lord of the Iron Mines."

"It's such a lovely day! Poor old Snap, I don't think we should have left him. I wish your father would take him to the vet and put him out of his misery."

"For heaven's sake, Mummy! I gave Snap a piece of my bacon this morning and he gobbled it." The girl was studying another book. "The temple itself was twenty-four by eighteen metres! That's quite big."

"Still, he's had a good life. Jolly good gun-dog."

"This must be the ambulatory which was three metres wide."

"Poor Snap. He would have loved it here."

"Mother!"

An energetic figure came climbing up the hillside, a florid faced man with iron-grey hair, open shirt, and corduroy trousers. He reached the summit near to where we stood and was greeted by the woman: "Oh, there you are, darling! Trust you to come up the steep way!"

"Sweet chestnut, the fellow said."

"Wouldn't Snap have loved it here!"

"Not in his condition, he wouldn't. So long as he enjoys his grub I'm not taking him to the vet. So what have we here?" he asked, joining his daughter.

"It says in this book that the name Lydney comes from 'Lydan-eg', meaning 'Ludd's Island'."

"Ludd? Never heard of Ludd. Are these stones the reason why you've dragged us all this way?"

"They're Roman, Daddy."

"Mr. Ludd's old home?"

"Daddy, do be serious! Look, this is where the old temple was. And this is the dormitory."

"Could have fooled me. Think I'll take a recce while you get inspiration from Mr. Ludd's stones." The man left his daughter and walked up the back of the ruins where he stood looking out at the view.

Harry twiddled the knobs on his binoculars to get a clearer focus. "It must be quite something to see the Severn bore sweep up from the estuary," he remarked.

I'd forgotten the Severn bore, and Harry was right. At certain high tides, the rising water was forced upstream in a tidal wave causing a rapid rise in the water level as it went. This phenomenon began at the curve of the Severn we were actually looking at, to which the temple was aligned, and the tidal wave continued on upstream for some twenty miles. Was this location for the temple of Nodens at Lydney Park chosen specifically for this reason? I began to think it must be. To me the hill and river were unique, and I could understand the ancient desire to honour the god with whom water and well-being were associated.

A reconstructed illustration in the booklet made the whole Roman complex look something like a medieval village; I would never have recognized it as a religious centre as there were none of the customary columns and architraves of a classical temple. The Romans had developed this temple site in the late fourth century, not long before they withdrew from Britain in the early fifth. They roofed and enclosed the temple against the elements and surrounded it with an ambulatory, or a processional way, now grassed over, but still traceable by the remaining ruined walls.

The young girl smiled at me and said: "Are you a Roman expert?"

"I'm afraid not. I'm more interested in ancient Greek and how the Romans adopted their old pagan gods. And here, of course, how the Romans tied their gods in with the Celtic ones."

"It says here there were chapels. Do you think that means Christian chapels?"

"I don't think so. Possibly it means smaller sanctuaries."

"I'm only wondering because Nodens was worshipped here till the late fourth century, long after Christianity had been recognized by Constantine the Great."

"Interesting," I said.

The girl's father by now was standing beside Harry gazing out towards the Severn. I heard him say: "Spot any foxes?" Harry lowered his binoculars

"I should have brought my own glasses, but what with mucking out the stables and feeding the horses, I clean forgot."

"Here, take a look."

"That's very good of you, if you wouldn't mind." He took the glasses and raised them to his eyes, adjusted the focus, then scanned around the panoramic view.

"Must be hundreds of foxes since the blighters banned fox-hunting," he commented. "So much drivel spoken about cruelty, don't you know! The damned fox gives as good as he gets. Got all of my ducks one night. I wouldn't have minded if he'd been hungry, but he frightened the life out of them, and left the dead bodies for me to pick up. Bring back fox-hunting I say!" He scanned the countryside, and said: "Good God! I never knew the Severn was so wide!"

The girl said to me: "So what gods did the Romans tie in with Nodens?"

"Apparently Mars was one of them," I said. "He was the

equivalent of Ares, the Greek god of war, which is odd since Nodens was a god of healing."

"He healed the wounded, perhaps?" the girl suggested.

"Maybe that was it," I agreed. "They also equated Nodens with their Roman god Mercury. He was the equivalent of the Greek Hermes, who guided the souls of the dead to Hades. I suppose that makes sense if he failed to heal the wounds."

I noticed the girl's father handing the binoculars back to Harry and turning restlessly back to his family. "Right! Marching orders! Have you seen enough of Mr. Lludd's ruins?"

"And, of course, there was Neptune," I put in quickly, "god of the sea, and equivalent to the Greek god Poseidon."

"I'm afraid we have to leave," the girl said apologetically.

"Are we going now?" asked the woman. "It's been so lovely sitting here. I hope poor Snap hasn't had another of his turns."

"Don't worry about Snap, I gave him his pill. Damn dog's costing me the earth with vet bills."

"Darling, please! You know you wouldn't have it any other way."

"Well, come along then. What are you women waiting for?"

We nodded our goodbyes as they set off down the track, and I turned my attention back to the ruins. Maybe it was because Nodens was a healing god, that his cult here had continued to flourish after the departure of the Romans. The pilgrims who'd come to be cured had been housed in a large dormitory, or abaton as it was called. There they spent the night hoping to be miraculously healed by morning, or sent a dream revealing what curative remedy to adopt. An interpreter was on hand to help the patient work out the exact meaning of the dream.

At the famous and much earlier healing centre of Asclepius, son of Apollo, at Epidaurus in Greece, Asclepius had also worked miracles on those who'd slept in his sanctuary overnight. He had also sent remedies in dreams, or he'd used his sacred snakes to work their miraculous cures. It was said that these snakes only existed within the Asclepian sanctuary; they would slither up to the patient under cover of darkness and lick (I didn't know snakes licked) the afflicted part.

At Lydney Park they had sacred dogs who licked wounds or sores to help the healing process.

"I'd rather have a doctor than a snake or dog, thank you!" Harry said, when I told him about Lydney Park and reminded him of Epidaurus.

"And you think they didn't have doctors in pagan times? People only resort to divine intervention when they've tried everything else possible without success," I said. "Old Nodens responded in his day just as much as you'd say the Almighty does today."

At some time in the development of Christian thought ill health was regarded as the consequence of sin. Incubation in a church was thought the best means of bringing about a miraculous cure, and the relics of a saint were believed to help also. If no cure came about, well, it had to be that there'd been no true repentance, that the patient was too steeped in sin, and the Almighty too displeased.

While I was examining the temple complex, Harry took himself off and began scrambling in and out of the Roman Baths whose ruined walls nearby rose from the turf north-west of the main temple. Cleanliness and purification would have been a part of the ritual for healing as well as for the well-being of the Roman soldiers.

"Where did the water come from?" Harry demanded.

We found from the booklet that the answer was uncertain, but there may have been springs up there which had since dried up, or it could have been piped up somehow from the valley down below.

In its heyday, when it was richly endowed in the later Roman period, there had been a number of mosaic floors. The main one had been in the cella and had depicted dolphins, fish and sea monsters. A great many artefacts excavated from the site had had reliefs depicting fish, fishermen and Tritons (mermen).

I kept returning to the view of the Severn in the distance. The river looked like a gleaming crescent moon reclining on the earth. I felt I should bow down to this silver arc of water glimpsed through the trees two miles away, in the same manner that I would bow to the new moon in the sky. Pure superstitious nonsense but one that I inevitably did when I glimpsed a new moon, believing it might bring me luck.

As we took one last look at the distant waters of the river Severn, I remembered that Nodens, the Celtic river god who was father of Ludd, or Lud or Nudd, or Nuada, had in fact, or so I'd read, displaced the earlier goddess Tamesis, goddess of the river Thames.

"So what?" came the response when I told Harry this interesting bit of information. He then told me I shouldn't take these pagan gods so seriously. Pagan gods, Harry said, didn't amount to a row of beans as they never had existed. To which I replied that undoubtedly the pagan gods should be taken seriously, because people had believed in them then just as people believed in God today. Or did he mean no god should ever be taken seriously because the whole God idea was a figment of human imagination?

"Of course not!" came the response.

"Of course not what? That they're not a figment of the imagination or not to be taken seriously?"

"That the pagan gods are a figment."

"But God isn't?"

"No."

"How can you be so sure? If the pagans are with hindsight, how do you know that with hindsight in a thousand years the same won't apply to God too?"

"Because I know."

"You really know?" I asked. "How do you know? Gut feeling? To know through your guts, isn't knowledge, it's an instinct, and that's different," I said with amazing confidence.

By this time we had walked up the slope behind the temple, to its westernmost limit. There the hill fell away steeply, almost sheer, to a tortuously winding stream way below which took our breath away and made us forget our confrontation about gods and return to the question how water could be got up here for the Roman baths. Undoubtedly the Romans had been wizards at overcoming all obstacles by engineering, pumping, sluicing, or doing whatever they found necessary to get water where they wanted it.

Soon after the departure of the Romans, when nature had reclaimed the site for itself, the hill had been rumoured to be inhabited by 'little people' such as dwarfs and hobgoblins. Apparently Tolkien as a young man had taken part in a dig up there under Sir Mortimer Wheeler who'd been conducting his excavations in the nineteen twenties, and had drawn on such fairy beliefs for his book The Lord of the Rings.

The 'little people', or 'fairy folk' as they were sometimes called, were mischievous and humans were wise to be wary of them. They might steal babies from their cots and substitute a changeling child; or they could curdle milk and cause other upsets. Shakespeare's Puck in his A Midsummer Night's Dream was drawn from such 'fairy folk'. Not only Puck but Titania, Oberon, Peasbody, Cobweb and all the fairies.

My reveries of 'little people' living in their secret domain beneath my feet were interrupted by Harry saying he was hungry. "Let's go down this way," he said, leading the way to another path which we could see took us to the car park and so on to the house.

Food first, then the museum.

We sat out on the terrace overlooking the sloping lawn with stone steps beyond going down to an out-of-sight lower level. Nearby a stone fountain in the centre of a large round pool gave the pleasing sound of splashing water. The sun shone, the air was warm, another pink magnolia was in flower, and the racemes of a wisteria against the house showed their first hint of blue. Three plump hens came to the lawn from around a corner - peacocks would have been more appropriate to this stately home - but no, these light brown hens were pecking their way over the lawn. If there were foxes, then they hadn't yet discovered these hens.

Lunch over, and it was museum time. I tried not to feel mesmerized by the numerous small exhibits as we passed from one showcase to another. There was a display of votive offerings, small ornamental dogs in stone, bronze or bone, the major specimen being a bronze wolfhound with its head turned towards what? His master calling him, or Nodens giving a command to lick the wound of an invalid? The dog's body suggested he was ready to spring instantly to action.

Harry was at a glass cabinet displaying the coins which had been recovered from the temple site. "Interesting," he commented. "From the heads on these coins they know the Romans were here from the time of the Emperor Augustus."

"You mean Christ's Augustus?" I asked stupidly.

Harry put on his spectacles and bent his head nearer to the glass showcase. "The Emperor Augustus from 63 B.C. to 14 A.D.," he read. "And the last recorded coin was from the time of the Emperor Honorius, from 384 to 423 A.D. Never heard of him," he added.

"If he was the last, then he was the one who couldn't cope with Britain, so abandoned us," I said, having just read up the matter from the booklet over lunch.

I looked at a damaged mosaic depicting writhing sea monsters and fish, maybe leaping salmon. There was also a lead curse tablet requesting Nodens to bring ill health to a family named Senicianus unless a ring (presumably stolen) was returned to Nodens' temple. Another inscription on a bronze plate assured Mars Nodens that the inscriber would fulfil his vow. I tried to empathise, but in my post-lunch semi-stupor didn't give a toss if he'd fulfilled his vow or not.

I took myself to another room where there were antiquarian books to look at. I asked about the temple and the god Nodens and was handed an ancient looking tome to read. I scribbled in my notebook bits and pieces which seemed relevant, i.e. 'Deus Nodens', if correctly written in the original language, would be 'Deus Noddyns' which meant 'God of the abyss' or 'God the preserver' from the verb 'noddi', 'to preserve'. The latter made far more sense for a healing god. Yet another Celtic scholar thought the incomprehensible 'God of the abyss' would be better interpreted as 'God of the deeps' which made considerably more sense as Nodens was god of water as well as healing.

So much in translation could change the entire meaning of a sentence. A scholar could easily use a word and mistranslate a passage in order to support his personal beliefs which, unless challenged, would become accepted fact over time. I could hear Harry telling me not to question but to accept with faith what others said and wrote.

"You never know, it might be true!" I could hear the words. Well, maybe it might. But maybe it might not. I closed the book and returned to the museum.

❧⊛❧

We took our leave of the god Nodens' sacred and not much known site. It was my turn to drive, and Harry's turn to map-read. We decided to return a different route which would take us down the Wye valley, somewhere we'd neither of us been before. We drove in and out of Wales again, but were soon firmly back in England.

The high, steep wooded slopes of the Wye valley stood proudly displaying their fresh spring colours. Here and there a house revealed itself in a clearing where from its vantage point it looked down over the river which meandered and glinted in the late afternoon sun. We passed rocky cliffs descending sheer to the river, then more wooded slopes. On the ouskirts of Tintern village the land opened up to reveal the soaring ruins of Tintern Abbey, its high Gothic, dark-with-age stone walls with their pointed arched windows were all that remained of the Cistercian monastery. Its monks had worn white habits and had led austere lives in prayer and manual labour until the dissolution under Henry VIII had put an end to them.

'Dust to dust, ashes to ashes,' came to mind. It was a shame because in Greece the earliest monasteries still existed, many having risen naturally from earlier pagan sites. There'd been continuity of worship even though the gods had changed which I found interesting.

Harry was in a hurry to get home now, so we didn't stop at Tintern. Soon we were passing Chepstow race-course with its stands and railings and immaculate green turf. Racing in England was something of a religion amongst those who loved horses. We'd just had the Grand National, and in a week or two there'd be the Badminton Horse Trials held nearby. There'd been a Celtic goddess of the horse named Epona (her name meant 'divine mare').

Soon we were on the M-road, and crossed the Severn bridge with its rugby goal posts and its suspension cables - not to mention Nodens' river flowing underneath.

"Good! Now we know where we are," said Harry with a satisfied sigh. "Soon be home again!" he said contentedly and felt confident enough to close his eyes knowing that with every rotation of the wheels we were getting nearer home.

I began thinking about my next trip in search of gods in Britain. From now on they needed to be hunted further and further afield. Scotland was high on the agenda and I didn't think Harry would need much persuasion to go to the Western Isles, or to walk Hadrian's Wall in early June. It wasn't, after all, a foreign land. He was in fact half Scottish, so I would work on that.

CHAPTER SIX

HADRIAN'S WALL

The two-carriage train was antiquated with its narrow central aisle, and its pairs of seats on the left facing one way, and those on the right facing the other. It rocked and rattled along in an on-its-last-legs sort of manner. We'd left the red-stoned suburbs of Newcastle, and were following the river Tyne wending its way through the Northumberland countryside. We had flown in to Newcastle early that day, and had spent all morning at Segedunum, the first fort of Hadrian's Wall at Wallsend - well, in truth the last fort of the wall since it was 'Wall's end', but the first one we'd visited.

The Picts and Scots had been despised by the Romans not only because they were uncivilized barbarians and illiterate, but because they didn't drink wine. When Hadrian had become emperor in 117 A.D., he'd decided to sort out these trouble makers once and for all, and had come in person to the wilds of Northumbria, the northernmost frontier of the Roman Empire, to see matters for himself. He'd realized at once what was needed to subdue the barbarians: nothing less than a seventy-three mile fortified wall from the Solway Firth near Carlisle, to the Tyne estuary at Newcastle. Carlisle's earlier name was Luguvallium, thought to have derived from Lugus, a Celtic god who was later identified with Lugh. By the eleventh century 'Lugus' had been shortened to 'Luel' to which the word 'caer' (meaning city, fortified place) was added hence Carlisle.

The landlady of our B&B where we were booked in had assured us that she would collect us from Haltwhistle station, and just to ring her on our mobile when we were on the train. I now did this, but there was so much creaking and clanking and people chattering in the carriage that I could barely hear the ringing tone, and then wasn't sure if the voice speaking was the landlady or an answer phone. At any rate, I informed whatever or whoever (if anybody) that we were on the train and would arrive at such and such a time. Repeat: such and such a time.

Harry wasn't encouraging. He thought that landladies doubling up as taxis were suspect. Obviously she had no guests or she wouldn't have the time to pick us up.

The train arrived and we got out. When the other passengers had dispersed, a smiling blonde stood waiting for her new arrivals. Oh, yes, she'd got our message, she said. How nice that we'd brought fine weather. Had we had a good journey? Could she take our luggage?

"Well!" I said to Harry when the door was shut on our comfortable room with its T.V., private bathroom with every luxury thrown in, "what more can we possibly want?"

"All that smiling! She has ulterior motives. She'll pile it on the bill when we leave. You just wait!" came the reply.

❧

Breakfast the next morning consisted of strawberries, blueberries, cornflakes, fried bacon and eggs, sausages, tomatoes and mushrooms. I was conscious of the fact that everybody eating was bursting with good health, and wore walking boots and hiking gear. The couple at the table beside ours told us they had walked all the way from Wallsend (where we'd been the day before in Newcastle) which had taken them three days. Others said they were walking the Pennine Way (of which Hadrian's Wall was a part) and were doing fifteen miles a day. We ourselves kept silent about the mere three and a half mile walk we planned to do that afternoon; we weren't even sure we could do that.

"Just give me a ring if you find yourselves stuck anywhere, and we'll collect you," said our smiling landlady as she put us down at the Vindolanda Fort. She had made a special trip on our behalf because the first bus was too early and the next one too late.

"You're so kind," I said.

"It's my pleasure!" came the reassuring response.

Harry spoiled it all by warning me that she wasn't doing it for love. There was no such thing as a free lunch, he declared.

I had come armed with information regarding the forts on

Hadrian's Wall, and had made a note of the chief sites which I felt were of interest, Vindolanda being the first on the list.

Vindolanda had been built as a Roman fort forty years before Hadrian ordered his wall to be built. Situated midway between Carlisle and Newcastle, its purpose had been to guard the east-west supply route. Later, when the wall was built, it was incorporated into its construction.

The Vindolanda site was extensive with views to distant undulating hills, and green fields hedged about by trees. We gravitated towards a wide area where archaeologists were working. A man with a clip-board stood beside the cordoned off ruins talking to someone who looked like an official photographer. He was pointing out various things of interest at the site. When the photographer left I approached the man who turned out to be the director of the Vindolanda excavations.

"The Romans were quite relaxed about their religion," said the man, when I asked him about the gods there. "So long as festivals honouring the emperor were observed, religious beliefs were an entirely personal matter. You'll find in our museum many inscriptions of gratitude to a god for granting a wish or bestowing good fortune."

Harry, who'd been leaning on his stick with his eyes on a distant reconstructed fort, suddenly spoke with what I thought quite unnecessary pride. "My mother was half Scottish."

"The Scots put up a good fight against the Romans," said the director obligingly.

"I have a kilt and jacket and sporran somewhere in an old tin trunk," Harry went on.

"Have you really?"

"Full of moth-holes when I last looked at it," Harry added.

"Were there Roman Christians here at Vindolanda?" I asked, determined not to get side-tracked from the main purpose of our visit. But Harry was into his Scottishness.

"I have a marvellous old dirk," Harry went on. "We have it hanging on a beam by our old fireplace. The silver needs polishing, of course, but it has a large stone like a garnet on it. Terrifying blade, and I'd use it on a burglar if I had to."

"So what pagan gods did they worship here?" I asked, trying to get the conversation back on track.

"And it has a small knife and fork with silver studs and garnets - they used them to eat haggis, I suppose. Or if they'd killed a stag, to eat the venison."

The director, uncertain who to turn his attention to, said first to Harry: "Remarkable workmanship went into dirks."

"And a skindoo, but that's a bit battered. It's something you stick in the top of your sock."

"How interesting."

"That's hanging on the beam also."

"Very decorative."

Having reminisced, Harry turned to look at the undulating landscape. I could see the photographer returning, so quickly seized my opportunity to ask the director again about religion at Vindolanda. I repeated my former question: had there been Roman Christians at the site?

"We believe there was almost certainly a Christian church built here at the beginning of the fifth century," said the man, drawing himself back to his duties as director of excavations. "In the courtyard of the Commanding Officer's Residence you can see the semi-circular apse we think must have been the sanctuary." He indicated the walled ruins a little distance from where we stood. "For the pagan gods you'll find altars and dedications in our museum. It's worth spending some time there."

The photographer now wanted his attention, so I thanked him for his information and we continued on our way. We paused by the ruins of the fort's headquarters where Harry asked me if I knew where the old tin trunk containing his moth-eaten kilt was? I said I hadn't a clue but we'd hunt it out when we got home. We then went on to the Commanding Officer's Residence where we saw the semi-circular apse of what might have been the early fifth century church.

"Isn't it odd," I said, "that there was no whiff of Christianity here before the fifth century - no mention of the Jewish God although the Romans had conquered Palestine and must have known all about him. After all they weren't averse to tying their own gods in with others, yet never once, as far as I know, did they have a Jupiter-Jehovah, or Jupiter-Yahweh."

We moved on to the reconstructed fort. We climbed to the top and looked out at the gently rolling landscape with its trees and fields. There was a cooling breeze and a coverlet of light cloud with patches of blue sky visible. From there we made for the museum, visiting on the way a replica of a Nymphaeum (a small Temple of the Nymphs) beside a stream, a reminder to all of the importance to honour the water nymphs as without water there could be no life.

❧⟐❧

"There was an altar to the Celtic god Moguns," I told Harry, reading from the brief notes I'd made while in the Vindolanda museum. We were in the café eating salads. "The inscription on it went - " I moved my finger along the scribbled words in my notebook, "'For the god Moguns and the Guardian Spirit of This Place, Lupulus deservedly fulfils his vow'. Don't you find that interesting? The 'Guardian Spirit of This Place' - I mean where would we be without our Guardian Spirit?"

"Dead and gone," said Harry with conviction.

"Exactly. Well, if not dead, then in wheelchairs, or dragging ourselves around on crutches. Or inert and unconscious being fed through a tube, or something quite horrific."

If I believed in little else, I paid considerable lip service to our Guardian Spirit - well, I called it our guardian angel, or angels. How else could I or Harry have survived during our farming years if we hadn't been protected from disaster by some unseen hand? There'd been the occasion when I'd fallen on my head on concrete among the stampeding hooves of four panicking bullocks whom Harry had been trying to drench (trying to get liquid down their throats). I'd foolishly been sitting on a gate gripping the yard rail in an attempt to pen them in but couldn't hold them. Or on another occasion when I'd been letting down the back of a cattle truck and the springs had failed and it had crashed down on me, yet I'd somehow dived beneath it and had emerged unscathed. Or the other time when Harry had his leg pinioned between the metal upright of our hay barn and the metal lathe at the back of our hay trailer, and before he passed out I'd managed to lever a metal-handled pitchfork between the two uprights so he could ease his leg out leaving just his gumboot hanging.

"Do you remember?" I asked Harry, reminding him of these occasions. "Yet some people aren't so fortunate. Some people don't seem to have guardian spirits or angels, and consequently have terrible lives or die young." I speared a piece of tomato together with some shredded lettuce, and a morsel of chicken. "To be able to eat!" I exclaimed, putting it in my mouth. "To be able to chew!" I added, with my mouth full. "You just have to say 'thank you!' over and over again to whatever it is that keeps us well."

"And keep on the right side of the Almighty," said Harry with a warning look as he devoured some chips and a sausage. "In other words, don't go knocking God."

"God would have clobbered me long ago, if he existed." I said, with the usual mild anxiety I felt when putting God to the test. Harry gave me another warning look and changed the subject.

He told me of the numerous writing tablets he'd seen in the museum consisting of Latin script written in ink on thin sheets of softwood; documents, reports, inventories, and a personal invitation to a birthday party.

I returned to my notes and said: "And there was an altar found in the Commanding Officer's Residence with the inscription: 'To Jupiter Best and Greatest, most immortal among gods...' There! People believed then as much as others believe now!" I read on: "Here's a good one. 'To the spirits of the departed Cornelius Victor, Singularis Consularis...' whatever that means. Don't you like the words 'spirits of the departed'?" I took another mouthful of chicken salad.

"I mean, these 'spirits of the departed' must mean the unseen inner voices tussling with conscience, pulling you this way or that with the pros and cons of what you should or shouldn't do. Everybody has a conscience - well, to a greater or lesser degree. Some, I suppose have no conscience at all. They don't care what they do."

I turned back to my notes. "And there was a carved relief of a Celtic god called Maponus whose name means 'divine son'. Isn't that interesting? Divine son! In niches either side of him were Apollo and Diana. Apollo was a divine son, and Diana, I suppose, was a divine daughter. Anyway, Maponus as a Celtic god under the Romans became equated with Apollo. Divine sons - like Jesus."

Harry broke in. "Do you want to catch that bus, or do you want to stay on here?" I looked at my watch and saw the next bus for Housesteads Fort would be leaving in ten minutes. From there we planned to walk back to our smiling landlady.

"Better go," I agreed, "unless you want to ring your blonde to come for us."

"No, I do not!" came the positive reply.

Unlike Vindolanda, Housesteads Fort was on high ground with spectacular views to the distance across fields bounded by dry stone walls. Sheep and black Aberdeen Angus cattle grazed the hillsides. The light clouds sometimes drifted apart revealing blue sky and sunshine.

We walked up a long path to the small museum and ruined walls of the Housesteads Fort, but we both felt saturated by the museum we'd just seen at Vindolanda, and disinclined to exercise our minds further; physical exercise was more like it. The walk, I understood, would at times take us on the wall itself, or the Military Way alongside it.

The views from the Housesteads Fort were limitless; no Pict or Scot could have got near except under cover of darkness. The Romans had, in fact, been quite alarmed by the Picts who'd been in the habit of cutting off the heads of their enemies and galloping away with them as trophies. They painted their bodies and often fought naked, screaming like maniacs as they attacked. To have them coming out of the darkness at you at night must have been extremely unnerving.

We followed a path to a wicket gate beyond which was a stony track which took us through woods with the stone wall a few metres away on our right. We found a trail which took us up on to the wall itself. A footpath ran along the top which Harry found exhilerating.

"Look at that!" he said, staring down through trees. I looked, saw the hundred foot plummet to the ground far below and instantly looked away. Idiot! Of course I could look at THAT. I grew accustomed to the mighty drop and looked beyond to the far distant cattle quietly slumbering in the warmth of the June afternoon.

After several hundred yards the wall petered out and we followed a track to the Milecastle 37. Milecastles were fortified gateways through which troops and goods had passed; they were spaced at regular intervals along the wall. The blocks of stone here were large and immovable. In its heyday there would have been double gates at the front and rear of the Milecastle in order to keep the enemy at bay.

We tramped on, occasionally meeting others coming from the opposite direction. Sometimes they just smiled in passing, occasionally we spoke. "I guess that must be Scotland?" asked a mild American, pointing in that direction. He must have noticed I thought it a ridiculous question, and added: "I mean those hills in the far distance."

The Military Way along which we tramped rose and fell with the contours of the hills. We met a couple with two small fat terriers.

They had come from the Twice Brewed Inn and told us we had two more miles to walk. The terriers were old and portly. "Oh, they love it," we were told. "One has just caught a mole and the other chased a rabbit." Neither looked as if they could do anything more than waddle obediently with their owners.

We strode on where the view became more and more spectacular. We climbed steeply up and saw rocky crags to our right which we were told by some booted and spurred individual was Cuddy's Crag. Further on there was a long loch. After another hour we came to the spectacular Highshields Crags, or was it Steel Rigg? By now we just kept walking - one foot in front of the other as the Roman infantry had done, or the small fat terriers. How the Romans marched such distances they did, and in all weathers, was amazing. The Roman army consisted of Legions in which Roman citizens served. They were skilled and well disciplined soldiers, and it had been they who'd been responsible for the building of the wall. There were also the Auxiliary, made up of non-Roman individuals, many of them from Gaul or Germany. They were rewarded with Roman citizenship when they retired.

The Romans might have had to endure the hardships of the English/Scottish climate and, no doubt, became all the tougher for it, but we ourselves were enjoying the day. It was bracing, neither too hot nor too cold with a light, fresh wind. Another stretch of water to our right we took to be Crags Lough (lough was the word used here for a Scottish loch, or an English lake).

After two and a half hours we reached what was known as Sycamore Gap. Here a majestic sycamore with a straight trunk and shaped like an ace of spades, was in full foliage in shadowy shades of green. It stood in the cleft made by two hills sloping down towards it. The tree had been pointed out to us by a young man the evening before when we'd been leaving the Twice Brewed Inn. It was, he'd told us, the location for the first Robin Hood film. It was also where a television celebrity had crash-landed a helicopter and had miraculously survived - a guardian spirit?

Never mind what had occurred there in the past, at that precise moment what mattered most was that we were near our final destination and could now see the Twice Brewed Inn and the Visitor's Centre on the main road.

We deviated south along a grassy pathway to a gate beyond

which was a side road. Another fifteen minutes and we were back at our lodgings.

"Have you had a good day?" asked our smiling landlady who was seated at her computer near the entrance.

We told her we'd walked from Housesteads. "You've done well," she said. The small cubby hole of her reception area prevented her from watching as we crawled the last twenty yards along the corridor back to our bedroom.

We propped ourselves up on our beds with mugs of tea and watched the Wimbeldon championships on T.V. A match was in progress between two unknowns, a match in which the fifth set could only be settled by a tiebreak and was to pass into the record books as the longest ever. As we sipped our tea the score stood at 17-17. By the time we'd finished it was 19-19. I got off the bed and felt cripplingly stiff, so ran a hot bath and wallowed. When I got out I felt totally refreshed, so Harry did the same and by the time we were ready to walk to the Twice Brewed Inn for supper, the score was 24-24.

At the Inn we found ourselves seated near to where the match was continuing on television. By nine that evening it was 59-59. We were still watching when it was decided that the light was too poor for play.

The following day we were out when the match continued and finally ended at 70-68.

After several miles along the dead straight and undulating B6318, we were put down at the side of the road at Brocolitia Fort. There was no indication of any fort, and the only sign of civilization in that open, desolate landscape stretching away to the south was a lay-by on the other side of the road where a white van was selling refreshments to a few individuals who'd parked their cars.

"Why on earth have we come here?" Harry demanded.

"For the Brocolitia Fort," I said, hurrying across the road and making for the small group of people gathered by the van - I hadn't yet told him that the next bus left in thirty minutes, and if we missed it we'd have to ring our landlady or wait several hours.

A fellow who looked like a hairy biker wearing a leather broad brimmed hat, broke from the group and I intercepted him to ask if he knew where the Mithraeum and Coventina's Well were.

Speaking in an incomprehensible northern dialect, he indicated the path we should take.

"We've less than thirty minutes before the bus," I now told Harry. "Thirty minutes to see the temple. We need to hurry." To which he remarked that from the look of it five minutes would be enough.

Following a track for about two hundred yards amongst quietly grazing sheep, we came unexpectedly on the stone ruins of the Mithraeum in a shallow hollow on our right. The low walls enclosed a rectangular area, and at the far end were three stone altars with dedications inscribed on them by commanding officers at different periods, and on the left hand one a figure of Mithras with sun rays about his head. The rays were deeply incised so that a lamp placed behind would have caused the rays to glow. Behind these three altars there would once have been a depiction of Mithras like the one we'd seen in London: Mithras in the act of slaying the bull with his eyes averted, and with the figures of Cautes and Cautopates either side of him, the one pointing to the heavens, towards the light, the other to the earth and darkness.

Within the stone-walled interior were a series of slender broken pillars (these were now concrete, replacing the original wooden ones). Centrally placed among the pillars on the right was a well-weathered stone figure of a mother goddess.

In the pre-Mithras creation legend, there had been a powerful creator god who'd had an even more powerful wife who'd become the mother goddess when she'd given birth to a son, Ahura Mazda. Ahura Mazda was the power of light and all that was good, and a second son had been the opposite, the embodiment of darkness and the forces of evil. It had been very similar to the Celtic idea of light and darkness, good and evil, not unlike God and Satan, I supposed.

Harry pointed to his watch. "The bus," he warned.

"Oh, God, the bus!" I saw we only had fifteen minutes, and we had yet to find Coventina's Well.

We moved on to where the grass petered out and rushes took over in an extensive boggy area. I noticed a couple treading carefully and pausing beside something of interest and commenting on it before heading on.

A splash of bright yellow flowers brightened the rushes on our way there. Further on a semi-circle of these brilliant yellow flowers grew around a small swamp of water. This was Coventina's Well.

Coventina had been a Celtic water goddess, and had been a favourite with the Roman military. Here she had had a simple shrine, a small temple with the well at its centre where Romans from all levels of society had come to honour her.

The sun momentarily shone from between the clouds, spotlighting the bright yellow plants before it hid again. I had no time to study them, to see if they were marsh marigolds, yellow vetch, or some other flower. I merely noticed that nature here was free to do as it liked. It was nature at its most peacefully sublime.

I picked my way through the rushes to get closer, avoiding the water-logged patches of bog. The well, I'd read, had been seven feet deep and lined with stone or gravel. Its simplicity was enchanting.

Apparently more than thirteen thousand coins had been found in the well, presumably representing thirteen thousand prayers and wishes. Other objects retrieved from it had been altars, pots, incense burners, pearls and carved stones. The images on the coins revealed that the well had been going strong at the time of Caesar Augustus and had continued into the late fourth century. It was thought that, as with the Mithraeum, the Christians in a gesture of intolerance had desecrated the site.

The Emperor Theodosius I had in the last decades of the fourth century issued a decree forbidding sacrifice, and had closed down all pagan temples in his bid to advance Christianity. By the fifth century pagans were excluded from all government positions which presumably encouraged anyone with ambition to get himself baptized.

"Don't you think it's odd," I said, "after all the religious tolerance of the Romans to suddenly wham! turn their backs on all the old known gods under whom they'd gained their empire, in favour of the God of the Jews? It's really quite extraordinary, since the Romans had been at war with the Jews and had even destroyed their temple."

"If you want to catch this bus - we've less than five minutes."

Bother the bus! I remembered that Hadrian had not only been responsible for the wall and its forts here, but had during his reign rebuilt Jerusalem, renaming it Aelia Capitolina with a shrine to Jupiter on the Temple Mount where Solomon's temple had been, and a temple of Venus over the Holy Sepulchre, the tomb of Jesus. But, before I could tell Harry this interesting bit of information, I saw him heading for the road, then striding along to the bus-stop. I hurried after him and could see the white bus cresting one of the undulations of the dead straight road. Our next destination was Chesters Roman Fort about eight miles on. I was only just in time as the bus arrived.

◦❧◦

The usual mental fatigue after seeing Chesters Roman Fort ruins and visiting its museum required another brisk walk along Hadrian's Wall to clear the head. We were faced unexpectedly with an almost vertical climb and it was a challenge. I took it in one stupendous climbing burst and reached the top triumphantly. Harry did it more sensibly, ten steps up, then a rest before starting again.

The views from the top were spectacular, north to Scotland and south to England across dry-walled fields. The sun shone spasmodically as clouds drifted gently on their way to wherever clouds go.

My thoughts went back to Chesters, the Roman cavalry fort, where we'd just been. Its landscape had been in sharp contrast to the desolate one at Brocolitia where we'd seen the Mithraeum and Coventina's Well. At Chesters the setting was the grounds of a stately home belonging to the Clayton family. The first owner, Nathaniel Clayton, had bought the property in 1796 but had absolutely no interest in its Roman ruins. It had been his son, John Clayton, who'd become excited by the archaeological remains on his doorstep, and had first organised the digs at both Housesteads and Brocolitia where he'd discovered Coventina's Well and the Mithraeum.

At Chesters we'd sat on a fallen tree trunk beside the river Tyne which bordered the property. We'd eaten our packed lunch made up for us by our smiling landlady which, no doubt, would be another extra bonus for her on our final bill. On the far bank of the Tyne we'd spotted the remains of Hadrian's Wall where it had once crossed the river.

The far bank of the river had been fringed with tall trees: oak, sycamore and alders, all reflected in the still waters downstream, while upstream had been fast-flowing shallow waters rippling and eddying around rocks.

We'd already tramped the various points of interest at the fort - the barracks, the head-quarters, the commandant's house, the granary and bath house, but it had been the museum with the treasures John Clayton had acquired over his lifetime which had most interested me.

There had been at its entrance a large relief of the god Mars. Mars had been the Roman counterpart of the Greek god Ares, god of war. To the Romans Mars had initially been a god of vegetation and the protector of livestock. As the first enemies of Rome had been rabbits and predators, mice and caterpillars, Mars had been called upon to save them from such pests. In due course, as Rome had expanded her empire bringing with it many wars, Mars had reverted to his god of war role. The word 'martial' comes from the god Mars.

There at Hadrian's Wall Mars had become equated with various Celtic gods also, such as Cocidius, a woodland hunting god (Mars Cocidius); or Alator, a Celtic deity meaning 'huntsman' (Mars Alator); or Condatis, the Celtic god of the confluence of rivers (Mars Condatis), god of water and healing.

Among the numerous altars and sculptures there'd also been a statue of Neptune, which had been found in the commandant's house. To the Romans Neptune had been god of the sea and of horses and, therefore, a very suitable god to be honoured by the commandant of a waterside fort garrisoned by the cavalry.

The museum had also contained several dedications to the goddess Coventina. Unfortunately, a sculpture of her reclining on a water lily leaf holding a plant in one hand had completely spoilt the image I'd conjured up of her. The sculpture portrayed her as an ugly creature with a small round head, a long nose, closed eyes, and hair like the petals of a daisy.

Harry arrived up the steep track and stood staring at the view while he got his breath back. I tried not to think that what comes up goes down and hoped that any downward gradient would be gradual. As we neared the bottom of one slope we saw three people with a Scotsman in tartan trousers wearing a navy blue Tam o'Shanter with a long feather in it. I thought I heard him talking in his Scottish accent about Hadrian being a keen footballer. As the four-yearly World Cup was under way, and daily matches were being played, football was very much on everybody's mind.

"Hadrian was a footballer?" I joked as we drew near.

"A keen, fine builder, that he was," said the Scotsman.

"Oh, fine builder! Yes. Are we right for Cawfields?" I asked.

"Aye. You've a way yet."

"No very steep descents, I hope?"

He eyed me speculatively. "Nooo. Just a wee drop."

We strode on feeling confident. We passed a great clump of wild flowers huddled together on several feet of wall, yellow and purple vetch and thyme. Soon we passed a rise of rough tufted grass on our left where skylarks rose into the air trilling, before descending.

We were met by four athletic men with long trekking sticks. They were breasting what I took to be the 'wee drop'. They seemed glad to pause as we greeted them. They turned out to be ex-army individuals walking the Pennine Way in aid of the Help for Heroes charity set up to rehabilitate those who had been wounded in Afghanistan.*

"We have one week to do it and it's murder," said one.

"I've got blisters on blisters, and my feet are bound up. But we have to do it,"said another.

"Two hundred and seventy miles in one week. We can't give up."

"We get up at three thirty every morning and start out."

I was caught up by their commitment and involvement, and said spontaneously: "I'd give you money but I don't have any on me."

"Oh, just give something when you get home," said one of them.

To meet these vigorous ex-British army individuals, with their energy, enthusiasm, and determination seemed amazingly appropriate for Hadrian's Wall where the Roman army had once done battle with the Picts and Scots. It was all very well walking it in peaceful conditions with the sun shining, the skylarks singing and no fear of the enemy lurking below the next rise. But in Afghanistan men went about in perpetual danger, conscious of possible death or mutilation around each corner from a roadside bomb or landmine.

We watched as the ex-soldiers, using their trekking sticks, strode away and disappeared.

"I feel inspired," I said, as we crested the next hill.

"You need to," said Harry, as we looked down at the 'wee drop' which seemed to plummet to a great depth.

"I'm not doing that!"

"We're not turning back now! I'm not, anyhow. Come on! Say your prayers! I'll go first."

Harry led the way. "Great stuff!" he said. "Look at the view!" He used his stick in one hand and held on to the stones of the wall with his right.

"Bloody hell!" I dug my stick into a grassy patch between the slabs of stones which marked the descent, and sat on my bottom as step by step I eased my way downwards. I didn't once look at the view

*At the time Britain was still at war in Afghanistan attempting to oust the Taliban regime.

for fear of swooning. I said my prayers in a sort of desperate 'Oh, God, help me!' non-committal way.

Slowly, slowly, slowly.

I heard voices higher up behind me. The wretches were descending, and I was still in my 'Oh, God, help me!' state. Near the bottom a man with a buxom red-haired girl in shorts, with a puce face and strong pink legs caught me up.

"That's some drop!" I said. "Do, please, give me your hand!" The man turned and held a hand out to me.

"No problem! Easy does it!" he encouraged.

I joined Harry at the bottom who appeared embarrassed at my wimpishness. "She doesn't like heights," he explained.

"I was glad of a hand myself," said the man nobly. "We've already done fifteen miles today."

"Fifteen?"

"We aim to get to the Milesend Cross Inn and then by bus to Haltwhistle," he said, and he and his buxom girl strode on.

Without anyone else to ask we found ourselves having to make decisions regarding the various possible paths to Cawfields and to the Milesend Cross Inn. As I was the worst person at finding my way anywhere and inevitably went in the wrong direction, I left it to Harry to make the big decisions. Whether it was a fluke or navigational skills taken from the sun and various landmarks, we eventually arrived at the inn where we saw the man with his pink-legged girlfriend thumbing a lift. We watched as a lorry stopped and they climbed up into the cab and went on their way.

But it was the ex-soldiers walking the Pennine Way in aid of the Help for Heroes who came repeatedly back to mind. There was something indomitable about them, something unbeatable and heroic. The noblest of humankind, out to help those who had suffered misfortune.

We are back at Housesteads which we visited on our first day here. At the time we didn't explore it because we'd already been saturated with ruins and the museum at Vindolanda. Some people could easily do both in one day, but we are limited in our ability to concentrate before interest dims like an electric light bulb when the power supply is failing.

I am seated on a stone step in the Fort's Headquarters, looking south across the ruins of the Commandant's House to the fantastic view beyond.

I am very conscious that where I'm sitting is the entrance to the Chapel of the Standards where once the standards of the regiment were kept, and where there was a shrine for the worship of the emperor of the day.

I've just been to the museum where I copied from a notice board the religious practices of the Romans. It said something to the effect that Roman soldiers could honour any god they liked so long as they participated in the '...festivals celebrating the birthdays, accession days and victories of the Deified Emperors...' It also said that the statue of the current emperor was kept in 'the shrine of the standards in the Headquarters Building...'

I find emperor worship sort of interesting. Emperor worship! To worship a man seems to me infinitely easier than something unseen and intangible like a deity. Emperor worship first began with Caesar Augustus who was deified after his death. Subsequently emperors were regarded not only as gods but as messiahs and saviours also, appellations which were used for Christ. After Constantine, emperor worship gradually petered out, though the emperor's person was still regarded as sacred. Instead of being honoured as a god, the emperor was then regarded as God's deputy on earth, God's vicegerent.

I see Harry standing in the south-east corner of these ruins staring at the Latrines, of all things. At every fort these are always on the hillside - for easy drainage, I suppose.

In the museum here I saw an altar to Hercules, an understandable role-model for soldiers as he was noted for his strength, courage, and endurance. Here Hercules was depicted performing three of his twelve labours, one with the Nemean lion, another destroying the monstrous Hydra, and the third killing the dragon, Ladon, who was guarding the apples of the Hesperides.

I also saw in the museum the usual altars to Jupiter, 'To Jupiter, Best and Greatest...', as well as an altar to Mars together with Victory, and another to the Mother Goddesses.

The slope outside the Fort Gate to the south is called Chapel Hill. There was once a Mithraeum there also which had in it a sculpted relief of the birth of Mithras. According to legend Mithras was born in a cave in the same humble conditions as Jesus. Oddly enough Jesus was visited by three wise men from the east, and these were none other than priests of Mithras, known as the Magi.

I feel inspired while sitting here on this step leading up to the Chapel of the Standards. Maybe I mean I feel spiritual. Perhaps it's due to the ancient ruins and their associations with divinity and worship, or because the weather is neither too hot nor too cold, but pleasantly warm with a soft breeze and just right for putting me in this reflective mood. I have to admit I can see no real reason for worshipping anything. What is this word 'worship' anyway? The dictionary I have of word origins says that the verb 'to worship' wasn't used until the twelfth century; it began originally as a compound noun meaning 'worthiness' formed from the adjective 'worth' and the suffix '-ship' which denoted 'state' or 'condition'; it was first used to mean 'distinction, credit, dignity' before changing to mean 'respect, reverence'.

I do have 'respect' and 'reverence' for nature and the spiritual energy that comes with it. But the word 'worship' now seems to have connotations of prostrating oneself before God. The Christians over the centuries have made God so pure and holy, unlike the God of the Old Testament who was a jealous God (God's own admission) that I wonder why Christians turned to the Old Testament at all.

What pagan god ever gave his son to be crucified? Christians have come up with the idea that he was crucified for us, for our sins. Why? It is something I really cannot comprehend.

Humans are so complex! We don't just live, we have this inner world which is vast with its streams of ideas, its sudden unexpected springs of inspiration, its rivers of thought –

Harry is approaching. Real life is encroaching on reflection. Oh, well. I must now come back to reality where action is required. It's time to say our last farewells to Hadrian's Wall before catching the bus back to our landlady who will by now be totting up our bill.

Harry doesn't believe her many small kindnesses won't be accounted for. No such thing as a free sandwich or a taxi ride, he repeats for the umpteenth time.

I am decidedly in the real world now, seated in the same somewhat antiquated two-carriaged train with its line of two seats facing one way, and line of two seats facing the other. A bunch of boisterous, over exuberant young men are seated all around me, and Harry is by the door guarding our luggage.

We have said goodbye to our smiling landlady who dropped us off at the station. Harry paid the bill without comment which has to mean there were no outlandish extras, no deceptions hidden behind her smiling face.

There are wild wolf-whistles as one of the young men comes prancing down the passageway with a self-conscious grin, wearing a cowboy hat and a short pink gauzy girl's dress over his jeans.

There's a lot of unleashed energy around us and I sit silently, attempting to keep a low profile while my ears are barraged by shouts, guffaws and wolf-whistles.

I am unexpectedly poked on the shoulder, and turn to see a large red face looking at me through the gap between the seats. I am asked if I have a pair of scissors. My instant reaction is to say no, I haven't. The red face with its beer-smelling breath withdraws, and I now remember I do have nail-scissors in a zip compartment on the lid of my suitcase. It's my turn to look through the gap, and I ask if nail-scissors will do. I fetch the nail-scissors and Harry wants to know why I want them. When I tell him, he makes a face at me of 'careful what you're doing, you don't want to get knifed'. He doesn't relish the idea of having to step in to rescue me.

In an odd sort of way I'm quite interested in the 'real world' of these boisterous fellows. The one in the gauze pink dress returns as I make my way to my seat. I let him pass and hand the scissors to the red faced smelling-of-beer chap, then watch as he and his mate cut eight inches off the legs of a rather nice pair of dark brown velvet trousers.

When the job is finished the nail-scissors are returned. "Yer a star!" I'm told, and he offers me his open can of Lager. I decline politely but feel curiously pleased to be regarded as his friend.

I wonder how the day will end for them. For us when the day ends we hope to be in Mull. That anyway is the plan.

MULL AND IONA

From the battlements of Duart Castle I looked out over the Sound of Mull to the hills beyond. Walking further round I saw Loch Linne from its vantage point, and further still the Firth of Lorne. Built on a high rocky ledge at the end of a promontory the castle held a commanding view of the seaways. Duart was the ancestral home of the Clan Maclean - the name 'Duart' is from the Gaelic 'Dubh Ard' meaning 'Black Point'.

On the landward side from these battlements I could see more hills, the highest being Ben More. To the south of that would be Loch Scridain, with the small port of Fionnphort at the westernmost point of the Ross of Mull. It was from there that a ferry-boat made regular crossings carrying pilgrims from Mull to the small island of Iona where St. Columba first set foot around 563 A.D., and where we also would set foot in a day or two.

Less than twenty miles south-west of Duart Castle was the ruined Castle of Moy with its nearby ancient stone circle which we had visited that morning. The stones stood upright in rough pasture amongst clumps of rushes. The centre of this Lochbuie stone circle was aligned with an outlying stone which marked the position of the setting sun at the winter solstice, and with another outlying stone marking the sun at the winter quarter days in early November and early February. Like all standing stones, I can admire the ability to erect them, but have a mental block regarding the reason why. Astronomy and alignments remain for ever a mystery to me, though clearly they mean a great deal to those today who know about such things, Harry included, and to the pagans all those millennia ago who went to all the bother to set them up. I find it amazing that people then had the time to study the sky and glean enough knowledge to fix stones as markers, and with such conviction. I'd have thought their lives would have been so occupied with the problems of survival - with growing food, raising families, hunting, felling trees, chopping wood and lighting fires with sparks from flints or rubbing sticks together, that to look up at the stars and moon at night would be just a momentary wonder before falling asleep. And at that time there was no literacy so their findings weren't recorded; any new discovery had to be accurately remembered and handed on by word of mouth. How many generations did it take before they could be certain about the annual recurrences of sunrises and sunsets at specific points on the horizon, or the variations in the rising and setting of the moon throughout the year?

Down in the Great Hall the present Chief of the Clan Maclean had spoken to me, and I was trying not to let it go to my head. He told me that a pagan wedding had been held at Duart Castle a few months back. How the subject had come up I couldn't quite remember, but he'd been most charming and had been standing in for a member of his staff who'd gone to lunch. I think he must have asked what had brought me to Mull, and I'd said something about my interest in pagan gods and how Christianity had ousted them. Far from dismissing me altogether he picked up on the subject as though it were the most interesting one in the world, and told me of a pagan wedding which had been held there in the castle grounds.

There had been a priestess, he said, smiling at the memory. A priestess? What had she been like, I asked? She'd had piercing green eyes and red hair, and she'd worn a long feather head-dress which he'd warned her would blow off in the gale coming round the headland. But the priestess had been unperturbed and said she could perform the ceremony quite well without it should that happen (and it had). At the end of the ceremony they'd drunk mead out of cow horns.

"I wish I'd been here to see it," I said.

I came down from the battlements, circling around the very narrow stone spiral stairway to a lower floor, and on down to the Great Hall - the laird had gone. I still had time to walk around the castle grounds. As I passed the wooden hut beside the gravel driveway where visitors had their tickets checked, I saw the laird emerging from it. "Hello again," he said.

"Good heavens! You pop up all over the place!" I found myself remarking.

"Yes, I have to take over when people go to lunch. If you'd like to see where the pagan wedding took place, it's through this small gate here."

With impeccable good manners he opened the gate for me and pointed to a flat area of grass, a few hundred yards beyond which was an outcrop of rock and the Sound of Mull.

"I must get back to my duties. Enjoy your walk," the Chief of the Macleans said, and left me to my musings about the easy grace and attractiveness of lairds, before returning to the more serious subject of modern pagans. The description I'd been given of the priestess fitted well with what I would expect one to look like. 'Loonies and weirdoes,' Harry would say. I'd once challenged him on those he considered 'loonies and weirdoes' by suggesting that perhaps we were the loonies and weirdoes and they the normal ones, and we just didn't think it. But he wasn't having any of that.

The wind caught me as soon as I rounded the castle walls and, had I worn a feather head-dress, or any other head-dress for that matter, it would have blown away instantly. The Caledonian MacBrayne ferry-boat was crossing the Sound of Mull on its way from Oban to Craignure. Down by the water's edge was the castle's slipway for its own private boats. The scenery all around was of hills and mountains, groping inlets and sea.

I wondered what drove people to join a pagan group. At heart I supposed that I was one myself since I was in awe of nature, and aware of some divine energy at work, but I couldn't see myself ever praying to the earth as Mother-Goddess, or the sun as Father-God, or the Horned God. To enrole as a Druid or a Wiccan? Harry would be gone in an instant, leaving me wearing my robe with my floral head-dress and my wooden staff. If I wanted to attend spiritual gatherings, what was wrong with the local church and the vicar in his robe, or the bishop with his pastoral staff, would be his comment.

I strolled down to an outcrop of rocks, then followed a path around to the back of the castle on the seaward side. Looking up at its fastness made me realize how the enemy from the sea would balk at the prospect of attacking it. Its high stone walls had small windows, and its turrets had arrow slits; the castle walls here were between five and eight feet thick, and those on the landward side ten feet as there was greater danger from overland attack.

Behind the castle bracken grew up to the craggy basalt rock on which the castle perched. The wafting smell of bluebells in the warm sunshine rose from where they grew amongst the bracken and strayed out to the footpath. I looked out to a point where eddying waters washed over a submerged rock revealing where a Maclean ancestor in the sixteenth century had marooned his wife (a Campbell). He'd hoped she'd drown when the tide came in, but a fisherman had saved her, and when the Campbells learned about it they'd pursued and murdered him in his bed in Edinburgh, stabbing him with a dirk - 'Dirked in bed' was the term used.

I saw it was time to meet up with Harry at the castle shop. The next shuttle-bus from Duart Castle arrived at Craignure in time to connect with the early evening bus to Tobermory, a small fishing port on the north-east corner of Mull. It was a shame to have to leave the castle with its historic past; but Scotland was full of inter-clan battles and feuds and legends. Its history could be palpably felt as soon as you set foot across the border.

The scenery was spectacular in the late afternoon light as the bus took us alongside the Sound of Mull to the small fishing port of Tobermory. Voluptuous grey-white clouds boiled over the high Morvern hills casting their reflections in the waters, and their shadows on the slopes. Small sailing boats sailed quietly in a light breeze. There were long-horned Highland cattle and sheep grazing on the lush green grass going down to the water's edge. Here and there were spruce forests.

"I spoke to the Chief," I told Harry, trying to keep pride out of my voice.

"What chef?" Harry asked.

"Chief. Chief! The Chief of the Macleans!"

"Oh, him. I spoke to him too." Harry took the wind out of my sails, and my great announcement fell flat. "He told me about a Hector Maclean who fought for King James and was killed at the Battle of Flodden in 1513. Their motto was 'To Conquer or to Die'."

"They had a pagan wedding at the castle the other day," I said, pursuing my line of thought.

"And his grandfather was Fitzroy Maclean, the fellow who parachuted into Yugoslavia in the war. They had some of his things on show. Nice man, your laird. Very friendly."

I gave up on my pagan wedding information and, as I looked out of the bus at the long stretch of water between Mull and the mainland, at spruce forests and the grazing Highland cattle, I thought how quickly the scene was able to change in the Highlands with its mists and lochs and clouds and light. That morning I'd woken early and, whilst sitting up in bed with a mug of tea, I'd looked out at Tobermory Bay. The sea had at first been a brilliant sheen with many small sailing boats lying still in the water, their myriad masts reflected like sticks as though in a looking-glass. Amazingly, ten minutes later they had vanished in a thick sea mist which had drifted in (known as a 'haar' in Scotland). Another ten minutes and it had begun to lift, and the numerous small vessels could be seen as ghostly spectres before they finally became boats again. It had been remarkably dramatic, as though it had been a deliberately planned stage effect for my entertainment.

My thoughts drifted on to the future. The following day we were moving on to the Ross of Mull in order to visit the tiny island of Iona, made famous in the sixth century by St. Columba. As it had been impossible to get accommodation at Fionnphort, the port from which the ferry took pilgrims to the island, we'd booked a room at a small croft a few miles inland. It was a working croft which Harry would find interesting. The only drawback was there was no bus so we would be dependent on the one and only taxi in the area to collect us and take us to the port.

Harry resigned himself to this expenditure, but cheered up when I told him that to hire a car would cost much more.

❧⟨◈⟩❧

The trip from Fionnphort to Iona took less than twenty minutes on the ferry-boat. There was a strong wind and the sea was choppy, but the sun shone and there were only a few unthreatening clouds in a blue sky. From up on deck we saw the tiny island with its rocky shoreline, and its tranquil grassy slopes where sheep were grazing. The great Abbey founded by St. Columba could be seen near the foreshore and I tried not to think that its squat and solid structure looked dour, sombre and somewhat - and I hated to admit it to myself - disappointing.

I'd been told by several people how they felt surprisingly spiritual while on the island, and I was looking forward to my own spiritual levels rising once I stepped ashore. I expected Dr. Johnson to be right when he wrote in 1773: 'that man is little to be envied...whose piety would not grow warmer among the ruins of Iona.'

Iona's geological make-up was of a very ancient and enduring rock known as Lewisian gneiss which led people to believe the island would exist for all eternity. There was an ancient prophecy which said that seven years prior to the Day of Judgement the ocean would sweep over both Ireland and the Isle of Islay, but Iona, this island of Columba, would be spared the inundation and would float on the waves for ever.

Columba was born around 520 A.D. in Donegal, Ireland. He was of royal lineage and his family was probably pagan. At an early age he'd been fostered by a priest who, so it was claimed, on his return from prayers one day saw his 'house bathed in a bright light' and a 'fiery ball of light over the face of the sleeping child'. He was aware then that the young Columba was destined for great and holy things.

It is thought that Columba had come to Iona in 563 A.D. because he'd had to flee Ireland due to a dispute over a rare copy of the Vulgate (the Latin version of the Bible translated by St. Jerome 342-420 A.D.) which he'd obtained, and which he'd refused to hand over to the High King who'd demanded it. The quarrel had somehow resulted in a bloody battle in which three thousand people lost their lives. Columba had then either been banished from Ireland, or had been so mortified by the many deaths that he'd gone into voluntary exile as a penance.

The story goes that Columba sailed from Ireland in a coracle (in Scottish Gaelic a 'currach'), a boat shaped like half a walnut shell made of woven willow or withes, over which hides were stretched, the whole being then coated with bitumen to make it watertight. As a vessel it was very light, which presumably made it soar and plummet on the huge waves for which the Irish Sea is notorious. But the advantage of its light structure was that it could be carried overland with ease, to be used for fishing on rivers and lakes.

Columba arrived at the southern tip of Iona at Port a Churaich (Port of the Coracle) with twelve companions (the mystical twelve). One coracle for twelve men? Or did each have his own?

Having arrived on this small eternal island, Columba set about founding his monastery and converting pagan Scotland. Because of his royal connections he had access to the king of the northern Picts, King Brude (or Bridei), and in 564 A.D. he was given permission by him to preach Christianity throughout Scotland.

It is possible that Iona had always been thought of as a holy island, and that pilgrims had come there from Mull and the mainland for pagan festivals. What have been thought to be the remains of ancient standing stones erected along the Ross of Mull, have given rise to the idea that they were deliberately raised and aligned with Iona for the benefit of pagans millennia ago in order to direct them to the island. There were signs that there'd been Iron Age inhabitants who would have observed their own religious rites on Iona. Some say that Druid priests had fled the mainland to Iona when the Romans came. In fact, there was another name for the island 'Innis nan Druidh- neach' translated as 'Isle of the Druids'. On one of the hills on Iona it was thought fires had been lit at Beltane (May Day) and cattle driven through them as an act of purification.

Our ferry-boat was coming in to the small harbour and its bows were lowered like the mouth of a whale opening to spew out God- fearing devotees like Jonah. Soon we were disembarking and walking up the quay past fishing nets and lobster pots. Some passengers turned left to Martyr's Bay, others right to the line of small terraced houses, while others like us continued up the street past the shops, and turned right at the top for the Abbey.

We came to the first high standing cross, over sixteen feet high, known as St. Martin's cross. It was a fine example of a late eighth century Celtic cross carved from a single slab of stone brought from Argyll. There had once been many high standing crosses set up by the monks, each one to mark some significant event which had taken place. In the seventeenth century, however, they'd been violently overturned and demolished by the Puritans who'd regarded honouring stone or wooden crosses and the calling upon saints as idolatrous

"Really odd," I said to Harry as we paused by this tall, remarkable stone cross richly carved with biblical scenes, "odd that Christianity, which is supposed to bring love and peace to the world, also spreads such violence."

"People have strong views, I suppose," said Harry easily.

"Well, yes. But that's what's so odd. They are all acting in opposition - on collision courses with each other in the name of God. Explain that!"

"As I keep telling you, it's nothing to do with God."

"But you can't say it's nothing to do with him! God is at the centre of it all. He is the reason for it."

"It's to do with men and their opinions."

"But why is it the fault of men, when they are merely acting on what they are certain are God's wishes? Is God so supremely aloof - or indifferent? Or is he, in fact, supremely non-existent?"

But I was on Iona to feel spiritual, not to be controversial. If I started using reason and plain common sense, then I might as well go home. "No! I won't say another word!" and I shut my mouth firmly. I thought immediately how a priest would tell me God was all powerful, all merciful and loving, and immediately opened my mouth to air the fact that if he was all powerful then why didn't he act on miserable situations when everybody cried out to him? But, I kept silent. If everybody else's spiritual temperatures soared on this holy island, then I must give myself a chance to feel its holiness, not to argue points.

We continued along the road. There were Aberdeen Angus cattle and hills to our left with a few small houses, and on our right larger houses with gardens and views to the rocky shoreline and blue sea. A few small boats bobbed at anchor.

We came to the Abbey ticket-office. There, a grey-headed man with a good honest Scottish face, a good Scottish accent and wearing tartan trousers, sold us entry tickets for the Abbey.

"Do the Orthodox Church hold regular services here?" I enquired. I had heard from someone that one of her most memorable experiences had been on Iona when she had by chance been there for a Greek Orthodox service in St. Oran's Chapel. She thought such services were held there once a week, and I rather hoped that fate had brought me to Iona on a day which coincided with one.

"Och, aye," said the Scotsman, "there's sometimes a gathering of the Eastern Orthodox community here on Iona."

"There's not one every week?" I asked

"The last one was at Easter," came the Scotsman's answer.

I was disappointed. If anything gave me that extra spiritual awareness it was the Greek Orthodox Church services.

The Scotsman must have seen I was disappointed by his answer. "If you're wanting St. Oran's Chapel it's that wee building there," he said pleasantly: "Enjoy your visit to Iona."

We took the path heading for the Abbey and came first to the replica of another high standing cross, the cross of St. John which stood before St. Columba's shrine, a small high gabled stone building to the left of the west entrance to the Abbey church. It had two arrow-slit windows and a locked wooden door set in a stone archway. It was thought that it was there that St. Columba had originally been buried.

From there we headed for St. Oran's Chapel where the Orthodox celebrations had been held. The building was very similar in design to St. Columba's shrine, but larger. The wooden door, which was set in a stone pillar-flanked archway decorated with chevron was open, so we entered. Two plain windows either side of the sanctuary let in light.

There was a strange story regarding this building. It was said that the original monastic church was unable to be built because the walls kept collapsing, so it was thought necessary to consecrate the ground with a living person's burial. Oran, possibly a brother of Columba, volunteered to be the human sacrifice - was this a left-over from Druid practice? It was thought that just before his self-sacrifice, Oran had been arguing with Columba regarding the nature of heaven and hell. At any rate, twenty days after Oran's burial, Columba felt so sad that he had the earth removed so he could have one last look at his brother/friend. To his dismay, Oran's head poked up and said that heaven was not what it was said to be, nor was hell. He went on to declare that neither were the saved for ever happy, nor were the damned for ever lost. That was such a severe shock to Columba that he ordered the earth to be immediately thrown back over him again.

To hallow Oran's memory and, no doubt, to wipe out his shocking pronouncements, the chapel was built in his memory, and honouring him with a sainthood must have clinched it.

On the right wall of this small building was an ornate late medieval tomb recess, thought to have been constructed to take the body and effigy of John of Islay, last Lord of the Isles, who died in 1503. Before it stood a wrought-iron stand for candles. To the right of the small plain altar was a crude wooden cross to which were pinned scraps of paper with written prayers from those seeking a miracle. I read one that stood out glaringly: 'Please prefix every use of the word 'Israeli' with F..K...!' Good God! God's chosen people! Humans on a collision course again.

"Finished here?" asked Harry. He was getting restless in this somewhat bare-walled chapel.

We wandered out to the burial ground known as Reilig Odhráin.

Odhráin was yet another variant of Oran, and Reilig meant graveyard.

It was here that the early kings of Scotland had been buried. Most of the graves were now unnamed but it was thought that Macbeth had been buried there, as was Duncan I, killed by Macbeth. It was said that their graves had been side by side but that their ghosts had quarrelled so much that the islanders had felt it necessary to separate them.

I told Harry about Macbeth.

"You mean Shakespeare's Macbeth?"

"Yes, of course," I said. "I've read that Macbeth was actually a good monarch, not at all what Shakespeare made him out to be. He was a Christian and did a lot for the Church," I said, as though that explained his goodness. "And you know the three witches in Macbeth?" I went on.

"Everybody knows the three witches," Harry said vaguely. He was staring at the pristine grave slab of the recent Labour Party leader, John Smith, who'd died in 1994, and whose body had been brought to this, his favourite island.

"Well, in the play the three witches are sisters, like the three sisters in ancient Greece known as the Moirai, who were responsible for the fate of men. The point being that Shakespeare repeatedly used the word 'weird' regarding his witches, and Wyrd was a concept in Anglo-Saxon times of Fate. Interesting?"

"I suppose so," said Harry who, I suspected, wasn't really paying attention.

"Not forgetting the mystical 'three', the triple mother goddesses. I mean, the early Christians were good at speaking in derogatory terms about things pagan, and by medieval times what had been acceptable words to the pagan mind had become unacceptable to the Christian. The Fates had become witches and were looked on as evil doers."

"Well, if you say so."

"And do you know that the etymology of 'wizard' is 'a wise man'? Originally it was used for a sage or philosopher. But with Christianity wizards were frowned on. St. Paul tore his hair out over the wise, or those who thought themselves so, because Christianity could only be practised by faith, so he said that it was better to be foolish. Christians were good at turning the meaning of words on their heads." I felt I was beginning to lose the thread of what I was trying to say regarding witches and wizards. Harry had lost the thread a long time before, and merely said: "So where to now? We'd better enter the Abbey, I suppose? Or we could eat first and then do the Abbey?"

Food first.

Over lunch at the Columba Hotel, with views to the sea, and the hills of Mull beyond, I told Harry about St. Columba and wizards. I had recently read the Life of St. Columba, a biography written by an abbot, Adomnán of Iona.

In the book a wizard had challenged Columba regarding the power of God; his own pagan gods, he claimed, could prevent Columba sailing across Loch Ness which was what Columba was planning to do, and the wizard summoned a thick mist and gale force winds to prove his point. But St. Columba with fearless faith stepped into his boat and ordered the sailors to set sail into the gale and the mist, at the same time calling on Christ's protection. Immediately the gale died down to a gentle breeze which filled the sails of his boat, and in no time Columba and his crew crossed the loch and reached their destination.

"The miracle was rather like pharaoh's wizards who tried to prove the power of their gods against Moses," I said.

"What happened to the thick mist?" Harry enquired.

"Well, presumably that lifted too."

"That's faith for you," said Harry confidently.

"Another story in Adomnán's biography," I went on, "was when St. Columba frightened off the Loch Ness monster."

"With faith you can do anything," said Harry.

I found Harry's new-found confidence in faith irritatingly pious. "Faith doesn't always get you what you want," I said. "The monks must have had faith that God would protect them when the Vikings came, but a number of them were murdered, and the Abbey was plundered."

"Um. They didn't have the faith of St. Columba obviously." I saw Harry eyeing the remains of my bread roll.

"So what about the Loch Ness monster?" he demanded, taking the remains of my roll and buttering it. How did he know I didn't want it, but I let it pass.

I told him how the monster had apparently devoured some wretched unfortunate who was in the loch, and St. Columba had immediately ordered a man to go into the loch and swim across it to fetch a boat from the opposite bank. "I think he might have swum it himself," I remarked, "instead of sending someone else."

"Perhaps he couldn't swim."

I eyed Harry for a moment. "Of course he could - with faith,"

I said, throwing the confidence-in-faith idea back at him. "Anyway, the poor chap who set off had every reason to be petrified because the monster at once felt the water disturbed by movement, so rose up and with a great roar, went to devour the swimmer but, in the nick of time, St. Columba called on God and the monster fled as though ropes were pulling it away. I like the description."

"And all the heathen onlookers were converted?" enquired Harry, who I was beginning to think would make a good missionary.

"Well, they were impressed certainly," I answered.

Harry used the last of my roll to wipe around his soup bowl. "Have you had enough to eat?" he asked.

"Enough to keep up my strength. We've got the Abbey to see, and other places - the museum, I suppose."

After idling a while longer, enjoying the views from the sheet-glass windows of the Columba Hotel, we paid our bill and left.

We sat in the choir stalls in the church and took part in the Iona Community's afternoon service. The Iona Community was an ecumenical movement consisting of lay and ordained men and women who'd come to this holy island for their various reasons to work for the common good, and to pray together in order to promote justice and peace in the world.

The interior of the church was sombre and grey with stone columned archways and dark flagstones. The carvings on the capitals, and the stone effigies of past abbots, didn't exactly raise my spiritual levels. Dour from the outside and dour from the inside was how I saw it.

The present service was being conducted by two Community men in open shirts and sandals. Prayers were said by a grey-headed one, and general assistance given by the second with a ponytail. The theme Justice and Peace was a worthy one, because without justice (or should the word be fairness?) there could never be peace, only dischord.

Grey-head gave a short address which, for some reason was about Jesus' words regarding salt: "'Salt is good; but if the salt have lost its savour, Wherewith shall it be seasoned?...'" (Luke 14:34). I supposed he was alluding to those who needed a sprinkling of Christian salt to enhance their spiritual well being. I was feeling disappointed because I felt totally unspiritual, even dispirited.

After the address Ponytail carried a small bowl around the congregation, and I noticed that all in turn put a hand into it and then put their fingertips to their lips. I wondered if the bowl was to put money into and there was a certain Community ritual attached to it like kissing the fingers afterwards but, as it drew near, I saw it had a small amount of white substance at the bottom. It could have been cocaine for all I knew, or maybe caster sugar. I knew Harry would be suspicious of whatever it was and, as expected, he handed it straight on to me. I took a pinch and found that it was salt which hadn't lost its savour. Why it had been thought necessary to pass salt around, I wasn't sure. It might have been kinder to have passed sugar, or a gift of sweets.

Music from a C.D. was then played. It was of soprano voices singing in harmony like an angelic choir, and was quite pleasing. It was almost spiritually uplifting but I remained earthbound like a kite which couldn't fly because it was on the end of too long a piece of string.

A few final prayers regarding justice and peace and the service drew to a close. They had done their best; I had done my best. We all went our separate ways, each of us perfectly happy having said prayers, or not having said prayers, while the world, no doubt, continued with as much injustice as it had always had. Or did prayers really shift the minds of those in power?

We left the Abbey and I noticed not far from its entrance a woman seated on top of a grassy hillock reading a book. It was the Hill of the Abbot on which St. Columba had had a wooden hut, or a woven wattle one, where he'd slept and devoted himself to writing and copying manuscripts.

We climbed to the top and looked around at the various Abbey buildings, and to the sparkling blue sea, and the hills of Mull beyond. A few Aberdeen Angus cattle grazed peacefully. They reminded me of a miracle performed by St. Columba, done with every good intention, but which struck me at once as having caused many more problems than the miracle warranted. Columba had been given hospitality by a poverty stricken peasant and to thank him he'd asked the man to bring him his five cows. Horror of horrors, when the saint increased them, not to double the number which might have been a blessing, but to a hundred and five. When Harry and I had farmed we'd had more than enough problems with forty-five milking cows, such as twice-a-day milking, making enough hay or buying in food for the winter, not to mention the calves that were born, the inwintering sheds for the animals, and the disposal of dung. For the poor peasant who'd been used to five, to be suddenly faced with a hundred and five - and in those days there was no electricity, so every cow had to be milked by hand - must have been a nightmare.

"A hundred and five blessed cows!" I said to Harry as we stood on the hillock and I reminded him of this miracle.

"I'm sure Columba miraculously solved every problem," Harry said with his new-found confidence in faith.

"I very much hope he did!" I replied.

We stood on the knoll and felt the warm breeze on our faces. The woman who'd been enjoying her silent solitude with her book, got up and gave us what I thought was a reproachful glare before departing. We sat down on her vacated rock and were pleased to have the knoll to ourselves.

"Do you know," I said to Harry after a while, "that there is an old prophecy saying that Jesus will come again to Iona which means that Jesus has already been?"

"I doubt that somehow."

"Off the west coast of Skye there's a small island called Eilean Isa which is the gaelic for 'Island of Jesus'. So he may well have been there too."

"Um."

"AND! Hold your breath! There is a suggestion that when Jesus came here he brought Mary Magdalene and they had a son!"

"One of these half-baked stories," Harry remarked, picking a daisy from the grass by the rock.

"Well, to add to the half-bakedness of it, and listen to this! Iona was once known as the Isle of John, and the name of Jesus and Mary Magdalene's son was John."

"Who says?"

"Well, whoever - those who know, I suppose."

"Absolute rot."

"And the reason why Iona is called Iona is because the Hebrew for John is 'Johanan', in Greek Ioannes. And just for your interest, the first part of the Hebrew 'Johanan' means Yahweh, God, and the second means 'gracious, or the giving by someone to another in need'. Isn't that interesting?"

"It could as well be called after John the Baptist, or John the

Evangelist, or in anticipation of John Smith, the Labour chap who's buried here."

"But the whole point is that Mary Magdalene came with Jesus."

"Oh, bosh!" said the authority on faith and belief. "You need to use your imagination on positively proven facts, not allow it to range around like an animal on the prowl for scraps. Get your teeth into the real thing."

"Maybe I will in time," I said. "Meanwhile, another fascinating scrap is suggested by a tombstone of the last prioress of the convent nearby - now all gone - which had on it an effigy of what looked like the Virgin and Child, but because of certain give-away features, it is now thought it was Mary Magdalene and THE child."

But Harry had had enough. "We'd better get to the museum," he said, getting himself up with difficulty from his sitting position and dusting off his trousers.

"There's also a stained-glass window in a church on Mull - whose name I've forgotten - which shows a pregnant Mary Magdalene. So explain that!"

Harry exploded. "What's wrong with it being the Virgin Mary, for God's sake! Come on!"

It was mid-afternoon and we were back in the Columba Hotel having afternoon tea. A polite occasion with deep armchairs, and white china, elegant teapot and milk jug, scones and strawberry jam, and murmured conversations all around us.

Nearby I could hear an American holding forth in a dreary monotone, snatches of which I caught: 'I received strength from Our Lord...'

I glanced around and saw that the man was middle-aged, well built, wearing a dark suit. He had a neat moustache and rimless spectacles. Two elderly women sat across from him leaning forward earnestly with expressions of compassion.

The sky outside had become ominously overcast with a volcanic dark cloud. The view to the Sound of Iona had become a glinting grey, with the hills of Mull hidden by a squawl.

"It's going to rain," I said. "What luck we're here and not still rambling about outside."

'...and died with a smile on her face...'

We'd visited the museum in which were the pieced-together broken parts of the original St. John's cross. "Lots of St. Johns!" had been Harry's comment, "and absolutely nothing to do with Mary Magdalene's phantom child!"

We had also seen St. Columba's stone pillow with a cross on it, which he preferred to straw. No doubt he had Jacob and his 'Stone of Destiny' pillow in mind. As with most museums I'd felt bog-eyed with over-concentration.

'...gotten strength from you good folk...'

As quickly as the rain had come, we could see the volcanic cloud sail on. There was an amazing clarity in the sky as the sun shone again and the sea sparkled and the hills of Mull were brilliantly green and shadowed.

"When St. Columba died," I told Harry, "his soul was seen in Ireland ascending to heaven like a pillar of fire. Don't you think that's remarkable? He died here on Iona before the altar in his church and, although it was night, his soul ascending lit up the whole world like a summer's day."

"Says who?"

"Say those in Ireland who saw it, and says Adomnán the abbot who wrote his biography."

"Irish blarney," came the comment.

"The death of a holy man," I said, surprised how Harry could swing from belief and faith, to disbelief and scepticism.

"So are we going to Staffa tomorrow?" Harry demanded.

"God willing," I said. Harry cast me a sharp look, as though surprised that I'd used the name of the Almighty.

Was I falling under the influence of the American? I heard him say: '...and the Church of the Holy Sepulchre...'

"It depends on the weather, but we're booked with whoever it is who does the Staffa trip, probably Mac something or another. We have to look out for a brown wooden boat."

'...then on to Galilee where Our Lord walked on water...'

"I'm looking forward to sitting on a boat and not having to traipse around churches and chapels, and hillocks and museums," Harry announced.

'...and up Mount Tabor where Our Lord was transfigured, as I recall...'

As we left I glanced at the American who had one hand on a knee, and was sitting upright in his armchair with the self-assurance of one who believed in himself. I noticed that one of the women, although leaning towards him, had her eyes almost closed, while the other had a handkerchief out. As we passed I heard, "…lost a beloved wife but found Jesus…'

The sea was rough and I chewed crystallized ginger to ward off seasickness. We were in the stern of the wooden fishing boat wearing zipped up anoraks against the strong wind and the spume carried on the air when the boat hit a wave. The boat trip to Staffa was only to be undertaken 'weather permitting' (the words were written on the conditions advertising the boat trip). To me, a non-sailor and non-swimmer, the weather didn't permit but the trip was being done anyway.

The skipper, a competent looking Scotsman in whom we had no option but to have complete faith since our fate was in his hands, told us that now we had left the Sound of Iona and had passed a few other small islands, there was nothing, but nothing at all, between us and America. It was a sobering thought. The boat pitched and rolled on the waves, and the thin overcast of grey cloud seemed uncertain whether to thicken to storm clouds, or to shred itself to reveal blue sky. The skipper spotted some black seabird skimming the sea but, by the time it had been pointed out and Harry'd raised his binoculars, it was gone.

Long before the forty-five minute trip was completed, Staffa could be seen on the horizon whenever the pitch or roll of the boat didn't hide it from view. As we got nearer it looked like a grass-carpeted hill with a railway tunnel cut into its centre.

Slowly, slowy we advanced towards it; then the boat changed course and rounded the island so the cave was nowhere to be seen, only the strange grey-black columned rock formation of the cliffs, and above that a great layer of rough-textured basalt over which lay its carpet of grass. Spread-eagled around the base of these tightly packed columns were grey-black blocks like chimney-stacks also densely massed together.

There was an air of expectation among the passengers as the boat eased its way towards a small concrete jetty. A young man leapt ashore and was thrown a rope to make the boat fast, before he offered each of us a strong arm to jump ashore. To get to Fingal's Cave, we were told, we must go to the top of the first precipitous flight of concrete steps, then follow the cliff face to the left.

Well, we had arrived. We were reminded by the skipper that we had only one hour to explore Staffa. Few of the passengers seemed interested in the prospect of seeing the cave and continued on up to explore Staffa's grassy summit. Harry and I found ourselves alone with a young foppish looking photographer whom I'd noticed sitting silently in the boat with a tripod. He was already ahead of us, edging along the uneven basalt stepping-stones. We clung on to the cable hand-rail on our right, fastened intermittently to the rockface with metal rings, and tried to ignore what looked like an excessively uncomfortable drop to our left.

Now we were on Staffa it was ridiculous to consider opting out of seeing Fingal's Cave; clearly it could be done or they wouldn't have put up this safety device to hang on to. If the young fop ahead of us with his camera equipment and tripod could do it then of course we could do it too.

Always nervous of precipices, not to mention the sea, I mumbled one of my many silent prayers to God to keep me from slipping or swooning or having a fit as we stepped from one uneven volcanic stepping-stone to the next along the rockface. My nerve was sorely tested when I found one of the metal rings holding the cable had come off its anchorage to the rock, and I had to creep past it and on to the next secure one.

After about two hundred feet, the cliff curved around and there before us was the mouth of the cave, its entrance and interior lined with compressed basalt columns rising from what seemed like a mound of massed basalt chimney-stacks and the sea. The cave roof also appeared covered by these closely packed chimney-stacks but inverted ones. Over the millennia these stacks and columns were the result of erosion from the sea and the tides and the winds advancing and receding from its interior. I noticed that the sea below us just within the mouth of the cave was a pale amethyst blue etched with white where crested wavelets hit the rocks and backed off. The cave was roughly sixty-five feet high, and over a hundred and fifty feet in depth. Ten feet or so beyond where we stood there was a wider ledge already occupied by the photographer with his tripod and equipment.

I suspected he didn't want us on the scene. Well, I didn't particularly want to be there either; I was too anxious about the clinging-to-the-cable walk back. But now we were there it was ridiculous not to make the most of it.

Unfortunately, my anxiety made me witless, and I forgot everything I'd wanted to remember while there. I forgot to listen to the music of the waves and the echoes of the sea on rock, as immortalized by the poets and composers who had come to the cave in years gone by. Mendelssohn's Fingal's Cave overture had been inspired by the melodious sounds in the cave. Wordsworth had gone into raptures over it: 'O for those motions only that invite/The Ghost of Fingal to his tuneful Cave...'

"Who was this Fingal anyway?" Harry asked.

"Fingal? He was a giant," I replied. And I told Harry how these basalt columns and chimney-stacks were similar to those at the Giant's Causeway in Northern Ireland, the result of a violent volcanic eruption millions of years ago.

"The Giant's Causeway was occupied by the giant Finn McCool," I began.

"I've heard of him I think."

"It's all a bit confusing because it's not certain whether the Scots at first had a giant and then adopted the Irish Finn and called him Fingal."

"Oh. Why?"

"I've no idea. It was centuries ago. I think perhaps because they wanted their own mythology - Ireland had Finn, and England had Gog and Magog. Anyway, the story goes that Fingal one day shouted insults at Finn McCool, and Finn McCool responded by hurling great clods of earth across the sea at him which prompted Fingal to fling huge rocks back. Finn's clods of earth created a causeway, whereupon he dared Fingal to cross over and confront him."

"And did he?"

"Yes. But Finn McCool pretended to be a baby asleep in a cradle, and his wife told Fingal that Finn was away, and then showed him the sleeping child saying it was their son. When Fingal saw the enormous infant, he was thrown into a frenzy, fearing that if their son was that large, then the father must be horrendously more so. So he fled back across the sea to Staffa, tearing up and flinging away the clods of earth which made the causeway as he went."

"Is that all?"

"That's all I know about Fingal. There's quite a lot about the Irish Finn McCool."

The blustery gale buffeting the waves on the rocks at the mouth of the cave was not exactly warm, and Harry was keen to get back so he could look for puffins which we'd been told had colonies on the island.

I was, in truth, slightly disappointed with this cave which had sent poets and musicians into raptures, or maybe more disappointed with myself for not being in raptures about it also. I had been spoilt for caves having seen the spectacular Diktaion mountain cave in Crete where legend had it the supreme god, Zeus, had been born. There the cave had glowed with different hues of sombre colours, and had depth and width and temple-like columns, as well as stalagmites and stalagtites, and a small crystal-clear lake which overawed and filled the visitor with wonder.

Here at Staffa we turned about gingerly, and step by step, clinging to the cable - letting go where it was loose, and regrasping it where it was fixed again - we made our slow way back to the concrete steps where at last we could relax.

We climbed the remaining steps and reached the grassy top of the island where we were free to walk in whatever direction took our fancy. With no particular purpose in mind except puffins, we headed north over the undulations. Now we were on land with no hazards to occupy our minds, Harry said: "So what about Finn McCool? You said there was more about him."

"Finn. Well, as well as being a giant, he was a great hero also and gathered warriors around him. He was admired for his valour and killed hostile giants, goblins and serpents. He was also able - and you'll like this! - to change his shape by wearing a magic hat which, when cocked at different angles, changed him either into a dog or a stag."

"Typical Irish jargon!"

"Not just Irish," I replied. "In ancient Greece there was a sea-god called Nereus, who was endowed with wisdom and also had the ability to change himself into different shapes if anyone pursued him, although he didn't have a magic hat to do it. His daughter married a king and their son was Achilles."

"I suppose these stories were built up from hearsay. The Irish probably traded with Greece - like Joseph of Arimathea traded in tin and came to Glastonbury spreading Christian stories."

"In case you're interested, they say that St. Patrick interceded for Finn McCool and his band of warriors, and so saved their souls."

"St. Patrick drove away the snakes from Ireland," Harry remarked.

"Yes. So that was one up on Finn McCool who only destroyed serpents if he came across them. And just for the record, it was thought that Fingal, and I suppose by association that means Finn McCool also, was descended from the Celtic god Nodens. You remember? We saw his temple at Lydney Park?"

"Oh, him. I remember he was something to do with the river Severn." Harry raised his binoculars and scanned the northern shores for puffins. Gulls glided on the gusts of wind. The black basalt chimney-stacks with the waves breaking over them were spectacular.

Saturated with Scottish and Irish legends, I expected to see mermaids seated on the rocks, combing their long hair, their tails draped over the rocks. Or perhaps a Kelpie, the Highland mythical water-sprite which took the shape of a horse.

Instead, we saw two people from our boat walking briskly towards the east of the island as though they knew that puffins could be seen there on the shore. We followed in their tracks with fifteen minutes left before we were due back at the boat.

By the time we reached the east side of the island the couple had left by another route. There the basalt rocks curved gently to the sea like the rotting planks of a long disused wooden boat. Somewhere on this side was a cave called Clamshell Cave, but we saw no sign of one. Harry scanned the shoreline, and then the sea for puffins, but saw only what he thought might be a kittiwake and a few cormorants. He was enjoying this trip to Staffa where nature was wild, and there were no churches, chapels or temples, synagogues or mosques, but deity in the raw - well, I supposed really I meant humans in the raw with nature.

Time was against us. We didn't want to be marooned and left combating the elements, scrounging for food and eating grass and insects like the holy hermits had done in the past whom I'd always thought a bit demented. We didn't want to save our souls, living like the early Christians had in caves. Rather were we determined to keep body and soul together in as much comfort as was possible.

We hurried back to the boat, well pleased with our expedition.

"No puffins," Harry told the skipper as he was helped back on board.

"That's a shame," said the man. "I've a mind they'll be in the water somewhere. They're safer that way."

"Safer? Why's that? Are there predators?"

"Och aye. Ye'll find the - " I thought he said 'razorbill', at any rate it was some vicious sea bird, but his voice was lost on the wind, "...swoop down and slit their throats."

"Good God! Not nice," said Harry.

"They're safer bobbing in the water, than sitting out on the rocks there. If I spot one I'll give you a shout," he said.

All passengers were accounted for, and the boat pulled away from the jetty and turned about. Soon we were sailing away, heading for what looked like a dark cloud - on Staffa the sun had shone which was amazing.

"Look there!" shouted the skipper. "You see the wee heads bobbing out there where I'm pointing!"

All eyes turned to look. "They're puffins for you!" he called.

Harry stood, his binoculars raised, his sea-legs not as steady as they might be as the boat rose and fell or rocked from side to side like Finn McCool's cradle. I clutched his anorak to keep him from falling in the wrong direction. Eventually, Harry lowered the binoculars, and said: "I can see better without these damned things!"

I stood beside him and saw what looked like bobbing corks, but no orange beaks, or white clown-like markings. Still, we had seen puffins, if only just.

I sat back on the wooden seat and gave silent thanks that the sun had shone on Staffa. Our landlady at our B&B croft had thought it quite likely that our trip would be cancelled. She always listened to the weather forecast because her husband was a lobster fisherman. She'd told us how some years before she and a party of schoolboys had made the trip to Staffa on a wild day. She'd expected the boys to be seasick on that roller-coaster trip, but they'd all loved it, and they'd arrived in a thick sea mist which had made the cave look eerie and mysterious. Suddenly the island had appeared at them through the mist. Whether they'd seen the cave from the boat, or crept along the lethal stepping stones to see it, I wasn't sure; but she'd described how the mist had been swirling in and out of the cave mouth, and how it had been a never-to-be-forgotten experience. She would never try to persuade people not to go there in bad weather as it was more spectacular that way, she'd said.

I'd been aware for some time of the two women seated at the table close to ours in the pub. The younger of the two was energetic and lively looking, and the other I thought could be her mother. They were both wearing dresses and bead necklaces, and had clearly made an effort for their evening's outing to this pub at Fionnphort. They had finished their meal and were having coffee when the younger woman smiled at me. "Are you here on holiday?" she asked.

"A working holiday," I replied.

She seemed interested, and enquired what the work was, and I told her about my interest in pagan gods and Christianity.

"How strange," she said. "I'm fascinated by that too."

It turned out she was a school teacher from Yorkshire and, yes, that was her mother whom she'd come on holiday with. The mother smiled but said little, allowing her daughter to continue with her enthusiastic prattle about Celtic gods and heroes.

She said suddenly, twisting in her chair and pointing. "You see that huge boulder down there on the sand?"

I stood up to look. "That," she said, "is known as Fingal's Rock. It's said to be one of the rocks he threw at Finn McCool."

"Really? I must go and look at it," I said at once.

"I'll come with you," she said.

Harry wanted to finish his dessert, and the mother said she'd stay where she was till we got back.

There was a vivid sunset, the sky and clouds were streaked with reds and pinks and orange. The colours were reflected in the waters of the Sound and glowed on our skin. As she and I walked over the grassy dunes to the damp sandy shore which also reflected the sunset, she told me about Finn McCool and the Fianna who were his warriors.

"Of course, those Irish legends which are recounted in the famous Fenian Cycle were what inspired the King Arthur legends," she said. "Have you read them?" she asked.

I supposed she was referring to the Fenian Cycle, and I had to admit I hadn't. I may have heard of the title, but that was all.

"It's sometimes known as the Ossian Cycle - Ossian, as you probably know, was Finn McCool's son. Their names are in some way related to deer. Finn was said to be an incarnation of the Celtic antlered god Cernunnos. I'm sure you've heard of Cernunnos, the forest deity?"

"You know so much!" I said.

"I'm probably boring you, but I'm fascinated by these folk heroes and their legends and the gods."

"Tell me more!" I invited, as we jumped across a small pool of sea water to a stretch of damp sand beyond.

She stooped suddenly and picked up a small white shell. "I collect these for the children," she said. "They use them in art class for decoration. So where was I?"

"You were telling me about the antlered god Cernunnos, and Finn having some sort of association with deer."

"Oh, yes. He had a son called Oisin or Ossian meaning 'small deer'.

"And who was the mother?"

"Her name was Sadbh meaning 'Doe'. Oh, it's a long story. They are all enchanted, all magical - typically Irish. Finn is out hunting with his two hounds one day when they come across a beautiful red deer, but the hounds refuse to attack it. Finn is mystified, and the red deer follows him home before revealing itself as a beautiful woman. Till meeting Finn McCool she'd been under a curse put on her by a Druid who, because she'd refused his advances, had been so angry he'd transformed her into this deer. Meeting with Finn the curse lifted and she and Finn fell in love and married and had a son, Ossian. I like the story, don't you?"

"It's a fairy story," I said.

"Of course. It's quite unbelievable but it has magical qualities, like religion. I just love the stories, although I don't believe them. Like the Salmon of Knowledge story when Finn was given the task of cooking a salmon but on no account was he to eat it. But while it was sizzling he touched a blister on the fish which popped and burned his finger which he then sucked and acquired the knowledge and wisdom of the fish. Don't you think that's interesting? By imbibing or ingesting something that has certain qualities, a person can acquire those qualities - like taking the Christian sacraments which are the body of Christ."

I was astonished at this young woman. Her enthusiasm was infectious, and I thought her young pupils were lucky to have her as their teacher.

"Of course this salmon story has a parallel in the Welsh one about Gwion and the fertility goddess Ceridwen," she went on. "Gwion is asked to stir her cauldron of inspiration and knowledge but on no account to let the liquid touch him. But three drops splatter him and he sucks the drops from his fingers and so acquires its magical powers of knowledge. Three drops! The magical three. In Celtic lore the number three was mystical. And when Christianity arrived with its Trinity, it attracted the Celts to it as they could identify with this mystical three."

The sun by now had set, though the sky was still on fire. We reached the great rock whose grey blackness I could see was covered with yellow lichen.

"This is it - one of Fingal's missiles intended to kill Finn in Ireland."

"He wasn't much of a shot," I said.

"Oh, this one was thrown back by Finn," said the teacher with confidence. "It's quite lovely here , isn't it?" she went on, gazing across the Sound to the silhouetted outline of Iona and the dying orange colours streaking the sky.

"The end of the world - Armageddon," I murmured.

"Funny you should say that. They say that Iona will survive into eternity, while all else goes up in the final conflagration. Oh!" she laughed, as we turned and walked back to the pub. "I feel exhilerated after our long talk! It's been so interesting. I'm so glad we met!"

"And so am I," I said. "Thank you for showing me the rock."

Our B&B working croft wasn't the most upmarket but it was by far the most interesting. As well as the paraphernalia required by a lobster fisherman, there was all the necessary junk required for farming: a tractor, sheep troughs, wooden posts etc., not to mention livestock running loose such as lambs with black-speckled legs, a couple of sheep, speckled hens and mandarin ducks, all wandering freely over the so-called lawn.

A wire fence kept out several long-horned Highland cattle and a handsome bull with even longer horns and a ring in his nose. When working outside our landlady, who must have been in her fifties, wore long boots and a boiler-suit and carried a stick. There were a lot of adders on Mull, she told us. Once when she'd been getting the cattle down from the hills she'd been bitten by one. At first she'd thought it was a bee, but then had seen there were two puncture marks. By the time she'd got back home her head had felt painfully swollen as though she had a bad migraine, and she had pins and needles in her right arm and down her leg. It had taken six weeks to fully recover.

As for vets, well, if a vet was needed he had to come from Oban by ferry and the cost was over a hundred pounds before treatment even began. So they kept as much medication as possible for the animals there at the croft.

I imagined she had just a few acres, but I was quite wrong. She had two hundred around her, and four thousand acres of hill farming. The latter entailed going up with the dog and calling to the cattle. They always came to her voice. She only had trouble when there was a calf, and then she would have to put a halter on the cow and lead it in and the calf would follow.

No, they had no television because the reception was bad. Her teenage sons had to make their own entertainment. One played the fiddle, and the other an accordian and they and their friends, when they were working in the hay fields, would sing Highland songs to lighten the work.

Our landlady turned on a recording of Highland music, with fiddles, accordian, flute and drum. Harry's hand was soon beating the time on the arm of his chair, and my foot was tapping the floor. It was astonishing how rhythm had such an instant effect on the human body and could also arouse a variety of emotions. After what must have been an energetic Highland fling, the fiddles and flute played a slow and languid melody which changed the mood instantly - one which the fertility goddess would surely approve.

It was time to take our luggage to the gate to be ready for the taxi when it came. There was only one taxi in this area, a husband and wife team who had great patience as Harry and I tried to decide what time to be collected from the pub at Fionnphort in the evenings, or the time to be taken from the croft to the ferry-boat in the morning.

As we waited for the car we heard the cuckoo. I'd heard one on the day we'd arrived at the croft, its clear alto tone coming repeatedly on the air: 'Cuckoo. Cuckoo. Cuckoo!' We hadn't heard the bird down south for several years, and the sound brought with it instant optimism like a good omen.

The taxi came and I was relieved to see the driver was in good humour. I suspected he was making up for a momentary loss of patience with us the day before when Harry and I had been unable to decide what time to be collected from where we planned to eat that evening. 'Seven-thirty? No, nine o'clock. No, eight-thirty. Perhaps eight-fifteen?' He'd suddenly gripped the steering wheel, and dropped his head down on his arms tearing at his hair. "Are you all right?" I'd asked. "Yes, I'm all right," he'd replied, clearly indicating that it was Harry and I who weren't.

"To the bus stop?" he now asked pleasantly, handing us our bill with an itemised list of the journeys we had made with him.

As he took us to the nearby village for the bus, Harry looked at the bill. It was his turn to fling his head down on the steering wheel, except he wasn't driving. Instead, he sat bolt upright as we bumped along, and counted out the money.

We were put down at the bus stop, and the driver unloaded our bags cheerfully. Harry was ready with his money. "There you are," he said, handing the driver several twenty pound notes. "You'd better keep the change," he mumbled.

"Oh, well, that's very generous of you," said the driver. He then himself counted the notes and I saw him briefly frown as he thumbed and flicked the last one to make sure two weren't stuck together. Nevertheless, he hid his disappointment well and shook hands and wished us a good journey.

Soon the bus arrived and we were taken along the only road going east to Craignure; past rough pasture dotted with bob-cotton (wild grass with small white fluffy heads), past the mauve blooms of wild rhododendron, past yellow gorse and spruce forests, past the waters of Loch Scridain and the high hills of Ben More.

Suddenly from the bus I caught sight of a large stag standing still beside the loch amongst the bob-cotton, its head raised and its antlers held aloft, its eyes on the passing bus. A handsome beast. It could be the Celtic antlered god Cernunnos, I thought. Or a descendant of the legendary family of Finn McCool or Fingal.

I drew Harry's attention to it, and told him what I thought. "Good God!" was his instant reaction (maybe he was right about the god part). "What a beauty! Just waiting to be shot! Nothing like a haunch of venison with red currant jelly!"

To eat the meat/the god, and gain strength from it? Well, why not?

All things were possible in the Highlands where mystery and reality existed side by side.

CHAPTER EIGHT

EDINBURGH

It is evening, and we are outside the main entrance to the Botanical Gardens in Edinburgh. It is one of those spectacular evenings when the early summer sun is warm, there is no wind, and all is tranquil.

A wedding reception is being held inside the building and taxis are sweeping in to the circular driveway, depositing the guests before circling around and departing empty. We have been drawn to this spot by the sound of bagpipes. To one side of this broad entranceway, standing below a pine tree, a strongly built young Scot in kilt, studded jacket, sporran, long white hose and black Gillie brogues, is standing erect, bagpipes tucked under an arm, his left foot beating time on the ground, his cheeks puffing in and out repeatedly as he keeps the skirl going. It is a uniquely evocative sound on this mellow evening.

Another taxi sweeps up and a fine looking silver-haired Scot emerges followed by his wife. Apart from the occasional beauty who arrives with the air and poise of a film star, most of the women who get out of the taxis look surprisingly drab, unlike their fine looking husbands in their tartan kilts and black studded jackets.

After a while Harry enquires: "So what are you planning for tomorrow?"

"Hopefully, Edinburgh Castle in the morning, and Rosslyn Chapel in the afternoon - the Dan Brown's Da Vinci Code chapel," I say. "You'll enjoy that. It's only seven miles by bus."

"Good God. I'd no idea it was so near to Edinburgh. Well, the book was all right, I suppose."

Harry started boasting about his Scottish blood as we sat on a wooden seat on one of the ramparts of Edinburgh Castle. "The Romans were quite unable to cope with the Scots!" he said with pride. "When they came they were forced back by them in no time - unlike the Romans in England!" he scoffed. I was proud of my Englishness, so immediately said that the Scots weren't so invincible since the Angles had defeated them in the seventh century.

"Pah!" said Harry. "The Scottish King Malcolm the something-or-another - "

"Malcolm III?" I prompted.

"Defeated the Angles in the eleventh century," he said.

"Only to lose again to the English in the thirteenth!" I added triumphantly.

"Until they were defeated at the Battle of Bannockburn, thanks to Robert the Bruce, so there!"

We were taking a break from touring the castle. I was already feeling bog-eyed with its super magnificence, its ramparts and high walls, not to mention its kings, heroes and heraldry. But I wasn't there so much for the castle as for its pre-castle pagan days, and its early Christian worship. It was thought that there had once been inhabitants living on the Castle Rock who'd worshipped the sun, moon and stars. Edinburgh was in the heart of the area known as Lothian, or Lleuthern, meaning 'the fortress of Lleu', the sun god. In 600 A.D. it was known as Din Eidyn (the stronghold of Eidyn). Some think that there was a legendary giant called Red Etin. Well, maybe.

Harry left me ruminating on the seat and returned to the nine cannons pointing through apertures in the dark-stoned, gently curving battlements of the Half-Moon Battery. I'd already peered through the appertures and had been amazed at how wide a vista could be seen. Looking north there'd been the city centre with the Scott Monument, north-east the Firth of Forth, and a few degrees further east the Palace of Holyrood and the hill known as Arthur's Seat. The name Holyrood, I'd read, came from 'holy rood' meaning 'sacred cross'. The palace had been built in the twelfth century by King David of Scotland, pious son of a saintly queen, St. Margaret, wife of King Malcolm III, the king who defeated the Angles - who also killed Macbeth and seized the throne.

Apparently, King David had gone hunting one day when a stag had startled his horse and he'd been thrown. He'd tried to grasp the stag's antlers - I wondered why he hadn't tried to hang on to the horse's reins or cling to its mane, as that would have been more normal - but, no, he'd tried to grasp the stag's antlers, and had instead found himself holding a cross. Perhaps the story reflected the Celtic antler-horned god, Cernunnos? What better legend than that to illustrate the switch from paganism to Christianity? On the night after that incident a voice had commanded King David to build a 'house for Canons devoted to the Cross', hence the Abbey of Holyrood which later became the royal residence, or Palace of Holyrood.

The rock on which the Castle perched, and the Royal Mile which ran down from it to the Palace of Holyrood, were created as the result of violent volcanic activity many, many million years ago. The area of this ancient extinct volcano is now the Royal Park, and the highest of the craggy hills is the one known as Arthur's Seat, called that less because of King Arthur than as a corruption of 'Archer's Seat', or even from the Scottish Gaelic 'Ard-na-Saidh', 'Height of the Arrows'.

Here at the Castle Harry was determined to stick with his cannons, and concentrate on military matters, so I took myself off to see the main purpose of my visit, the Stone of Destiny. I made my way to the end of a long queue waiting to get in to the Crown Room where the Stone was kept along with the Honours of Scotland.

Shuffle, shuffle, and the queue slowly advanced towards the small door at the base of what I took to be David's Tower and entrance to the Royal Palace where the treasures were kept. The queue was in what was known as Crown Square, a large open area around which were handsome buildings, and on my left the Scottish National War Memorial.

Shuffle, shuffle. Compared with the previous fine, warm evening, that day was gloomy. It was overcast, one of those non-weather days when there is neither sun nor rain, just dullness. I would have preferred a Scottish 'haar' with the Castle shrouded in a thick Scottish mist. That would have added mystery and excitement to the scene, how it had been once when I'd visited a convent on one of the Greek islands, and the mountainside had been in swirling cloud where sometimes the bell-tower could be glimpsed and sometimes not, and I'd had to grope my way around stone steps, and literally feel my way to the convent's various points of interest.

Shuffle, shuffle. We were at last inside and mounting narrow stairs which were dimly lit. At last I reached the small room with its centrally placed reinforced glass cabinets where the Crown and Sceptre, Sword of State and other royal regalia were on display under discreet lighting.

And there, together with these Honours of Scotland, was this lump of sandstone, this priceless Stone of Destiny. The word 'priceless' could be used to mean it was of such immense value no price could be put on it, or it was of no value at all, or it was priceless as in amusing.

Whatever its true worth it had been fought over, smuggled, stolen, retrieved from one kingdom to another since 1296 when the English under Edward I captured the Castle and took this 'priceless' booty, this Stone of Destiny, to Westminster. It was he who had then commissioned the Coronation Chair and had had it designed in such a way as to take the Stone beneath the seat for the crowning of a monarch.

The Stone had come to Scotland from Ireland, and the story was that it had been taken to Ireland from Spain where it had originally been brought from Egypt by Pharaoh's daughter named Scota. It was said to be Jacob's Pillow, and there'd been a prophecy that wherever the Stone was there the Scots would reign. When Edward I seized it and took it to Westminster he let it be known that because he now had the Stone he had supreme power over Scotland too.

The Scots then claimed that in actual fact THE original Stone had been hidden by the monks of Scone Palace on Dunsinane Hill. In other words, Edward I had taken a dummy stone. But that didn't stop those in high places revering it. It became regarded as the Stone which bound the British people, a sort of palladium or talisman which kept Britain safe. In 1921 Freemasons claimed it came from the altar on which Abraham had prepared to sacrifice his son Isaac - from THE Rock in Jerusalem around which King Solomon had built his temple, the Holy of Holies, no less.

But then in 1950 three young Scottish Nationalists with much daring stole the Stone from Westminster Abbey and took it back to Scotland. Four months passed before the police tracked them down, during which time it was suspected that several more copies of the Stone had been made, dummies of the dummy.

And there it was before me, a lump of sandstone with metal rings on either side to haul it around. Sceptics think it might originally have been a man-hole cover. In 1996 it underwent certain scientific tests which established that the Stone almost certainly had come from a quarry less than a mile from Scone. Dummy or not there was by now no turning back from its sacred indelible stamp of authenticity. If Scotland had twice fooled the English with a fake, then the English had now called their bluff when, after receiving it again after the theft, they returned the Stone to Scotland on loan as a gesture of extreme largesse with all the security, pomp and circumstance reserved normally only for a visiting head of state. Let these Scots keep it, on the strict understanding it is returned to Westminster Abbey for the coronation of the next monarch. Tradition and beliefs are the fabric of society and, whether true or false, must at all costs be maintained.

It was time to meet up with Harry at our pre-arranged rendez-vous in order to catch the bus for Rosslyn Chapel.

As soon as we saw Rosslyn Chapel we were struck by its diminutive majesty. If my hopes and expectations were high when we glimpsed its decorated pinnacles adorning each flying buttress, and the ornate stonework around its arched stained-glass windows, they positively soared as we entered the chapel. It was at once clear why so many writers and artists over the centuries had been captivated and inspired by it. As for Dan Brown's novel, The Da Vinci Code, he'd really set the world alight with his characters following mysterious clues which brought them racing to Rosslyn Chapel to unravel the riddle which would finally unlock the secret whereabouts of the long lost Holy Grail.

In a few minutes, we were told, a guide would be giving a thirty-minute talk about the St. Clair family whose property this was, and would point out the main features of the chapel with its myriad small stone-carved figures and faces peeping out from among whorls and scrolls, flowers and foliage, so if we would like to sit –

We took our places in one of the small wooden pews and stared at the elaborate stone work, and the attractive stained-glass windows.

"Would you like to hear why it's called Rosslyn?" I whispered to Harry. He bent his head down to me, and I told him how I'd read that the Celtic word 'ross' meant 'rocky promontory', and 'lynn' meant 'waterfall'. "It probably refers to the castle which was built on the side of a glen not far from here long before the chapel," I said.

"Is it open to the public?" Harry asked.

"I think it's open to the sky and is a ruin," I replied. "We can walk and see it later, if you like." There was another far more fascinating interpretation of Rosslyn and I plucked at Harry's sleeve. "And what is more," I began, "and you'll like this!" Harry inclined his head again. "Another theory of why it's called Rosslyn, or r-o-s-l-i-n as the village and castle are spelt, is because it's a corruption of Rose Line."

"As in railway line?"

"No. Line as in lineage. Rose lineage. Jesus was once referred to as the Rose of Sharon, and in the Middle Ages the Virgin Mary became Santa Maria della Rosa. And if Mary Magdalene was married to Jesus and they'd had a son, then the son was descended from the Rose Line. AND! Wait for it! Some think the St. Clairs were descended from this same Rose Line. Perhaps that's why they were Saints - Saint Clair. A sort of courtesy title because of the blood line from Jesus."

"Never heard such tosh!" remarked Harry.

"Well, I'm only telling you what the experts say - well, some experts," I added.

"Some nuts," came the retort, and he raised his head and sat upright out of earshot.

I plucked at his sleeve once more. "And some other so-called experts, or nuts as you like to call them," I said into his ear which had come down again, "those in the know about ley lines and meridian lines, and things which are a complete mystery to me, say there's a fantastically energetic ley line which is called the Rose Line running under the chapel here. Called that, I suppose because of the lineage Rose Line. Dowsers have gone into raptures over this ley line because whatever they use for dowsing positively palpitates over the altar here."

A man's voice behind said loudly: "The score's two-one to Germany so far!" which was immediately followed by muted cheers and groans from those who thought one goal was good, and others who thought one goal not good enough. The World Cup was entering a crucial phase and England was playing Germany that afternoon. Never mind Rosslyn Chapel and all its accompanying mysteries and legends; the World Cup was all that really mattered. An England victory would be a triumph. Scotland hadn't even qualified, something which so far I'd been good enough not to crow about to Harry.

A jolly, rather plump woman, dressed in loose flowing garments, came and stood before the small gathering waiting to hear her. She must have been in her fifties, and had a pleasant, smiling face. She announced loudly to everybody in the chapel that she was there to speak, and for those not wanting to listen if they could creep around noiselessly, it would help.

Rosslyn Chapel had been founded by Sir William St. Clair in 1446, she told us, and it had taken forty years to complete by which time Sir William had died, and she went on briefly about the earlier St. Clairs. The St. Clairs had originated in France and a former William St. Clair had been first cousin to William the Conqueror, she said, and had with other St. Clair knights fought with him at the Battle of Hastings. Some, though, had become disillusioned by William the Conqueror's cruelty and had come to Scotland, lured there by King Malcolm III (whose wife had been St. Margaret).

The woman realized she had to lighten her talk to keep us alert if we were not to nod off. She started telling us about the numerous figures which could be spotted among the whorls and scrolls of stone carvings, and used a pointer torch to draw our attention to them. Soon she had us twisting in our seats peering here and there at the many heads of the Green Man with foliage covering his head, or coming out of his ears or his mouth. There were over a hundred such Green Men inside the chapel, and more outside, she informed us. The torch picked out dragons and snakes, dance of death skeletons, the seven virtues and seven deadly sins, and the sculpted figure of an angel playing the bagpipes - a novel idea for an angel.

For a while she had us transfixed by the barrel-vaulted ceiling above the choir and sanctuary which was divided into five sections by carved stone ribs, each section containing its own particular decoration - four-petalled flowers, multi-lobed leaves with flowers, roses, lilies and stars. The little red light of her pointer torch flickered here and there as it picked out from among the stars the sun, the moon, then a dove and the face of Christ with a hand raised in blessing.

"Three-one to Germany!" a man said hoarsely behind me.

"What?"

"Three-one!"

"Oh, God!"

"Jesus!" The expletives, I thought, were appropriate considering where we were.

The woman next drew our attention to the master mason's pillar, and the far superior creation of the apprentice's pillar, done while the master mason was absent. The quality of the apprentice's pillar had so annoyed his boss that he'd killed him on the spot. More twisting of heads as the woman turned her pointer torch on stone faces looking down: the apprentice's head with a gash on it, his mourning mother, and the angry master mason.

"Which brings me to the Knights Templar," said the woman cheerfully. "You've all been waiting for me to tell you the secret hiding place of the Holy Grail."

I'd done my homework regarding the Knights Templar, and had read that they'd been a band of French knights who'd gone with the Pope's blessing to Jerusalem, supposedly to protect pilgrims travelling to the Holy Land, but it was later suspected, hoping to discover and bring home the lost Jewish temple treasures such as the Ark of the Covenant and ancient Jewish scrolls, as well as Christian treasures such as the Holy Grail, the True Cross, and possibly even the mummified head of Christ.

Whether the Knights Templar discovered the lost treasures is unknown; whether they were being paid vast sums of money to keep silent about something momentous they'd discovered is also not known. What is certain, however, is that the Knights Templar became so rich and powerful, that the Church and State became increasingly alarmed and summarily disbanded them.

"Certain features in the Chapel suggest the St. Clairs had connections with the Knights Templar," said our woman. And she beamed the red dot from her pointer torch towards two knights riding a horse. "Two knights on a horse are to be found on the official seal of the Knights Templar," she said. "After they were proscribed by the Pope who feared their power, it was the Freemasons who began to flourish in Europe. There are numerous stone carvings here in the chapel revealing signs that the St. Clair family had connections with the Freemasons. And her torch flitted here and there picking out this and that until I felt cross-eyed with little figures.

"For those of you looking for the hidden Holy Grail, or the Ark of the Covenant, then go through the door there where there are stone steps going down to the vault. A great part of it is sealed off, and the St. Clair family won't allow access to it. You can draw your own conclusions from that if you like, but I can tell you that radar scans have been used around the chapel and the results have all been disappointing." Her expression betrayed suppressed amusement as her audience waited for some revelation which would unlock the riddles and mysteries which had brought them there. But nothing came. The woman thanked us for our patience, and invited us to come up and ask her questions if we had any. I couldn't resist the opportunity. I left Harry sitting and managed to get to her first.

"I'm curious about the Green Man figures," I began. "You told us there were over one hundred heads inside the chapel, why is that, do you suppose?" I asked.

"The Green Man was a symbol of death and resurrection," she said. "The riot of carvings which you find here in the chapel are designed to make the worshipper aware of the tragicomedy of life. The frowns, smiles, ghoulish expressions of the Green Man do this admirably."

"Is the Green Man a pagan symbol? A pagan god, even?"

"Well, not exactly a god, but certainly he comes from pagan times. He is much the same as the death and resurrection of nature deities in antiquity such as the Greek Adonis, Dionysos or Persephone, or the Babylonian Tammuz. You could say Jesus, even. The Green Man has been found all over the world."

"So he's not just a Celtic idea?"

"Not at all." She smiled at me, then said: "You have to realize that the St. Clair family when this chapel was built was Roman Catholic, and the Roman Church was never afraid, indeed, probably encouraged, building churches on pagan sites and adapting pagan symbols to Christian use. Have you been to Roslin Castle yet?"

"No, we're hoping to go there now."

"I think when you see the glen, you'll realize why there are so many carvings of the Green Man. It is a positive riot of greenery at Roslin Castle. A sort of Garden of Eden. Archaeologists have found evidence of habitation there from the Bronze Age. And they've found certain Roman artefacts suggesting there might well have been the worship of Mithras there too."

"Mithras? Really?"

I became aware of others waiting to speak to her, and felt I had monopolized her for long enough. "Well, thank you so much. This place is amazing."

"Go down to the glen and Roslin Castle," she advised. "I think you'll be pleasantly surprised." She turned to a man who was coming forward, and I moved away.

"Roslin Castle," I told Harry, "I've been told we ought to see it."

We were directed along a footpath which soon passed through a wood. To the right of the path the ground fell away steeply and, after several hundred yards, we glimpsed the towering ruins of the castle through the trees. Another two hundred yards and we crossed a long bridge to it.

From the unseen depths of the glen tall trees grew in profusion, their different hues and shapes of green leaves deeply shadowed in the late afternoon sun. The bridge had once been the drawbridge to the castle. What a fantastic setting! No wonder poets had been inspired by it.

I looked down from the bridge to the tree-filled abyss. The intensity of nature was astonishing. The immense power required for the growth of all these huge trees reaching up to the light from the dark depths was due to what? Was it the ley line responsible for such energy and growth, the Rose Line over which some think the castle, and later the chapel, had deliberately been built? I could imagine Green Man faces peering from the shadowy foliage, grimacing and smiling.

A mobile phone rang musically, and a woman nearby quickly answered it. "Four-one to Germany? It is true? We beat England!" she shouted to her companion.

"We have beaten England? We beat England four-one? Ach! I am so proud! Tonight we celebrate!" said the man.

"I knew England hadn't a hope," Harry said. "So much for England! Bad luck!"

I couldn't let that go, and blurted out what I'd so far left unsaid: "At least England qualified which is more than Scotland did!"

"Much better not to qualify than to lose 4-1 to Germany!" was the final comment. And I could think of nothing more to say that would put England out on top.

༈

The following morning found us walking down the Royal Mile heading for the new Scottish Parliament building and the Palace of Holyrood.

"Scotch oak," said Harry approvingly, when I commented unfavourably on the new Scottish Parliament building with its windows screened by what looked like fencing stakes set at a slant. He would have defended what I saw as a monstrous eyesore at the bottom of the Royal Mile, till I reminded him it had been the brain child of a Spanish architect so his immediate comment was 'foreign maniac!'

We passed the Palace of Holyrood, approached the Royal Park, followed the road around, and began the ascent of Arthur's Seat along the rough track which wound steeply up the flank of the hill. It was hard going so every now and again we stopped and sat on a rock to admire the view. To the east we could see across to the Firth of Forth and the North Sea. Further to our left was a hill with an unfinished monument on its summit which the guide-book said was modelled on the Parthenon. It had been built to commemorate those who'd fallen in the Napoleonic Wars, but money had run out and it had never been completed.

I'd always thought Edinburgh had been called the Athens of the North because of Edinburgh Castle perched on its rock like the Parthenon on the Acropolis, but I was wrong. It was because of this unfinished nineteenth century 'Parthenon' on Calton Hill.

"Do you know St. Andrew is patron saint of Greece as well as of Scotland?" I asked Harry, as we sat on a rock enjoying the vista. "Apparently, he was crucified at Patras, a port in the north of the Peloponnese. He was given the choice of being sacrificed to the Greek gods or being crucified, and he chose crucifixion."

"Not nice," said Harry.

"He chose to be crucified on a diagonal cross, bound to it by thongs. It's why the Scottish flag has on it a diagonal cross. And, if you'd like to know why he came to Scotland, it was because a Greek monk, or some say an Irish one under St. Columba called St. Rule, or Regulus, or something, was told in a dream that he was to take St. Andrew's relics to the 'ends of the earth'. Being a good, obedient monk, St. Rule or Regulus set sail with a tooth and other relics of St. Andrew, and arrived off Scotland where he was shipwrecked. You'd have thought God wouldn't have wanted him shipwrecked and have intervened, but no. Anyway he got to shore which is why the town St. Andrews is called what it is. It's funny to think we're walking on the 'ends of the earth'."

We continued along the track and were glad of our walking boots and trekking sticks because the path was rough shale and we'd seen several people slip on it. "And because St. Andrew was fixed to a diagonal cross," I went on, "it took him three days to die, and all the while he was praising God. Isn't that odd?"

"Well, he was a saint."

"St. Margaret, the queen who was married to King Malcolm III, died praising God. She died of grief four days after her beloved husband and son had been killed in battle. God could have saved them but he didn't. He could have saved her but he didn't do that either. All that praise, and he didn't move a muscle. But, then, if he isn't there he can't, I suppose."

A woman who looked Filipino came jogging up the track with a big smile on her round olive-skinned face. She paused beside us and said: "I catch my breath! Huh, huh, huh!" When she'd caught it enough, she said: "I do this every day for my health."

"Every day? You must be fit!"

"Ah. My work is in a care home with old people. It is good to get out and run." She sized us up as though she thought we too should be in a care home, and said: "You go up all the way to Arthur's Seat?"

"I thought we were on it," I said.

"This is the beginning only. I think it will be hard for you to go up to the top. I think when you go back down it is better that you take the other path. Soon you will see it. This path is not good if you fall. So many where I work have the broken hip. But you have the sticks, that is good." By now she had caught her breath. "Ah, I must keep running." She gave us a wide, happy smile. "Have a nice day!" she said, and jogged on up the track, her ponytail of raven black hair bobbing with every step she took.

We continued trudging. The weather was fine, the sky was blue with large white clouds sailing the heavens. We soon had a view to the west, across the city suburbs to distant hills. A road far below was busy with cars driving away from the city or coming into it.

We saw Arthur's Seat, a much higher crag ahead of us. As we were flying home that afternoon we had no hope of getting up and back again in time for our flight. We came to the much easier narrow track which the Filipino woman had recommended for our return. It cut through a broad open space of long coarse grass with hills either side. After a while we could see St. Margaret's Loch, and a young man jogging up another path some way off.

"You know," I said to Harry, "I've read that on Calton Hill where that Parthenon monument is, Neo-Pagans have started to celebrate the ancient Celtic festival of Beltane. In it the May Queen, the Green Man and Horned God play a role in some sort of ritual. The Horned

God is killed off only to be resurrected as the Green Man. It's a sort of self-sacrifice for the rebirth of nature."

"A nonsense thing."

"Except they take it seriously."

"Of course they do. Crackpots always take their ideas seriously."

"And I've also read that hundreds climb up here to Arthur's Seat on May Day to re-enact the ancient fire festival in honour of the sun god."

"More crackpots."

"And, not to be outdone by the Neo-Pagans, Christians come up too to say prayers at dawn on May Day."

"Hm."

"And this will interest you! At the ancient Celtic Beltane fire festival, the custom was for Druids to extinguish all fires from the previous year and then rekindle them from a new flame. Perhaps it's only coincidence but with Christianity, on the night of the Resurrection - in the Greek Orthodox Church at any rate - the priest on the stroke of midnight appears with a newly lighted candle, the new 'light of the world'. Isn't that interesting?"

Harry made no comment. He was enjoying the scenery in this prairie-like former volcanic crater, with its high surrounding crags, St. Margaret's Loch ahead, and the sky above. Another jogger was making his way along a goat track in the distance, and a cyclist was heading our way from afar.

A proverb suddenly popped into my head, and I found myself quoting it aloud: *"Plus ça change, plus c'est la même chose,"* I said.

"Plus ça what?"

"Nothing changes, nothing remains the same," I told him. In fact, I later discovered that the proper translation should have been: 'The more things change, the more they remain the same'. But Harry didn't speak French, and the fact that I'd got it wrong didn't matter because my own translation exactly summed up my thinking so far as religion was concerned.

ST. MICHAEL'S MOUNT AND TINTAGEL

As we drove in to the small town of Marazion we caught a glimpse of St. Michael's Mount which made us both shout: 'There! Look!' It was a diminutive, cone-shaped granite island rising from the sea several hundred metres offshore with a castle perched on top.

Ten minutes later we exclaimed again: 'Look the Mount! Look! Look!' We'd just been taken to our room in our B&B accommodation. From our bedroom window the Mount rose spectacularly in the distance, an imposing bulk looming from the calm, steel-blue seascape. Workmen's houses ringed its base, and evergreens filled the gap between the houses below and the castle above.

Apparently, Julius Caesar had been made aware of it as a trading centre and port for exporting Cornish tin. The Sicilian historian of the first century A.D. (the one who'd hinted that Stonehenge had been a sacred enclosure in honour of Apollo) had described how tin was worked in Britain and was taken to a tidal island named Ictis (believed to be the Mount) which was at the time a trading post from which tin was shipped to Gaul. It was one of the reasons Julius Caesar's interest was awakened in this far distant northern island of Britain.

Later that afternoon we walked down into the town to its fine stretch of sandy beach. St. Michael's Mount as ever dominated the scene from the distance. An elderly woman stood near to us as we stared out at the scene. She seemed to want to speak and smiled at me and said: "Is this your first visit here?"

"It's most impressive," I said. "Yes, we've just arrived. And you? Are you here on holiday?"

"No, dear. We're here to scatter the ashes," she said.

"Oh, I'm sorry."

"It's my mother, dear. She died in the spring and it was her wish. I've my Aunty Edith's ashes too. She wanted to be scattered here like her sister."

"How sad," I said.

"We've had a hard time these last few years," she said, and proceeded to recite a list of fatalities in her family. "...And he died of cancer six months ago... And my nephew was stabbed to death last year in Birmingham... Then there was a helicopter crash when Arthur's cousin lost his life..."

"It sounds too awful," I said, my face transfixed to my most commiserating.

"And Arthur - he's the one over there, dear - " She indicated a florid-faced man with sparse grey hair staring morosely out to sea. "He's got angina."

"Oh, dear. But he looks so well," I said, trying to inject a touch of optimism into the conversation.

"He has an aortic aneurysm," she confided. "He could drop dead at any moment," she went on. "But you know, dear, tragedy makes you stronger. I'm a stronger person now than I was."

"Yes, I suppose so," I said, floundering hopelessly as I tried to find something suitably sympathetic to say.

"But I mustn't burden you with my troubles, dear," the woman went on. "You enjoy yourself here while you can. Is that your husband?" She indicated Harry who was watching several intrepid figures kite surfing, their bright coloured sails catching the wind, causing them to skim over the waves on their water-boards.

The woman said: "I'd better get back to Arthur. He looks well, but you never know. Make the most of what you have while you have it, that's what I say. Goodbye, dear."

"It's been nice talking to you," I said, not certain if that was the right thing to say.

I watched her join her husband and together they wandered off. I remembered then that St. Michael was guardian of the souls of the newly deceased. I supposed it was in keeping for the woman to come to the Mount to scatter the ashes of two of her close relatives. St. Michael's Mount was called that because the archangel had been seen there in a vision on an outcrop of rock by some fishermen in 495 A.D.

He had taken over the escorting of souls from the Roman god, Mercury. In ancient Greece it had been the god Hermes who'd accompanied the souls of the dead to Hades for judgement. St. Michael was often depicted holding scales in which he weighed the good against the bad deeds of the deceased in order to pass judgement.

Before St. Michael took charge of the Mount there must have been pagan worship there, though little has been reported on the subject. I imagined the Celtic sea god, Llyr, would have been honoured by those living on the Mount or in the vicinity, and also Llyr's son, Manannan, as he'd been protector of seamen and fishermen. Another of Llyr's sons had been the giant Bran, the one who'd requested decapitation on death and his head buried on Tower Hill in London. The Celts revered the severed head as it was the seat of learning and wisdom. Bran had been part god, part giant.

White and pale grey cumulous clouds filled the late afternoon sky. A few children were still playing on the sands, several watching their fathers flying kites to amuse their offspring or themselves. It was a joyful, far-from-thinking-of-death scene.

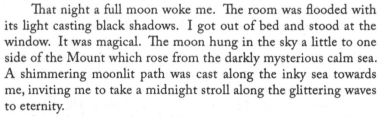

That night a full moon woke me. The room was flooded with its light casting black shadows. I got out of bed and stood at the window. It was magical. The moon hung in the sky a little to one side of the Mount which rose from the darkly mysterious calm sea. A shimmering moonlit path was cast along the inky sea towards me, inviting me to take a midnight stroll along the glittering waves to eternity.

I stood at the window and let my imagination take over. It was amazing the pull or power of the moon on the world. It affected the tides; it could turn minds so people became lunatics (from the French 'lune' meaning 'moon'); the crescent new moon heralded important events in the Moslem calendar; in Jewish belief the queen of demons stalked the earth at full moon looking for victims; and in Christianity the Church fixed Easter and the Resurrection for the first Sunday after the first full moon immediately following the Spring Equinox.

I wanted Harry to see St. Michael's Mount by moonlight, but his mound under the bed-covers was inert. In fact, he was so totally unmoving and silent I wondered if he was alive. I listened for the sound of breathing but heard nothing. Oh, God! Had St. Michael come for his soul? Another five minutes of dead silence, then a strangled snore reassured me he was still of this world. No need to worry.

✌⟨❀⟩❧

At breakfast the next morning a plump lone woman sat at a table near to ours. She was probably in her early forties, and had long dark hair with a white gardenia tucked behind her ear. She leaned towards us and asked: "Have you been here before?"

"No, it's our first visit," I replied. "And you?"

"Oh, I've been here many times," she said. "I come to recharge my batteries. It's the ley lines."

"Oh, yes?" I prompted, hoping that she'd elaborate.

"You know - ley lines?" she gave me a quizzical look to see if I knew what she meant. "Earth energy lines," she explained.

"Yes, of course," I said.

"The St. Michael line is unique," she said. She buttered her toast and used a long purple-black finger-nail to peel back the cover of her small packet of marmalade.

"Why special?" I encouraged.

"Oh, because it runs from St. Michael's Church on the Tor at Glastonbury straight through to St. Michael's Mount," she said. "Some people call it the Dragon Line because it undulates like a dragon. St. Michael killed the dragon, which of course you know."

"Well, St. George did too," I said.

"Yes. It's metaphorical, of course. Dragons represent evil, like the serpent in the Garden of Eden."

"I suppose so."

She deftly scooped a little marmalade from the small packet and spread it on her toast. Harry wasn't one to get involved in earth energies and ley lines, and probably felt wary because she had a white gardenia in her hair.

"Are you a pagan?" I found myself asking (it was the flower again). Having learned about modern Wiccans and Druids in my new world of dragons, horned gods, Green Men and fertility goddesses, I was beginning to think that more people were pagan than not.

She looked surprised by my question. In fact, I was surprised by it. I wasn't normally so forward with strangers.

"No, not really," the woman replied.

Harry threw me a sharp look of reproof, and I quickly backtracked to the subject of ley lines and earth energies again.

"Where else do you go for a ley line?" I asked.

"Oh, I only come here," she said. "But that's just me. There are ley lines criss-crossing the whole of Britain. Our ancient forbears knew all about the earth's energy, that's why they constructed barrows and beacons and standing stones which they aligned with solar and lunar events."

"Amazing," I said.

"They were the ones with the knowledge. We today think ourselves clever because we have our technology, but we've lost touch with nature and its energies. It was Alfred Watkins who rediscovered them. I expect you've heard of him?"

"I've heard of him," I said cautiously, remembering the name, though not knowing why.

"He climbed a high hill and from the top noticed that many famous landmarks fell in a straight line."

"Ley lines?"

"Exactly. But it's here I feel the earth's energy the most. It's here that I come to get revitalized."

"Do you do anything in particular to get it - to absorb it?" I asked, wondering what the proper phrasing should be.

"No. I just laze about," she said. "You don't have to do anything except relax."

"Astonishing," I said, hoping Harry hadn't heard because we had work to do that morning. "Well, we'll relax after we've been to the Mount," I said positively. "It's been really interesting talking to you." I scraped back my chair and got up, and Harry quickly got up too.

"Strange woman," was Harry's comment as we left. "Everybody knows that all you need for recharging your batteries is a good night's sleep. Ley lines! What piffle!"

It was drizzling as we joined others walking along the cobbled causeway to the Mount. The early saints would have taken this same route to visit this formidable stronghold dedicated to St. Michael. Cornwall for some reason seemed to have been invaded by early Celtic Christian saints determined to evangelize the people. They gave their names to such places as St. Ives, St. Austell, St. Mawes, St. Neot, and so on. But it was the vision of St. Michael the archangel, seen by the local fishermen on the Mount, that caused pilgrims in their droves to come, passing along the causeway to it as we were doing now.

In all probability there had been a pagan shrine on the Mount before the church was built in honour of St. Michael. The Mount and its location out to sea beckoned all who saw it. The fishermen who had seen the archangel would have been overawed by the vision and subsequently have paid close attention to what the many evangelizing saints in Cornwall had to say. What was their god, Manannan, protector of fishermen, in comparison? Some said that Manannan had become humanized, taking on the role of a Druid priest who'd even prophesied the coming of Christ; others that St. Michael was a reincarnation of Manannan.

There was a blustery cold wind driving the fine drizzle into our faces. It was autumn so what else could be expected but wind and storms? The trees on the Mount were evergreen and sombre through the mist. The sea was surprisingly calm despite the wind. Alongside the causeway were scattered rocks, seaweed and rock-pools. The granite base to what had once been an ancient standing cross marking the pilgrim way to the Mount was visible to our right.

We reached the workmen's houses at the bottom of the Mount and sat in a shelter waiting for the gates to open at ten-thirty. A party of Germans following their tour guide gathered close by. Their guide began to hold forth in German about something which was clearly of great fascination as everyone looked attentive. Suddenly the whole group exclaimed 'Oooooh' in one breath. The guide, encouraged by their collective gasp continued until the group with one accord went 'Aaaaaaah'. I wondered what they were being told. Were they being informed about Cormoran, the Mount's giant? Or about Mont Saint Michel across the English Channel whose giant had been attacked and killed by King Arthur, or so it was claimed by Geoffrey of Monmouth in his History of the Kings of Britain? The group moved on except for one who crouched before a red letterbox beside us and spent much time and trouble in taking a photograph of it. It was strange what foreigners found interesting.

At ten-thirty we went to the ticket-office, and were soon climbing the cobbled path which wound its way up the Mount between shrubs and trees. We paused by what was labelled the Giant's Well, a rather shallow looking depression ringed around by a stone wall. Legend had it that the giant Cormoran had built the Mount. From there he'd terrorized the people of Marazion by striding across and snatching cattle and sheep and even children which he then devoured. One day a brave young boy named Jack devised a plot to kill him. He dug this pit (the Giant's Well) while the giant slept then, when the sun was rising, he blew a horn on the east side of the pit waking the giant who, because the sun was in his eyes, didn't see the gaping hole as he came striding down and fell headlong into it, which put an end to him.

"Do you know that the giants in Cornwall were the result of thirty Greek princesses?" I asked Harry as we continued on up. "According to what I've read, each one was tall and beautiful, but they were sent into exile by their father for plotting to murder their husbands because they didn't like being bossed by them."

"I didn't know wives could be bossed by their husbands," Harry commented.

"According to the story," I went on, ignoring the remark, "they arrived in England - in Cornwall, I suppose - exhausted and famished because they'd been put to sea in a rudderless boat without food or water. But when they'd regained their strength after their storm-tossed voyage, their minds turned to the all important fact that they had no men in their lives. Their desires became so strong that little winged creatures called incubi magically turned themselves into men and in no time the Greek princesses became pregnant. And, because they were extremely tall, they all gave birth to giants. So there you are. That explains why there were giants in Cornwall."

"It just explains wildly imaginative minds, I'd have thought," came the reply.

On up, and we looked for the giant Cormoran's stony heart which was said to be embedded among the cobblestones. Neither of us could see it, but a tourist pointed it out - a surprisingly small three or four inch black stone heart.

"You want to look out for the giant's liver," said a man coming up alongside us. He looked like a castle official as he was dressed in a dark suit and carried a black zipped shoulder-bag. "It's that large granite rock there." He indicated a boulder with an amused smile. "He was an alcoholic and his liver got larger and larger," he quipped, as he left the cobbled path to take what I took to be a short cut to the castle up a narrow track to the left.

We came to a terrace near the entrance to the castle with cannons pointing through the crenellated walls. Harry and I parted company so that he could concentrate on battles, while I went on up to what interested me the most, the Church of St. Michael on the summit. I passed rapidly through the great open-to-the-public rooms with their St. Aubyn family treasures, pausing for a moment only by a narrow open window to stare down to the outcrop of rocks far below being thrashed by waves. The wind buffeted the castle walls and came in draughts through this narrow window.

I eventually came up to the battlements from where I could look down to the landscaped garden far below. Clearly visible was a high Celtic cross on a ledge facing out to the rocks and the sea. Did this mark the site where St. Michael had been seen?

I entered the fourteenth century church. It was a truly impressive ancient building erected on the site of a much earlier one. I sat down for a while to examine the booklet I'd bought. I read that on the right was an entrance to a small underground chamber where a very large seven foot ten inch skeleton had been found - the bones of Cormoran the giant?

An earthquake had totally destroyed the earlier church in 1275, but the priory which had existed there at the time had continued its business as before. The work of the Benedictine priory was linked with the one at Mont Saint Michel in Brittany where a vision of St. Michael had also been seen.

I inspected an exquisite bronze figure of St. Michael extending an arm to Lucifer writhing up from beneath his feet. Strange fancies! Lucifer (alias Satan, alias the devil) was more usually depicted as a dragon or a serpent. Serpents have had varied reputations over the centuries. Christians equate the serpent with the devil. Yet the Celtic god Cernunnos had often been portrayed with a serpent as a symbol of renewal because it shed its skin. Asclepius, the Greek god of healing, had sacred snakes in his temple because they were believed to heal the sick. And yet, the Python lurking at Delphi had been a symbol of evil and had been killed by Apollo before he took possession of his sanctuary there.

It seemed that humans could have their minds bent in any

direction depending on the era into which they were born. To me a snake was a snake, and when I saw one I was fearful, yet not so scared that I wasn't able to admire its graceful sinewy movement as it slithered away into the undergrowth. It was a symbol both of death, and by the sloughing of its skin, of rebirth. I never once equated it with Satan. I never said: 'Oh, there goes the devil!' The poor snake surely never brought upon itself its reputation? Only men with their imaginative minds did that. In fact, the serpent in the Garden of Eden persuaded Eve to eat from the tree of knowledge, which I thought rather a good thing.

"I thought I'd find you here." It was Harry whose hand on my shoulder made me jump. "Dragons and the Book of Revelation," he said mysteriously.

"What about it?" I asked.

"I've just overheard somebody talking about it. The twelfth chapter of Revelation, verse seven. I thought you'd be interested, so I've come to tell you."

"Really?" I'd never known Harry give me information of that kind before.

I went and asked a woman attendant if I could read from their bible in the church. She was very happy to oblige, and I opened it at Revelation, chapter twelve, and read: 'Now war arose in heaven, Michael and his angels fighting against the dragon; and the dragon and his angels fought, but they were defeated and there was no longer any place for them in heaven. And the great dragon was thrown down, that ancient serpent, who is called the Devil and Satan, the deceiver of the whole world - he was thrown down to the earth, and his angels were thrown down with him...'

The ability to conjure up imagery with words! The bending of the human mind to regard the serpent/dragon as an object of sinister evil. What amazing power words had!

"By the way, it's raining." Harry brought me back from the world of imagery to reality. I had already noted without giving it much attention that Harry's anorak was wet, and that people were wearing mackintoshes and entering with dripping umbrellas.

"Have you finished in here?" he asked. He was clearly ready to go. "We can take a boat back."

"Fine. I'm ready," I said.

The rain eased a little as we wended our way down the slope.

We were directed to the quayside where a boat was waiting with a few passengers already seated in it. We were helped on board and I sat beside a large rug of a dog with luminous eyes looking through an overhang of eyebrows.

"Hello," I said to the dog. The woman beside the animal put an arm protectively around it and pulled it closer to her. We sat silently with our anorak hoods up. The skipper cast off and the boat chugged out of harbour heading for Marazion which was seen through a veil of slanting rain. The boat ploughed through topsy turvy waves, and I noticed a few stalwarts walking along the causeway wading to their knees in sea water. I supposed it was the way the giant Cormoran would have gone when he strode from the Mount to get his victims for his daily meal. In one legend his wife, Cormelian, had been forced by her dear husband to carry white rocks in her apron from Bodmin moor to build their giant house while he snoozed and did nothing. Seeing her husband asleep she went and collected green stones from a nearby cove, hoping that he wouldn't notice the difference. But unfortunately the Giant spotted the substitute stones, whereupon his poor wife panicked and the stones fell from her apron and scattered along the causeway. In another version of the legend the Giant had been building the Mount with granite and his wife was bringing him the green stones in her apron, whereupon her husband, seeing the wrong colour, killed her on the spot and his wife dropped dead under her pile of green stones.

"Do you know where the pile of green stones is, where the Giant's wife was buried?" I found myself enquiring of the dog's owner. I hadn't seen any at all while on the Mount, in fact I'd forgotten about that part of the legend.

She looked at me briefly as though I was demented, which maybe I was, and turned away, her face hidden by her hood. But her dog turned towards me, snuffled my face and gave me a wet lick.

"The dog's a giant," I said to the hood as I received another slobbering lick from the creature seated beside me. Perhaps all these Cornish legends were affecting me? Or perhaps I'd become moonstruck in the night? "Are you a big giant?" I asked the dog who was determined to find my face for another lick.

The woman gave the animal a sharp tug on its lead. "Leave off!" she commanded. I wasn't sure if she meant me or the dog.

It was one of those occasions when Harry disowned me. He

would have liked to have slipped away but as there was nowhere to slip to except overboard, he could only stare at the horizon and pretend he had nothing to do with me.

We were soon back at Marazion and on dry land. Looking back towards the Mount I noticed the two flags flying from the battlements. One was the Union Jack, and the other the Cornish flag which consisted of a white cross on a black background. Later I learned it was the banner of the sixth century St. Piran, patron saint of Cornwall, and patron saint of tin miners in particular. I also read that symbolically the flag represented the white light of truth shining through the black darkness of evil. Another bending of the human mind to the imagery conjured up by words.

That night I was again woken by the moon. Looking out of the window once more I saw the fairy-tale scene of the Mount looming mysteriously from the sea, and to one side the dark but moonlit shape of the bay. A long dark cloud swept the sky below the moon. The soft swish of waves breaking on the shore was like a lullaby. I climbed back into bed and fell asleep.

The next morning the sun was shining. As it was September it was the time of the Autumn Equinox, the time when day and night would be of equal length. It was extraordinary the annual rhythm of the sun, its imperceptible increase until the summer solstice, then its decrease as the year drew on. It was never erratic - it never went on holiday or took a day off, not ever! There was never an unexpected loss of power, no absenteeism, but total reliability. Yes, clouds could pass across it, mists could blot it out. At night you knew it hadn't fallen out of the sky or been blown to smithereens, but that it would come up over the horizon in the east in the morning; it would move across the sky, and sink again in the west in the evening, except - except! - it wasn't the sun moving but the earth revolving - well, spinning. We were so much part of the rhythm and the harmony that we were unaware of this amazing daily, monthly, annual revolving of the spheres. We merely recognized the seasons and held festivals to celebrate them. Soon it would be Michaelmas (the mass of Michael), the feast-day of St. Michael held on the 29th September, a time for harvest festivals. We were entering the last quarter of the year, a period of dying before rebirth and resurrection in the spring.

Next morning Harry asked: "So where to next?"

"North Cornwall," I replied. "We have to see Tintagel."

"King Arthur?" Harry enquired.

"And Merlin the wizard," I said. "There are other places on the way I wouldn't mind seeing," I added. But I didn't elaborate knowing it was best to get into the car and just make sure I was the driver.

We sat on the tiered seats at the Minack Theatre and stared around us. It was midday, and Harry at last admitted that the detour to this small gem of a theatre hewn out of an outcrop of rock overlooking the Atlantic had been worth it. It had views along the Cornish coastline to slate grey cliffs and pale sandy coves. The sun shone brilliantly overhead and the sea was silver lamé. There was a light wind, and a flotilla of sea-gulls floated peacefully on the waves.

The meticulous work which had been undertaken to achieve maximum theatrical effect in this relatively modern theatre raised the spirits of all who came: the arched entranceways, the graceful curve of the stage whose two levels were reached by shallow steps, the small elegant balconies, all these were designed to delight - designed to 'bend the mind' of an audience to the unfolding drama on stage which might trigger tears or laughter.

When we returned to the car Harry beat me to the driving seat. After a short distance I mentioned that the Merry Maidens stone circle was close by and it would take no time to see it. But Harry shot past the turning saying that I'd seen stone circles on Bodmin Moor on our way down, and all stone circles looked much the same which was perfectly true.

After several miles I had another request.

"Land's End?" Harry queried. "Who wants to go there?"

"I want to," I said meekly.

"Why?"

"It has seven perpendicular rocks which are all that remain of a legendary lost kingdom destroyed by a cyclone," I said lamely.

"You'll see all the rocks you need at Tintagel," came the prompt reply, and he ignored the signpost to Land's End and kept on the main inland road running parallel to the coast. Cattle and sheep grazed the hills, and small granite farm houses were dotted here and there under their slate roofs. The sea could be seen in the distance.

"We're soon passing a village called Zennor," I said hopefully. "I'd quite like to stop there."

"Why?"

"There's a mermaid in the church," I said.

"A mermaid in the church!"

"And there'll be a pub there in the village," I added. "We have to eat," I said.

He turned off. There was a pub and we did eat. And I saw the mermaid in the church. She was carved on an end panel of a high-backed oak chair with a rich patina to it. She had long hair, but was otherwise somewhat featureless and bosomless but with a highly polished stomach, and wide hips ending in a long scaly tail with a couple of fins.

There was a notice on the wall which said that before the Christian era mermaids were symbolic of Aphrodite, goddess of love and the sea; that in the Middle Ages when Cornish mystery plays were performed, the mermaid had been used as a symbol to explain the two natures of Christ who was both Man and God, just as she was both woman and fish - a comparison I thought decidedly odd. The notice went on to say that the mermaid was a reminder that St. Senara (from which the name Zennor comes) had arrived by sea from Ireland and had founded the first church in the sixth century.

It was said that mermaids sat on rocks combing their long hair, and sang beautifully, so luring sailors to their doom. They were the Cornish version of the ancient Greek siren voices, beautiful women who enticed all who heard them to a fatal end. Here at Zennor church, however, it hadn't been the mermaid singing beautifully but a young man named Matthew Trewhella, son of the local squire, whose tenor voice had been so exquisite that when the mermaid heard him singing hymns at evensong on Sundays, she'd leave the sea to come and hear him in the church. One evening he'd caught her eye and they'd fallen instantly in love. She'd told him that her home was in the sea and he must follow her or she would die. He'd been so besotted that he'd followed her and was never seen again.

"That's true love for you," I told Harry when we were in the pub later and I told him the story. "Would you follow me under the waves if I were a mermaid?"

"No fear!"

We eyed each other. Harry began to realize that something more chivalrous might sound better, so added: "If you were a mermaid and I were a merman then of course I'd follow you under the waves." He almost convinced me.

As Harry had the car keys, he again made sure he got first to the car and into the driving seat. I could only make a suggestion.

"We're quite close to Zennor Quoit," I said. "An ancient chamber tomb. You'd like that."

"Why?"

"They are huge granite uprights with a capstone forming an inner chamber for religious ceremonies. Or you might prefer Chûn Quoit as there's also a Chûn Castle, but we'd have to drive back a little."

"We're not driving back and we're not driving sideways either," said the voice in command of the car.

I sat back in the seat, resigned. I tried one more detour. "We'll be passing St. Ives," I said tentatively. "In case you're interested, St. Ives was really a St. Ia who wanted to evangelize Cornwall and sailed from Ireland on a leaf."

"I don't care how St. Ives or Ia sailed. If we're going to Tintagel I'm not driving to St. Ives."

We shot past the turning for it.

There was nothing more I could do except enjoy the scenery of farmland, hedged fields, dead bracken, flowering gorse, ancient tin-mine chimneys, and the distant sea which was becoming slate grey as ominous clouds loomed over the horizon. A curious rainbow encircled a black cloud. A sinister foreboding, or a good omen, I asked Harry?

"Just a heavy storm cloud with the sun shining on it," said Harry practically.

Another half rainbow arched from the sea to the heavens. We could see a veil of rain blowing across the horizon.

We drove past wind turbines gracing the landscape. I thought them beautiful - the modern giants which in two thousand years might have legends spun around them.

Now that we'd left behind the long western tail of Cornwall known as the Penwith Peninsula with its numerous enticing landmarks, Harry thought it safe to let me take the wheel. He gave me a sharp assessing sort of look as we passed each other for the changeover. What he saw satisfied him that by now I'd had enough of sitting in a car and intended only to get to our destination, a village called Treknow a mile or so from Tintagel.

❧❦❧

Next day was stormy. We wore anoraks and boots and walked to Tintagel from our B&B along the coastal path. The coast was rugged with slate-grey rocks and high cliffs, the Atlantic waves pounding against them sending plumes of snow-white spume soaring into the air. It was a magnificent coastline, notorious for smugglers and shipwrecks. There were no boats or ships to be seen, nor smugglers for that matter, just the dark olive-green waves powering in from the Atlantic. The fields were divided by walls built with slabs of slate in various herringbone design, topped by closely packed thin slate uprights. There were wooden stiles for walkers to get from one field to the next. Not exactly made to keep the bull in, or the ram out, was Harry's comment, as we passed through sheep and then grazing cattle.

The walk took us first to the small Norman Church of Materiana on a hill overlooking the Tintagel site. St. Materiana was identified with a St. Madryn, princess of Gwent, who had evangelized the area around 500 A.D. The hill on which this church stood had been a burial ground for people of eminence, and it is believed that the hill had always been of some religious significance long before Christianity.

At the Tintagel ticket-office we were told that the north-east gale was on the borderline of safety regulations, and if it increased in strength then they would have to close the site. It didn't stop us buying tickets and joining the many others who were already there.

We began with a long-haul of steep steps up the cliff side to the top of the turf-covered promontory where the ruins of two castle courtyards could be seen. Fact, legend and speculation were interwoven on this summit: legend, that King Arthur had once lived here; fact, that the castle had been built by Richard, Earl of Cornwall, in the thirteenth century; speculation (thanks to an archaeological dig), that there'd once been an early Celtic monastery there, because fragments of pottery bearing Christian symbols had been found. Certainly there was ample evidence, from the fifth century A.D., that there'd been a prosperous community living on this promontory trading with the Mediterranean. King Arthur had been fifth century.

"This is where King Arthur was conceived, thanks to Merlin's magic powers," I told Harry. "His father was Uther Pendragon who fell madly in love with the wife of the then Duke of Cornwall who lived here. Merlin, being a wizard, cast a magic spell so Igraine, the duke's wife, thought that Uther Pendragon was her husband with the result King Arthur was conceived."

"She thought he was her husband!" Harry scoffed.

"It shows what magic can do," I said. "In fact, the duke died in battle almost immediately and Uther Pendragon married her."

The promontory was linked to an island by a narrow isthmus, long destroyed by wind and sea, and now reached by a bridge. For a while we watched the sombre sea from the bridge with its giant waves crashing against the rocks, then drawing back the spume on the swell as though it were a light carpeting of virgin snow. As an impenetrable stronghold Tintagel took the prize.

I stopped beside a notice and read words to the effect that the dramatic landscape of Tintagel was the result of an age-long struggle between land and sea. There'd been volcanic eruptions millions of years ago, then great earth movements which had pushed up the seabed to form mountains. The hardened layers of lava, ash and mud had been squeezed and folded to become the contorted bands of light and dark coloured rocks seen today. Atlantic storms had over the years gradually eroded the rocks to produce the spectacular coastline with its arches, caves and coves.

We crossed the bridge and again had to climb a length of steep uneven steps, this time against the full force of the gale. As Harry had gone ahead I seized the arm of a strong young man. I didn't fancy being blown away from dry land and plummeted to the storm-lashed rocks below.

"No problem," said the man who sounded Irish. He was quite slight and could himself have been blown away, though he had a certain sinewy strength as he held me steady and together we clambered to the top. "There you are," he said. "Any time, just you holler for me."

On the grassy uneven top of this island we found a well (water being an important commodity for any community) and, a little further along, a short underground tunnel which we entered. I read that it was believed to have been used as a cold store for perishable food. Inside we found the Irishman with his girlfriend.

"A cold store? I'm not believing that," said the Irishman, "it's too far from the castle."

"Then what is it?" I asked.

"I'm thinking we're in the womb of Mother Earth. Here's where they held fertility rites, for sure." Why was it that the Irish always spoke as though they had marbles rolling about in their mouths.

"Do you really think so?" I asked with renewed interest.

"It makes sense. There you have the holy well. You can't be having religious rites without holy water, can you now. By the by, have you seen what they call Merlin's Cave yet?"

"No, not yet."

"There's a treat for you! And while you're there, just you look up at the rock above and you'll see the horned god, Cernunnos. There's another fertility god for you. Look for the ram's horns. Or maybe you'll see his ram-horned snake of healing. The well here could be a healing spring. At least I like to think it is so," said the Irishman.

When he'd gone Harry said: "Irish men like to think all sorts of things, I wouldn't take too much notice of him! Sort of fellow who believes in leprechauns and things."

We left the tunnel/womb and walked along the uneven ground to the ruins of a chapel dating from the fifth to the seventh century A.D. It had been dedicated to a St. Juliot, a little known Celtic saint. The ancient font we'd seen earlier in the Church of St. Materiana on the hill, had originally come from this chapel. It had been an ancient looking stone font standing on four stone supports. The crude carving on the font itself depicted four heads of serpents whose tails curved up with the bowl of the font. I assumed its iconic message was the sloughing of the old skin (the old pagan body) to be reborn in Christ.

A sudden showery squall and we turned from the chapel and made our way back down the steps. This time Harry was the prop I clung to as we descended in the teeth of the gale.

We went on down to the cove to look at Merlin's Cave. Merlin had made his debut when King Vortigern, who'd ruled Britain in the fifth century, had wanted to build a castle on a mountainous area of Snowdonia in Wales. Whenever the walls reached a certain height, however, they'd repeatedly collapsed. In desperation Vortigern had turned to his advisers who'd told him he would never succeed in building his castle unless the blood of a fatherless child was first sprinkled over the stones. A strange tale, and not unlike the one on Iona where St. Columba had attempted to build a chapel but the walls of that too had collapsed every night until Columba's friend St. Oran had offered himself as a human sacrifice (a pagan idea to cure such ills).

Merlin had been the fatherless child because his mother, a Welsh princess (could it have been St. Materiana/Madryn?) had been impregnated by an other-worldly spirit. The boy Merlin, however, being a visionary, was saved from becoming the human sacrifice because he was able to give the king the reason for the walls continually collapsing. It was, he told the king, because two dragons were fighting every night under its foundations. Vortigern immediately commanded the excavation of the site, whereupon the dragons burst out and continued to do battle in the sky. One dragon was white and the other red, and Merlin prophesied that the red dragon (which symbolized Britain) would eventually be defeated by the white dragon (symbolizing the Saxons). This couldn't have been altogether displeasing to Vortigern since he'd already invited Saxon mercenaries to come over and assist him in his battles against the Picts and Scots.

Opposite the cave a waterfall cascaded down the cliff face. It was low tide so we could walk on the sandy floor of the cave, the roof of which was multiple hues of gleaming dark rock. The cave was more a tunnel than a cave as you could see right through it to the rocks beyond, the sea having pounded and eroded and finally bored its way through the neck of the land formerly connecting the promontory to the island.

Legend had it that Merlin had lived in this cave in order to be on hand to advise and tutor the young King Arthur. There was one story that the child Arthur had been washed ashore by the waves, and Merlin had been standing by his cave ready to receive him. Writers, poets and artists had seized on such unlikely tales, had added to them and, by the sheer force of their words, made them believable. Tennyson, in his poem Idylls of the King, wrote his powerful version of the arrival of the child Arthur:

> *Wave after wave, each mightier than the last,*
> *Til last, a ninth one, gathering half the deep*
> *And full of voices, slowly rose and plunged*
> *Roaring, and all the wave was in a flame:*
> *And down the wave and in the flame was borne*
> *A naked babe, and rode to Merlin's feet,*
> *Who stoopt and caught the babe, and cried,*
> *'The King!*
> *Here is an heir for Uther!'*

Before Geoffrey of Monmouth put pen to paper about King Arthur and Merlin, the latter had for long been a well-known shadowy figure. It is thought he'd originally been a Druid priest, whose fame had been passed on down the centuries; he'd been a wise adviser, judge, healer and prophet.

"Most of what is known about Arthur and Merlin comes from Geoffrey of Monmouth who was a bishop writing in the twelfth century," I said to Harry. "Being a bishop what he wrote ought to be true," I added.

"Hum."

"But I suppose it was also in his interest as a bishop to give King Arthur superhuman powers to show what Christian faith could do. It was never looked upon as lying but as pious fraud which made it all right," I said.

The sun came out briefly, lighting up the cave and brightening the scene. I asked Harry to go and stand like Merlin at the cave's entrance so I could take a photograph.

That done, I heard a voice behind me, say: "Will you be taking one of Maureen and myself, please?" It was the Irishman behind me holding out his camera. "You just press the button there and Bob's yer uncle."

I did as requested. They stood before Merlin's Cave, and he put his arm around the shoulders of Maureen and inclined his head to hers for the pose. With the photo taken, he said: "So have you seen the rock sculpture yet? The one of the god Cernunnos? Have you looked up there yet?" he asked. "You haven't? Come, and I'll show you."

I joined him and looked in the direction he was pointing. "You see the ram's horns, then?"

I tried hard to visualize a head, but was unable to conjure up anything looking remotely like a head, or ram's horns.

"So you can't see the face on the rock, that's a shame that is." He turned to his girlfriend. "It's a real shame," he grumbled, "she doesn't see the god."

"Not everybody sees what you see, Danny," she soothed. "Come away now. I'm after finding somewhere warm. It's freezing out here."

"Have you not been to Ireland?" asked the young man, apparently in no hurry to leave.

"Never," I said.

"You've not kissed the Blarney Stone?" he enquired. "There's luck for you if you kiss the Blarney Stone. They hold you over the edge by your legs so you can kiss the Blarney Stone, so they do."

"What's the luck?" I asked.

"You'll be granted the gift of the gab, for sure. If you've done something wrong, then you have to kiss the Blarney Stone so you can talk your way out of it."

His girl friend pulled him by the arm. "As you can see, he's kissed the Blarney Stone right enough," she said. "Are you coming with me now, Danny?" she said.

"Yes I am, I am." And he and his girl friend disappeared from our lives.

"Strange, imaginative people the Irish," was Harry's observation.

That evening we were seated on a wooden bench in a pub eating with others at a long pine table set on a flagstoned floor. The bar was busy, and four musicians were playing at the far end of the long room. The music was arresting; a man sang as two others played guitars, and a young woman in a long skirt (she could have been a mermaid under her skirt) also sang beautifully and played a sort of long-necked mandolin.

A couple of women sat on a comfortable sofa with a small woolly dog held by one of them in the crook of her arm like a baby. The dog's eyes shone with contentment as it looked at the diners and the musicians, its paws relaxed against its tummy.

"Well, maybe you're right," said Harry easily, "and maybe you're wrong." We had been discussing the difference between legends such as those woven around King Arthur and Merlin which didn't have to be believed, and legendary stories in the Old and New Testament which, though unbelievable, were regarded as undeniable truth and the word of God, and should be believed: stories such as the parting of the Red Sea, the Virgin birth and the Resurrection of Jesus in particular.

"I don't choose NOT to believe the unbelievable," I argued, "I don't believe because it's not believable."

"That's where faith comes in," came the answer.

"Faith?" I queried. "You're required to believe the unbelievable by making a statement of faith without giving it more thought? To me that makes no sense, at all."

"Free will," said Harry. "It's your choice."

"It's not my choice. It's what my brain tells me. I don't choose not to believe the unbelievable, I just don't believe because it isn't believable."

We were going round and round the believable and unbelievable circuit.

"Look at that dog over there," I said, changing tack. "It doesn't have legends that don't have to be believed, or religion that theologians say must be believed. It doesn't need God. It simply loves its mistress, who in turn dotes on it. It doesn't even say anything. It has no words to express its opinions on life, or speculate on the unknown. It just has body language by which it makes its feelings known."

The dog, with all the wisdom of a dog, turned its bright eyes on Harry, then on me. It shifted its gaze to the musicians, then back to me, then Harry again. The song being sung at that moment had a good beat to it with a frequently repeated refrain ending with: '...it has to be love, I suppose'.

But who loved who, or who loved what, whether it was the dog loving the moment, or God loving the world, or the world loving God, or writers loving legend, I really couldn't tell. I only knew for sure that the world was inextricably entwined in myth, legend and beliefs, and to understand its incomprehensible illogic was quite impossible.

CHAPTER TEN

ST. DAVIDS

"You can relax, this isn't Newport," I said, as the train drew in at the station. "It's Carnwydd - very Welsh sounding." The doors opened and a number of passengers got out. Harry suddenly spotted 'Newport' written as a sub-heading under Carnwydd.

"Oh, God! This is Newport!"

"It is?"

We sprang up, hurled our belongings into bags, and rushed for the doors, grabbing our luggage where it was wedged under others, and not waiting to put the ones which dislodged themselves back in place.

"Why call Newport Carnwydd?" Harry grumbled when we were out on the platform. Then muttered: "Ridiculous Welsh! What's wrong with English?"

Now we were in Wales railway announcements were given out in Welsh, before being repeated in English. We were where 'Ll' was pronounced 'Cl' ('God alone knows why!', Harry's comment); where there were male voice choirs ('About all they're good at'); Eistedfodds ('What's that?'); and Welsh border collies ('Wouldn't trust them with our chickens').

We caught our next connection on and, twenty minutes later, were streaking through the Welsh countryside. I began to understand why people talked about the hills and valleys of Wales. After we'd left Carmarthen I looked out of the window where I judged a town called Narberth would be a few miles off. There was an enchanted grassy mound at Narberth (named Arberth in antiquity, and the mound was Gorsedd Arberth) where legend had it the upper world met the lower. In ancient Welsh romance it was believed that if a nobleman sat on it he could expect to be either wounded or to see something amazing. Pwyll, prince of Dyfed, was eager to take his chance and, while seated on the mound, a woman wearing a shining golden garment of brocaded silk came riding by on a big white horse going at a slow pace. Nobody knew who she was but rather oddly, however fast they themselves went to catch up with her, her horse remained in front while never changing its slow pace. On several subsequent occasions they again saw the woman on her horse and, despite riding their swiftest steeds, they were unable to catch up.

Finally Pwyll called after her and asked her who she was. She reined in her horse and the result was a declaration of love. The woman was Rhiannon (whose name came from the Celtic goddess Rigantona, the Great or Divine Queen). Later she was equated with Epona, the Celtic horse goddess. She and Pwyll married and had a son and, after the death of Pwyll, she was given in marriage to Manawydan, the Welsh name for the Celtic god Manannan, son of Llyr, (the Celtic sea god). The story was recorded in the medieval Welsh tales put together in what is known as The Mabinogion.

Very strangely Pwyll's meeting with the beautiful Rhiannon was a friendly gesture arranged by Arawn, king of Annwfn (the underworld). The story of how the two of them met was as follows: Arawn had gone hunting one day riding his grey dappled horse, together with his pack of hounds who had gleaming white bodies with red ears (Arawn is similar to Gwynn lord of the underworld at Glastonbury), when he came across Pwyll also out hunting. To cut a long story short, they agreed to change places for a year, magically taking on each other's identity. While ruling the underworld, Pwyll slept with Arawn's wife but never touched her - something the wife thought a bit peculiar in her husband. After a year, as had been agreed between Pwyll and Arawn, they changed places again and became their true selves. Arawn was amazed when he learned from his wife that for the past year she had been untouched by Pwyll (whom she'd thought was him). What was more Pwyll had managed to defeat an enemy of Arawn and, in fact, all was better in his underworld kingdom than when he'd left it. And all was better also in Pwyll's realm. What the moral of the story was I wasn't sure, except that the goddess Rhiannon was Arawn's reward to Pwyll for his hands-off behaviour.

Harry said I was wasting my time looking for the Narberth mound, there were too many mounds, not to mention hills, to know which was THE mound. A herd of Welsh Black cattle grazed idly in a field paying no attention to the passing train.

At the next station we had to catch a bus on to St. Davids. To my surprise, everything had gone according to plan on this five hour journey, and I was beginning to hope that there would be time that afternoon to find a bookshop and, as well as see something of St. Davids Cathedral, glean more about the town's ancient past.

⚜

Despite a strong north-easterly wind, the sun was out and it was a surprisingly warm evening. The cathedral clock struck seven. From where we sat, the cathedral looked impressive in its hollow. The steep slopes of mown grass and tarmac paths, with intermittent tombstones going down to the cathedral were a change to the usual sacred edifices built on high ground. Up behind us through the eleventh century solid stone arched gateway, known as Porth y twr was the town of St. Davids, the smallest town in the U.K., or more properly I should say the smallest city because it has a cathedral.

We were seated on a wooden seat at the top of the thirty-nine steps which led up from the cathedral (symbolic it was said of the thirty-nine articles whatever they were). I've since learned they're the recognized Anglican Church doctrinal beliefs (drawn up after the Pope excommunicated Henry VIII in 1533).

The cathedral itself was a massive building built in dark shades of purple sandstone with a tall sturdy tower on which was a parapet topped by pinnacles bearing crosses.

On the slopes to the north and south of it were mature trees in full foliage. A colony of crows positively squabbled and squawked about, flying out from the trees in twos and threes, borne up in the air by the wind. Beyond the cathedral, across the river Alun, the medieval Bishop's Palace was stunningly beautiful despite its roofless state and ruined walls. During the Middle Ages bishops were extremely wealthy, they lived like princes and were regarded as second only to the monarch. The palace had massive thick walls and great arches crowned by an arcade where dignitaries had once been able to stroll along a walkway. Its upper level had weathered checkered stonework; it also had a magnificent glassless rose window whose tracery was clearly outlined against the sky.

"So what about St. David?" Harry asked, relaxing back on the seat with his eyes closed as he basked in the warmth of the evening sun.

"Well, he was Welsh," I said.

"Welsh, hum."

"In fact he was of royal blood. His Welsh name is Dewi Sant because his father was called Sant which means 'holy man', though he couldn't have been all that holy since he is said to have raped the beautiful Non who consequently became pregnant with David. Some say Non was the niece of King Arthur, no less."

"King Arthur?" asked Harry vaguely, his eyes still closed.

"Yes, King Arthur. While we're here we have to see Non's chapel and the well which sprang up when David was born. We can walk to it from here."

"Good."

I'd just read that before David came on the scene, St. Patrick had wanted to build a monastery here but had been stopped by an angel who'd told him that the spot had already been reserved for another who would come thirty years later. Slightly miffed, St. Patrick had only been mollified when the angel informed him he could have all of Ireland instead. I told Harry this. "Considering the angel was completely clued up on who was to build what monastery where," I said, "you'd have thought he might have told St. David right away to build his monastery here. But, oh, no, he allowed David to start building it several miles away which was a big waste of time as the walls kept falling down at night as fast as they were built by day - like poor St. Columba of Iona, remember?"

"Hopeless," said Harry.

"Anyway, the angel was eventually kind enough to let David know it was the wrong place and he was to build it here at - "I glanced at my booklet. "Glyn Rhosyn, which means 'the valley of the little marsh'," I read. "A marsh! To build in a marsh! Everyone knows a marsh is the last place to build anything."

"Well, if an angel tells you to - you can always drain a marsh."

"But what a bother!"

"It's a matter of faith," Harry said piously, with his eyes still shut.

I'd also read that before building his monastery there'd been a local Druid chieftain named Boia whom David had had to overcome. One day Boia had seen from his fortified settlement a fire in the marshy valley and smoke swirling over it. It was St. David making a ritual claim to his land. It is thought Glyn Rhosyn may well have been a sacred site long before Christianity. Egged on by his wife, Boia attempted to throw David and his companions off course by tempting them with beautiful naked women, but to no avail. Eventually several beheadings took place, including the beheading of Boia. Christianity finally triumphed as fire fell from heaven and destroyed everything pagan, or so the story went.

We wandered back up through the great stone gateway and out into the town. St. Davids was picturesque with its houses down the High Street each one different from the other in width and height and colour. Returning to our B&B via the centre we passed a tall stone Celtic cross, a reminder that Christianity had triumphed.

The weather for our walk around St. Davids peninsula was fine despite the persistent north-easterly wind. The path took us past several small farm houses, and round to the east side of Carn Llidi, a rocky outcrop visible for miles around, where the ground was rock-strewn with grassy stretches between gorse and bracken. Here and there a foxglove stood sentinel.

"Look! Arawn and Rhiannon!" I exclaimed, pointing to four or five wild horses on the landscape. Most were chestnut but one was dapple grey like Arawn of the underworld's, and another pure white like the one the goddess had been seen riding. There was no enclosure so they presumably were free to go where they wanted - at a slow pace.

Rhiannon (Epona in Gaul) was also worshipped in Rome itself as Regina where she was portrayed with horses and was honoured by the cavalry. Rhiannon was also known to have birds which sang to wake the dead, as well as to lull the living to sleep. They were thought to live on an island and their song was said to drift over the sea.

We clambered up amongst the rocks and boulders leaving the bracken and gorse below. By now Arawn and Rhiannon's horses and their companions had disappeared around a rise in the landscape. I'd read that on the way up to Carn Llidi we would pass two cromlechs, or burial chambers - capstone constructions. There were plenty of boulders but I saw no caps on any of them, and today it was life that concerned us not ancient burial customs.

We reached a high rocky elevation and turned to look at the

spectacular views all around St. Davids peninsula, to St. Bride's Bay and the long stretch of Ramsey Island. The weather was remarkably fine with light cumulous cloud. Unseen but somewhere beyond Ramsey Island was the much smaller island of Grassholm, a breeding ground for gannets. Apparently, the birds were so numerous that it looked like an iced cake from the distance when approached by boat.

It was on Grassholm that the severed head of the giant Bran (who, in fact, was Manawydan's brother and, therefore, Rhiannon's brother-in-law) had been left for eighty years following the seven years it had remained in Harlech, before finally being buried on Tower Hill in London. His decapitation, and where his head should be placed and for how long, had been ordered by Bran himself when he'd known he'd been mortally wounded by a poisoned spear. While his head had been at Harlech the birds of Rhiannon had bewitchingly sung to all Bran's companions causing them to sink into a blissful trance.

We retraced our steps and, as we rounded the slight rise in the ground we saw the Rhiannon white horse again, but now we took a path which would lead us to the coast. Further on, a large bird of prey hovered in the sky, its eyes on some creature it was targeting. It didn't, however, plummet down but came down swiftly as though on the cresta run and alighted on a gorse bush. Soon it had soared heavenward again and, as it rose, we noticed that its back was a rich chestnut colour. Others doing the coastal walk watched also. The tip of its outstretched wings seemed to divide and dip making full use of the wind to keep it hovering. Peregrine falcon, I heard somebody say.

Not long afterwards we came down to the café at Whitesands Bay. It was from there that St. Patrick was believed to have sailed for Ireland to become the patron saint of Ireland.

A salad lunch revived us. The thought of taking the bus back to St. Davids vanished as energy returned. Mystics have regarded St. Davids peninsula as an area of the earth's natural energies. We would continue the coastal walk and take the bus back from St. Justinian's Bay. It would take only forty minutes, or so our strong young landlord had informed us.

It took ninety minutes before we eventually rounded a point and saw a steep flight of steps going down to a white-walled, red-roofed building with a slipway to the sea, and a flag with the red dragon of Wales flying in the wind. Small boats were at anchor and passengers for Ramsey Island were waiting to embark.

We followed the path up to the road where I saw the ruins of the Chapel of St. Justinian on someone's private land beyond a stone wall.

"What's so special about it anyway?" asked Harry, when I commented that I wanted to go nearer. I had to admit that there was nothing special but I just didn't like to be thwarted.

St. Justinian had been a close companion of St. David, but their ways had parted and he'd taken himself off to Ramsey Island when he'd begun to think St. David's asceticsm and austerity too lax, even though St. David ate nothing but herbs and leeks. He was very attached to the leek and used them to identify the Welsh in battle who wore them in their caps. St. David's passion for the leek was the reason why it became the Welsh national emblem.

St. Justinian had lived on Ramsey Island with a few like-minded fiercely disciplined followers, till they themselves became fed up with his over-the-top abstinence and they cut off his head. Legend has it, however, that nothing daunted, Justinian picked up his head and carried it back to the mainland where he placed it somewhere near to where we were now standing and a spring had immediately gushed up from the ground. It was thought by some that the decapitation might have been because his companions had reverted to paganism, and it had been a form of Celtic sacrifice to the gods. Certainly skulls thrown into wells were not uncommon. Although the well was somewhere near the chapel I could see no sign of it and the chance of getting to it was negligible since it was on private property.

We are seated in the choir stalls in the cathedral waiting for evensong to begin. It is very relaxing after the day's long coastal walk. The choir stalls are intricately carved, and opposite us to our left is the enormous bishop's throne, a triple seated Gothic affair with carved spires, the centre one being the tallest.

There are misericords on the back choir stalls. I have at long last learned what a misericord is. It's a wooden ledge beneath which are intricate wood carvings such as entwined serpents, pigs attacking a wolf, a dragon, a fox and goose; but for me the most interesting one is the one of the foliaged face, in other words the Green Man. The idea for these misericords was originally for monks to be able to perch yet still appear to be standing while they chanted non-stop hour after hour.

The choir of small boys is filing in. They come in pairs, looking angelic in their white surplices over scarlet robes. Two clergymen take their places and the service begins. For the first hymn the choir master stands in the aisle and plays a small electric organ with one hand, while beating time with the other as he mouths the words at the choir. Afterwards there is a reading from the Old Testament. I find it difficult to understand why religion in Britain is not home grown but has come from the Orient through ancient Jewish scripture.

We are told to kneel or sit and God is beseeched by a priest I cannot see. He is intoning and sounding very much like a whining querulous child who is wanting his mother's attention. I admire the squares of floor tiles designed in patterns of yellows and saffron with black borders.

Soon the choir sings a lively syncopated anthem which the small boys clearly enjoy, and the choir master jerks his hand up and down to give the beat, ending with a cheerful syncopated A–a–a–amen!

When we come to the Nunc Dimitus it begins with a solo and I look around to see which boy is singing. I see one of the boys with his mouth wide open and think it is him, but his mouth closes and the solo continues long after the big yawn is over.

More prayers, during which the choir master makes a swift exit. I can hear the sound of something happening, the warming up of the great organ pipes above the stone archway to the nave, perhaps. Sure enough we have a full organ accompaniment for the last hymn. After the final prayers and a blessing, a man robed in black and carrying a wand leads the choirboys and clergy out. With the service over we all remain seated as though rooted to our pews; everyone appears to be in an end-of-day soporific stupor.

We've decided tonight to get fish and chips and take it to our room to watch television. By sheer coincidence the Cardiff Singer of the World competition is being held this week and will be on the box.

We return to our B&B with our supper concealed in a big plastic bag, and hurry past the office for fear of being spotted. Safely back in our room we are careful not to get grease from our fish and chips, or stains from our strawberries on the clean white duvet. We put our pillows on the ground and against the wall (there are no chairs) and seat ourselves comfortably for our picnic with a bottle of red wine which we pour into our tooth mugs. There's nobody about to frown or wag a finger at us, and I am surprised at how much I enjoy this louche behaviour.

The following morning, as instructed by our landlord, we took a short cut to St. Non's bay following a narrow path which threaded its way between fields, some of which had cattle in them. After about half a mile we eventually saw the small modern stone Chapel of St. Non with the creek-and-cove-indented coastline beyond, and the sea glinting in the sunshine. Many such chapels are to be found dotted along the Welsh coast as landmarks for pilgrims arriving overland or by sea.

We were directed to the nearby ancient St. Non's Well by a man mowing the terraced lawns before a house. The so-called well when we found it was a concreted rectangular area of water about a foot deep, covered by a low stone arch. A number of coins could be seen where wishes and petitions had been made.

This was the site of David's nativity. When Non was in labour legend has it that an unearthly light shone around her, and when the birth took place a spring gushed up from the ground - yet another spring. Maybe this spring (and St. Justinian's spring where he'd laid his severed head) had always been there but with Celtic deity associations, so it had been necessary for early Christians to smother the pagan connection with a good Christian story.

We left the well and came to the ruins of the original chapel in a field. From there we could look out at the sweep of St. Bride's bay, so named in honour of St. Bridgit of Kildare (the St. Brigid of Glastonbury). She'd been a contemporary of St. David and had been greatly revered here, though it is uncertain whether she actually visited Wales.

We planned that morning to do the coastal walk to Porth Clais where legend had it the great Druid chieftain Boia had been beheaded. We began walking. The word 'Clais' (pronounced 'Claesh' could mean a river valley, or in this case 'the harbour', from the ancient word 'clas'. Porth Clais was where the river Alun (which passed through the cathedral close) flowed into the sea.

As we drew near Porth Clais the path left the cliff edge and dipped down through scrub and stunted trees. Voluminous clouds sailed across the sky with ragged patches of blue between them; a lowering rogue slate-grey cloud seen first on the horizon swept nearer bringing the expected rain as we reached the harbour. We zipped up our anoraks and put up our hoods as we made our way down the rock-strewn path to the harbour mouth. The tide was out leaving a stretch of sand on which boats lay stranded at their moorings. Harbour walls lined the creek, and there was a slipway to launch small boats at high tide.

"St. David was baptised here," I told Harry. "And when St. Elvis, the bishop of the day, performed the baptism, water splashed into the eyes of a blind monk who was holding the baby and miracle of miracles, he could suddenly see. There! That's a wonder for you."

The dark cloud swept on and the sun came out again. We bought sandwiches at a small café, and sat outside at a table. We took off our anoraks, and folded them up to sit on because the seats were unpleasantly damp from the rain.

As we unwrapped our sandwiches I told Harry a King Arthur story concerning Porth Clais. "Another nice legend about this place," I began, "is that a nephew of King Arthur fell in love with the daughter of a giant who would only give him permission to marry his daughter if he managed to recover a gold comb, scissors and razor carried between the ears of a giant boar in Ireland. With great fortitude and perseverance the nephew, together with some of Arthur's knights, went in search of the boar who leapt into the sea and came ashore here at Porth Clais. Can't you just imagine a large boar with gold scissors, comb and razor on its head? How mad can legends get?"

"Did the nephew get his bride?" asked Harry.

"I expect so. All smitten knights and heroes usually win their loves. There wouldn't be a story if they didn't," I said positively. "And have I told you that Merlin prophesied the birth of David?"

"Did he?"

"He prophesied that an Irish preacher would become dumb while in the presence of a pregnant woman. And it came true when St. Elvis - the one who baptized David - was preaching in the church where the pregnant Non was, and poor Elvis found himself tongue-tied and unable to continue with his sermon."

"If only it happened to all preachers," Harry remarked, biting into his sandwich and scattering some of its contents on the ground.

"I've read that King Arthur might well have founded the Bishopric of St. Davids in 519," I said.

"Well, I suppose the Welsh want their share of King Arthur." Harry peered down at his bits of ham on the ground. "I suppose I'll have to leave it?"

"You certainly have to leave it." A nearby dog on a lead had already spotted it and was wagging its tail and drooling at the mouth. It was a hairy mongrel and could well have done with a pair of scissors, comb and razor between its ears. Harry bent down and threw the bits of ham to it and a mouth appeared between the whiskers and wolfed down the scattered ham pieces. Its owners smiled and nodded at us.

The cold offshore wind blew relentlessly as we returned along the coastal path which looped around creeks and coves. On several occasions we stood to admire the grandeur of the rock formations. There was a cove with caverns, and vertical jagged rocks; there was another where the cliff face had different coloured stratas of rock: charcoal, grey lime-green, burnt umber, with the clear aquamarine sea with its small crested waves on an incoming tide breaking on the massed rocks below. On narrow ledges half way down the cliff face two seagulls were seated on their eggs. Opposite them on a ledge where wild flowers grew out of the rock, we spotted a pair of dark birds with glossy ink-blue heads which we thought might be rock pigeons. Walking further, we came to a cove of steeply slanting elephant-grey rock with horizontal cracks in it plummeting to the sea. Further still, two grassy slopes bowed to each other and, on going close to the edge, we peered down and saw a mass of turquoise coloured oval pebbles washed smooth by the tides.

As we got nearer to the ruins of St. Non's chapel again, we saw several people in a field with inquisitive Friesian cows gathered around them. A young woman in jeans was stretched out on the ground her hip rising in the air. I thought that there must have been an accident and they were waiting for help to arrive. The others didn't seem too concerned, however, and some were concentrating on doing slow sinuous movements.

We had to pass through the field to reach the road. Harry went ahead and paid no attention to the people. A youngish woman in a homespun woolly hat, smiled as I passed. "What's going on?" I asked.

She had earnest honey-coloured eyes, a rather poor complexion, and wore a loose flowery blouse and jeans. "We are a workshop learning about Vipassana and Sumarah," she said.

"Vipas - Suma - ?" I asked. She repeated the words.

"What's that?" I'd never heard either of the words before.

She hesitated. It was clearly something which was being taken very seriously by everybody. "It's learning to be non-judgemental," she began.

"Oh, yes?" I encouraged.

"We try to reach out - to get in tune with nature." She brightened suddenly as she found the words she wanted: "To find the elixir of life," she said. "You must meet Seep... Seerya..." I couldn't make out the name. "He's from Indonesia. Come and let me introduce you. He's over there."

"Oh, I don't want to disturb anyone," I said cautiously.

"Come. He'll tell you about it. He'd be very happy to answer your questions."

I couldn't think of any off-the-cuff questions to ask but found myself being led to an elderly man seated in the lotus position on the ground with a boulder at his back. Before I could say anything he'd been introduced to me.

His voice was gentle, his Indonesian eyes were watchful. He wore a cap and had a thick white moustache stained yellow by nicotine at its centre. He was dressed to keep out the elements. Near to him was a young woman who might also be from Indonesia with her young daughter.

The guru, if that was what he was, told me what was going on, and what was the ultimate aim of these body movements. It was to reach a state of awareness - of touching nature - not just touching but wanting to touch - being at one with nature.

I couldn't really see the point of it all, as all these things I thought could be done without rotating, rolling or bending like a tree in the wind. He kept peering at me steadily, and I handed him my notebook so he could write down exactly what his work was. He printed his name along with his website so I could find out more. Something seemed to be required of me so I asked rather stupidly (having noted an unlit cigarette in the palm of his hand), "You still smoke?"

"Yes, I haven't yet given up," he replied without change of expression.

"And you're leaning against a boulder," I remarked. I felt a complete goof and could think of nothing better to say. But his answer jerked me back from my inanity.

"Yes, it is one of the many standing stones in this field," he replied.

Standing stones, and I'd been quite unaware of them! He pointed at different areas of the field and I saw a widely separated circle of ancient stones. But my mind remained blank, I only wanted to escape those penetrating eyes before they sucked me into his cult from which I might find no escape. I should have seized my opportunity, to have asked him his views on religion, spirituality and Life itself with a capital L. Instead, I smiled and nodded politely and told him that I must hurry after my husband who was waiting for me. He took my hand in a firm handshake, keeping his eyes on me as we said goodbye.

"Ah, there you are!" It was Harry greeting me from where he was hiding in the ruins of St. Non's ancient chapel, seated on the turf against a wall. "What are all those people up to?"

I sat beside him and told him about being one with nature.

"One with nature? What bunkum!"

"Of being non-judgemental," I warned.

Across from us was a large beige stone inscribed with a cross in a circle, the stem of the cross continuing beyond the circle. I wondered if it had been the Christianizing of a standing stone.

We were still seated there when one by one the members of the workshop filed past the ruins back to the nearby house which we were to learn later was a retreat. Lastly the guru came past, turned and saw us but said nothing. Instead, he solemnly put a hand to his heart and bowed twice to the stone with the cross on it (why not three times, three being the mystical Trinity?) Having done that he waved his hand in farewell, and went on up after the others.

Another black cloud and it began to rain. We hurried back to the Chapel of St. Non, the modern one with the roof on it. A swallow swooped through the open door to a rafter overhead where I could see its small clay nest.

A short middle-aged woman with a mop of mouse-coloured curls around a kindly face was in the chapel tidying books and cards and making neat piles of them. I took her to be the caretaker or cleaner of the chapel. She greeted us in a cautiously friendly manner, and told us it had been the Venerable Catherine McAuley, founder of the Sisters of Mercy, who had had this modern chapel built, and that she herself was of that Order and lived here at the retreat, the large house overlooking the terraced garden.

She told us how she had come to St. Davids several years earlier, and for many years before that she had worked in the east end of

London. God had called her for this work forty-five years ago, she said.

"How do you know that you are being called?" I asked. "And how do you know it is God calling you?" I added. I was really curious to hear her answer.

"Oh, you just know it," she said, looking at me levelly with her green eyes. "It's like when a young man woos a girl and she falls in love. In my case it was God wooing me. Once God has chosen you, you have to give yourself to him. No man gets a look in once you have a calling from the Lord. Oh, there she goes!" she said, following the swoop of the swallow as it departed through the open door. "We have to leave the door open for her."

"Don't you shut it at night?"

"Not at all. While she has her nest and her young we leave it open for her to come and go as she pleases. We have to put that newspaper down because of the droppings."

"Are you Irish?" I asked, detecting a slight Irish intonation.

"I am," she answered. "But, you know, it's not only the people of the Church who are called, we all have our calling in this world." The thought flitted through my mind that if that was so then I must have been called by God to write about the pagan gods. I often thought there had to be some sort of invisible force sparking the interest in me.

The woman continued speaking. "I was seventeen when I first had the calling," she said.

"Was it a surprise?" I asked.

"Oh, it was. At first I fought it, but it wouldn't go away. I was twenty-one when I gave in to God." She gave me a perceptive, penetrating stare, then said: "We're all equal in the eyes of the Lord, you know. We're all equal under the sun, the moon and the stars," she said with conviction. The sun, the moon and the stars I could believe in as I could see them, but God - ?

"Ah, here she comes again!" she said, and she smiled as the swallow swept back to her young.

The rain had stopped and now another couple entered, and the woman greeted them. On one of the window-sills I read a framed hand-written account about St. David's birth. Here there was no mention of rape. I was surprised to read that St. Non had been married to Sant, a Pembrokeshire chieftain. I supposed that in a Roman Catholic place of worship to admit to a saint having been born as the result of rape would have been too shocking. Born in wedlock was more seemly - a few Hail Marys for the lie, perhaps.

The following morning was dedicated to a serious exploration of the cathedral itself and the Bishop's Palace ruins. We crossed the footbridge over the river Alun - so named after the river goddess Alauna. While we were there five skewbald horses together with their mounts came splashing through a nearby ford led by their trek leader, a tough looking young woman in a hard hat. A plump youth looked anxious, his mount having decided to stand still mid-stream. I rather hoped to see the horse lie down and roll in the water to give some excitement to the scene. But the imperious woman in charge screamed instructions to keep going: "Use your heels! Grip with your knees! Keep him moving!"

We walked on to the Bishop's Palace which, although a ruin, never ceased to retain something of its ancient grandeur. We didn't want to pay for a ticket to enter, so stood and admired it from outside.

"So what is a palace?" A school teacher asked a party of school children waiting to pass through the imposing arched entranceway.

A small boy's hand shot up. "Somewhere posh," he said.

"Good answer. Somewhere posh," agreed the school master, and the group shuffled into what remained of this once posh palace.

We returned across the river to the cathedral. Exciting things were going on there. The nave was shut off to visitors because the B.B.C. was making a documentary on Richard II. A couple of extras dressed as wandering friars sat munching sandwiches on a wall. A man with receding hair and wearing chainmail, together with a royal personage looking like Lawrence of Arabia in a pale gold robe with a circular gold crown on his head under which was soft cream fabric framing a bearded face, were waiting outside the west door.

Raised arc-lights outside were blasting their light through the stained-glass windows faking sunshine. They were today's technology, the modern version of the Celtic god of light, the Welsh Lleu, Irish Lugh, or continental Lugos. The annual ancient fire festival of Lughnasadh, held in August, had been so-named after this god.

Harry hurried me past the actors before I could stop and talk to them, and we entered the cathedral by the south door. The interior was spacious and airy with the usual tombs, columns and archways leading to various chapels. We found ourselves in the Holy Trinity Chapel and stood before an arched recess in which was a large honey-gold and black wooden casket the size of a tea chest behind wrought-iron railings.

The casket was said to contain the bones of St. David and St. Justinian (who carried his severed head from Ramsey Island to St. Justinian's Bay). Whether the bones were really theirs or not mattered little. It was a focal point for reflection and remembrance. So many people were dead! So many millions more people dead than alive. It was a sobering thought, and made me suddenly appreciate the privilege of being on my feet and standing there. In an odd way memory brought the dead back to life.

The Welsh deities and their hero/god stories were numerous and complex. Many gods had Irish or Welsh names as well as continental ones. Shot through all their myths and legends, though, was this tussle between the upper world and lower, between light and darkness, good and evil.

We found ourselves in the south transept standing before a large icon in the Greek Orthodox tradition of Elijah being fed by ravens.

"Isn't it peculiar," I said to Harry, "that ravens which we don't much like today seem to have been of such importance in the past? They were sacred to the Druids who used them for augury and omens. And both Lugh and Bran were often depicted with ravens on their heads or shoulders."

"Ravens in the Tower of London," Harry said absently.

"Yes, because Bran's head was buried there, I suppose," I said. "But that doesn't explain why God had ravens feeding Elijah," I added.

"Ravens are carniverous." Harry's answer was spontaneous with no thought whatever for Jewish food taboos. "They were able to bring Elijah bits of meat from carcasses, such as dead rabbit. Ugh."

Our attention was drawn to the sound of voices coming through the closed door to the nave where the filming of Richard II was taking place - the living acting out the parts of the long past dead. Strange world!

Once again we walked up the thirty-nine steps from the cathedral. As before, the crows squawked and squabbled and rose out of the trees to let the world know they were still around and had their grievances. They were crows, not ravens, we were told.

From the wooden seat again I looked around over the trees to the hills beyond and the craggy peak of Carn Llidi where we'd seen Arawn's dappled grey and Rhiannon's white horse two days ago. It was curious that two thousand years ago and a thousand years before that men were worshipping the unknown and fighting to bring light to triumph over darkness by whatever mystical means they could. They harnessed nature to their will and named certain aspects of uncertainty as being a deity to be beseeched. Light and darkness; the annual cycle of growth and death. The ring of standing stones marking fixed points in the solar cycle of the year. Christ said he was 'the light of the world'. He lived when Palestine was under the Romans who worshipped Phoebus Apollo, Apollo the shining one. It seemed that nothing really changed, only the focus of men's attention. And so it would continue into eternity till the end of time.

CHAPTER ELEVEN

YORK

The wind hit us as we came out of Stonegate into the open space on the south side of York Minster. We positively had to battle against the gale. The weather forecasters had warned that the tail end of a hurricane would buffet parts of Britain and they were right. In Roman times Stonegate, now a narrow medieval pedestrian street lined with small shops and cafés, was known as the Via Praetoria. It was the main street which led directly from the south-west gate of the Roman fortress (now St. Helen's Square) to the Principia (the buildings for the command staff) where York Minster stands today.

We paused before a Roman column which had been found in the Minster during excavations undertaken in the 1960s. Roman artefacts had been discovered there which were now displayed in the Minster crypt in its Undercroft Museum, and we were on our way to it.

We were in York because in Roman times it had been the capital of the north. Founded in 71 A.D. it had been the base from which military campaigns had been undertaken against the troublesome northern tribes known as the Brigantes. The Brigantes had their goddess Brigantia who guarded all aspects of their lives from pastoral matters to fertility, healing and victory.

It was in York (or Eboracum as the Romans called it) that, on the death of his father in 306 A.D., Constantine was proclaimed emperor by the army. Near the column was a bronze statue of Constantine seated with an unsheathed sword pointing to the ground with the inscription 'By this sign conquer'.

Constantine the Great! St. Constantine! He had been the first Roman emperor to accept Christianity as a true religion.

Constantine's father, the Emperor Constantius, had already held the view that there was one supreme god which no doubt impacted on his son, although numerous gods still played a major role in the Roman empire - Britain being its westernmost outreach 'where it is appointed by a superior constraint that the sun should set' (Constantine's words).

"'By this sign conquer'," Harry said, peering at the inscription. "What's that supposed to mean?"

Constantine had been persuaded of the truth of Christianity (so it was claimed by Eusebius, bishop of Caesarea, and a great fan of Constantine) because on the eve of an important battle in 312 A.D., the battle of the Milvian Bridge, he'd seen a vision of a cross in the sky above the sun with the words 'By this sign conquer'. Another report said he'd had a dream in the night commanding him to 'delineate the heavenly sign on the shields of his soldiers'. I told Harry about the cross in the sky vision. "So Constantine put it on the shields of his soldiers and, against all the odds, won the battle of the Milvian Bridge," I said. "From then on the Chi Rho became a Christian symbol, a diagonal cross with an upright through it with a loop at the top right."

"High row?" Harry looked vague.

"Not high as opposed to low, but Chi," I said. "Ch as in Bach or in loch," I added. "In Greek Chi is written as a capital X and Rho is the Greek R which, just to be difficult, is written like a P. They are the first two letters for Christ, and the two letters together make the Christian monogram known as Chi Rho."

"Ah."

Another violent gust hit us. We turned from the statue of Constantine and battled our way against the gale to the south entrance to the Minster. The sudden stillness of the air as we entered the great building was like passing into the calm of a cocoon. Lofty columned arches, the high ribbed ceiling with gold bosses, and the immense stained-glass windows were imposing. But at that moment we weren't there for the Minster.

"The Undercroft Museum?" I asked.

We were pointed in the right direction and were soon descending a stairway to the crypt.

A notice told us we were now on the site of the Roman basilica, the ceremonial centre of the fortress where the Roman governor would have presided over court cases, or addressed the army on formal occasions. We were standing on the spot, or at least in the vicinity, where Constantine had been proclaimed emperor.

Interestingly, Constantine used the Roman basilica as the prototype for his Christian basilica churches. Its central nave flanked by columned aisles were for the congregation, and the curved apse at the far end where the governor would have addressed those come to hear him, became the focal point for worshippers with its altar. Such basilicas were aligned to the east so the congregation faced east towards the rising sun.

"You'd have thought that Constantine would have built his churches like the pagan temples," I said. "That surely would have been the more obvious way of honouring the Christian God. But no. No cult statue of Yahweh or Christ in the inner sanctum with their eyes to the east, as was the usual custom in pagan worship."

We walked on amongst the remnants of columns and capitals, and stood for a moment before what was called the Doomstone of Norman origin. It was a large limestone relief of demons pushing lost souls into a boiling cauldron with flames beneath it being stoked by grinning devils. The Celtic pagan cauldron of rebirth had now become a demonic object, intended to keep the illiterate in a state of fear at wrong-doing, to toe the line to Christian love, charity, and obedience to God's authority.

We left the Doomstone and sat for a while before the nearby shrine of St. William, a former Archbishop of York who'd died in 1154 and who, due to the sweet smell which wafted from his tomb, and various miracles which occurred in his name after his death, was canonized in 1227.

"Don't you think it's weird that Christianity had saints?" I asked Harry.

"Weird? I wouldn't call it weird."

"I think it's very peculiar that the earliest Christians had such a profound conviction of the truth of Christianity they were prepared to die for their faith," I said. "You never read about a fanatical worshipper of Jupiter or Venus. To fight to the death for your beliefs? Amazing!"

"Keep your voice down!" Harry whispered. He looked around to see if anybody behind was listening. Maybe he was afraid my words spoken aloud before the shrine of St. William might bring down a bolt of lightning.

Some years back York Minster had been struck by lightning which had caused a fire three days after the then Archbishop of York had consecrated David Jenkins bishop of Durham. People said it had been a sign of divine displeasure. David Jenkins had been notorious for speaking openly and controversially regarding certain Church beliefs. Concerning the Resurrection of Christ, the words 'conjuring trick with bones' had been used by him, or so the papers had reported, though David Jenkins complained his words had been taken out of context.

Harry liked to hold David Jenkins up as an example for me to follow. If a bishop could go along with Church doctrine, despite certain misgivings, then so could I, he said.

"St. Helena was Constantine's mother," I told Harry. We were seated in a restaurant in St. Helen's Square, and I was waiting for the right moment to put a money-no-object plan to Harry for the following day. He'd ordered a glass of wine and I thought I'd wait till he'd drunk half of it. "One unlikely story about her is that she was the daughter of King Coel of Colchester. King Coel - the 'Old King Cole was a merry old soul' King Coel."

"Oh, yeah?" Harry took the first sip.

"Or that she'd been a barmaid and had worked in an inn in Bithynia, wherever that is. Some say she was a prostitute and that's how Constantine's father met and fell in love with her."

"Go on." He took his second sip.

"Which, if true, might explain why she became a very pious Christian, like the prostitute who washed Jesus' feet with her tears and dried them with her hair and was forgiven all her sins."

Harry took another sip and eyed me steadily. I babbled on about Constantine sending his mother Helena to Jerusalem to find the True Cross which she miraculously discovered although it was more than three centuries since the crucifixion. And how she'd founded the Church of the Nativity at Bethlehem. And then I switched back to Colchester and prattled something about how, if Helena had really been the daughter of old King Coel, then she'd probably have known about Boadicea, queen of the Iceni tribe in Essex, who'd rebelled with terrifying ferocity against Roman rule calling on Andraste, the warrior goddess of victory and patroness of the Iceni tribe. Not that any good came from Boadicea's beseechings as her daughters were raped and she was eventually killed in battle and...

"So what are you wanting to tell me?" Harry asked, knowing that my gabblings meant I was hiding something. "What am I in for tomorrow?" he demanded.

I hung my head over my food and sawed at a tough bit of rump steak. "Tomorrow? Well." I played for time and began to chew.

"You presumably have a plan?"

"The museum," I stalled.

"All day?"

"Well, there is an ancient site at a village called Goodmanham," I ventured.

"How far?"

"Fifteen miles."

"Is there a bus?"

"No. We'd have to take a taxi."

"Fifteen miles in a taxi? Whatever for?"

"There's a church, the Church of All Hallows," I said.

"So?"

"It stands on the site of an old temple of Woden," I said. I suspected I'd already failed in winning Harry over to the idea of going to this remote village. His glass was still three-quarters full.

"What's so special about Woden?"

Saw, saw, saw. By God, the steak was tough. "He was the chief of the Anglo-Saxon gods," I said.

"And?"

"And in six hundred and something Edwin who became king of the Northumbrians worshipped Woden, but then he had a vision - there! Another vision! A stranger appeared to him and consoled him about his anxieties, promising him salvation before disappearing into thin air. The then bishop of York, a man called Paulinus, did the rest. He assured Edwin that his troubles were over and he had God to thank for it, and it was thanks to God too that he'd been crowned king. Clever. So Edwin was won over to Christianity."

"Which is no reason to spend fifty pounds to take a taxi to wherever it is you want to go."

"He was god of the dead, of wisdom and victory. Legend has it that Woden sacrificed himself on the world tree and was pierced by a spear. It sounds rather Christ-like, don't you think?"

"Absolutely nothing like," said he who knew best.

"A man called Coifi was the chief priest of Woden," I went on.

"And, when Edwin asked him his opinion on Christianity, Coifi said he'd long thought the old gods were baloney and that there might be something in this new religion."

"There you are!"

"Though how he knew it wasn't Woden who'd helped him sort out his anxieties, and got him on the throne, I'm not quite sure," I said. "The fact that Edwin was eventually killed in battle didn't come into it, it seems. They were so far gone in their Christian beliefs that they never supposed it might have been God's displeasure. Maybe it was Woden's?" I suggested.

"God's will," said Harry stubbornly. I stared at him for a moment but decided not to challenge him.

"To carry on with the story," I began, "Coifi himself galloped off from York and set fire to the Woden temple. And as there was no divine retribution from Woden or the other gods, he and his fellow pagans were also baptized into the Christian faith."

"Good for them. So as you already know all about it, and as there's nothing to see when we get there, there's no earthly point in taking a taxi at huge expense all the way there and all the way back again," Harry said with finality.

Chew, chew, chew. I'd lost the battle and the best thing I could do was to be gracious in defeat.

The following day, as part of being gracious in defeat, I suggested we forget about gods and take a bus to Castle Howard.

Castle Howard is a historic stately home built in 1699 for Charles Howard, third Earl of Carlisle. As the bus drew near, the landscape which had been flat for the best part of fourteen miles, began to undulate gently. Woods appeared on a slight rise of ground. Soon great weeping beech trees lined the roadside. We came to a high crenellated wall and the bus squeezed its way through its only-just-wide-enough entrance.

An amazing grandiose stately home of England! It was a long ornate edifice with a central dome and Parthenon like facade, set in extensive grounds of cut grass with focal points such as a lake, the Temple of the Four Winds, a Mausoleum, and a fountain with the figure of Atlas holding what looked like the world on his shoulders but presumably was the heavens. If this was being gracious in defeat it was worth every penny saved by not taking a taxi to Goodmanham to see a no longer existing temple.

The Howard family went back to 1483 when Richard III created John Howard Duke of Norfolk. Henry VIII's fifth wife was a member of the Howard family, Catherine Howard. After the Reformation many in the family remained Catholic and defied Henry VIII's break with the Vatican.

The motto of the Howard family was 'Sola virtus invicta' (virtue alone invincible). The day passed peacefully and very virtuously.

The morning was fine with a light breeze and fluffy white clouds in a blue sky. We walked along the ancient crenellated city walls from Micklegate to Lendal Bridge. The bridge spanned the river Ouse. On one side the river banks were tree-lined, on the other they were flanked by houses and office blocks. The Roman army in 71 A.D. had recognized that the hill on a triangle of ground formed by the river Ouse and the river Foss was an ideal place for a fortress. The building of Eboracum on the other side of the Ouse had then followed. London at that time had been regarded as the capital of what was known as Britannia Superior, and Eboracum (York) became the capital of Britannia Inferior. Roman government officials took up residence in this new town, and Eboracum flourished.

We came to the museum gardens where we saw the remains of one of the Roman fortress towers. Spectacular also were the ruins of St. Mary's Abbey, a medieval and a once prosperous Benedictine monastery, which stood proudly with its soaring ornate stone walls pierced by arched windows.

I bought a book on Constantine, and sat for a while examining it while Harry disappeared into the museum.

'We grant both to Christians and to everyone freedom to follow whatever religion they want to, so that whatever divinity there is in heaven may be appeased and made favourable to us and to all who are set under our power,' I read. They were words written by Constantine for circulation which became known as the Edict of Milan.

Unlike the Roman and Celtic deities who were honoured without anybody getting in a rage as to what should or should not be believed,

Christianity evolved largely by the rules of belief laid down by the Church Fathers (eminent theologians and bishops). Any heretical ideas, or deviation from their authority brought down their wrath.

Constantine didn't like disputes among the clergy and was good at calling the bishops to councils to resolve issues. The all important Council of Nicaea in 325, for example, was one of them, to which several hundred bishops were summoned to decide once and for all on the nature of Christ. Constantine himself wasn't too bothered about the nature of Christ, but was much more concerned that there should be unity in the Church. The decisions were made by majority vote.

Constantine would no doubt have heard of the Gnostics, a Christian movement which separated from what the Church Fathers called the true Church. Gnostic was Greek for 'knowledge' - its opposite being 'agnostic' (not to know). The second century Gnostics believed there was one true Divine Being existing on a higher level than the God of the Old Testament whom they regarded as a demiurge who had brought evil into this world. All men, they said, had a spark of the true Divine Being within them. They also claimed that Christ had not come to earth to save men from sin, but to guide them to a new spiritual understanding. In other words he had brought 'gnosis' (knowledge) to men.

A number of Gnostic gospels circulated together with many other apocryphal gospels. They all referred to happenings in the life of Christ, but all were damned and rejected by the Church Fathers except for the four gospels of the New Testament. How did we know that Christianity hadn't gone way off track due to the intransigence of those early Church Fathers, I'd once asked Harry? He'd merely shrugged and said that Christianity was what it was and of course it hadn't gone off track. And, after a little more thought, that if it had then it would have died out long ago, and much better to go with what we had than to keep wondering about what we might have had.

I began my tour of the Roman galleries in the museum and came first to a statue of Mars in Greek military dress which had been found near the Bar Convent where we were staying close by Micklegate. Mars had been greatly honoured by the Romans because the story was that he'd had it off with a Vestal Virgin who'd given birth to twin sons Romulus and Remus. It was Romulus who'd founded Rome, and consequently in those days Romans liked to think themselves descended from Mars.

There was also a temple of Serapis, a god resulting from Alexander the Great's conquest of Egypt. Like the Romans, Alexander the Great had also been tolerant of the religious practices of the countries he'd conquered, and Serapis was the result of several Egyptian gods such as Osiris and Apis fusing with the attributes of several Hellenistic deities, for example Zeus, Hades, Asclepius, and Dionysos.

I read from a notice that the Romans believed there were gods and spirits in everything and everywhere. They revered gods who could help them, and bribed evil spirits to leave them alone. Vows and bribes had to be regularly renewed through ritual and celebrations to ensure continued success.

So if today we touch wood, cross our fingers as we walk under ladders, bow to the new moon and feel fortunate if we find a four-leaf clover or see a black cat crossing our path, it is because our Roman forbears had that innate sense of being at risk and needing the encouragement of good omens, or the protection of whatever had the ability to help.

Exhibited were portable altars which allowed soldiers to practise their beliefs wherever they were, and I read the words 'Genio Loci Feliciter' (good luck to the spirit of this place). A notice said that because the Roman army depended on felling trees and using the wood for construction - and, apparently, twenty thousand tons of timber for the fortress had been used - so the Romans honoured the woodland god Silvanus.

There had once been temples in Eboracum in honour of Jupiter, Hercules, Mars, Serapis and Mithras though, unlike the indestructible marble temples in Greece and Rome which can still be seen today, because the Eboracum ones were constructed mostly in wood so only vestiges of them remain.

I went out into the museum gardens and settled down to read my book on Constantine again. I learned that coins struck in the early years of Constantine's reign had often borne the image of Mars on the reverse. Later he substituted Apollo together with the inscription Deus Sol Invictus (the unconquered sun god). During his reign he'd minted coins with his head on one side and Apollo on the reverse with a flaming halo round his head. Later the rays of the sun were shown around the head of the emperor also. The coins, passing from hand to hand, were making the point that the light from the emperor, like from the sun, encompassed the whole Roman empire. It was only very late in his reign that a few coins were minted with the Chi Rho on them. In those days images on coins were a means of spreading ideas of great significance.

In the early centuries of the Roman occupation of Britain, Britannia had been used on the reverse side of coins, Britannia being the protective goddess of Britain. The Romans identified her with Minerva, hence her helmet and shield the latter of which on modern coins bears the Union Jack.

My world of images on coins was interrupted by, "Oh, there you are!" Harry pointed to his watch and reminded me that our train left that afternoon and we'd better get back if we were to have lunch. I gathered up my things and we began our walk back along the city walls.

"Don't you think it strange that Constantine, while accepting that Christianity was a true religion," I told Harry as we went, "was never baptized until he was close to death?"

"Better late than never, I suppose," Harry said without too much thought.

"But don't you think it odd? Maybe deep down he was afraid of offending Apollo, Sol, Mars or Jupiter." York's street traffic ebbed and flowed below us as we walked along the city walls. We were approaching the railway station where a train was pulling out; skeins of railway lines spread away into the distance. "So he got himself baptized and had all his sins washed away. Considering he'd murdered his wife and eldest son, not to mention killing thousands when he went to war, he probably needed absolution. But then, if you think of it, God himself was quite good at killing those who angered him, and destroyed whole nations."

By now Harry was striding ahead. "What's that?" he shouted, "I didn't hear."

I wasn't going to shout back what I'd just said. I glanced to my left and had a mild attack of vertigo when I saw the height of the wall we were on. If God could destroy whole nations what was to stop him giving me a shove over the side? Fear of the unseen was never far away.

We came to Micklegate where steps took us down to the street and we were soon back at the Bar Convent where we were staying. Unlike the convents I'd stayed in in Greece, the nuns there didn't wear black habits. It was difficult to establish who was a 'bride of Christ' or who was an employee returning to her human spouse at night. I had expected to have sweet faced nuns robed in black praying over me, but there was nothing of the sort.

We sat out in a pleasant garden where we had a snack lunch. I picked up my book on Constantine again and began where I'd left off. I read: 'Nevertheless, it is clear from his own writings that Constantine did indeed have a strong sense of his own mission. In his Oration to the Saints, an address by the emperor delivered on Good Friday, in a year and location variously identified by modern scholars, and preserved in Greek translation, he says, "If therefore I dare great things, I ascribe my daring to my implanted love for the divine... the evidence (of God's work in the world) is that everything has turned out according to my prayers."'

I read on and came to a passage he wrote about himself: 'My whole soul and whatever breath I draw, and whatever goes on in the depths of the mind, that, I am firmly convinced, is owed by us wholly to the greatest God.'

But which God? The Christian God, or the Divine Being? Or did he mean Apollo, or perhaps Jupiter?

"Time to go!" Harry announced. "You can take Constantine on the train and read all about him there."

In no time we were hurrying to the station (within easy walking distance) trundling our luggage behind us. As we waited for the train, I realized suddenly I now had only Canterbury left to write about.

CHAPTER TWELVE

CANTERBURY

No one could lighten Theseus of his care
Except his father, old Aegeus, there.
He knew the transmutations of the world
And he had seen its changes as it whirled
Bliss upon sorrow, sorrow upon bliss,
And gave his son instructions upon this:
  'Just as there never died a man,' said he,
'But had in life some station or degree,
Just so there never lived a man,' he said,
'In all the world but in the end was dead.
This world is but a thoroughfare of woe
And we are pilgrims passing to and fro.
Death is the end of every worldly sore.'
On top of this he said a great deal more
To this effect, with wisest exhortation,
Heartening the people in their tribulation...

Geoffrey Chaucer
The Canterbury Tales - The Knight's Tale

It was Good Friday, the weather was set fair - unseasonably fair
for April - and we were on the train from London to Canterbury
as latter day pilgrims. Unlike the pilgrims in Chaucer's Canterbury
Tales, it wasn't a five-day journey mounted on a horse - I'd never have
got there had it been, as horses always bolt with me - but an hour and
a half by train passing rapidly through the county of Kent, past acres of
apple orchards in blossom, and fields of hops and oast-houses.

I had booked a room in a hotel well in advance, supposing that Canterbury at Easter would be seething with people. Because Harry was having trouble with his back he found it difficult to walk far. I used it as an excuse for booking into a hotel right there by the cathedral. There were certain advantages to be gained from Harry in that state as he was now only too willing to take taxis.

We took a taxi from outside East Canterbury station, and five minutes later we were put down before the modern arched entranceway to our hotel. The great medieval cathedral with its numerous pinnacled Gothic towers stood majestically a stone's throw away amidst lawns divided by tarmac paths leading to its various entrances.

❧❦❧

St. Augustine, who founded the first church here, the Church of Christ, had been sent to England by Pope Gregory in 596 A.D. to evangelize the pagan Anglo-Saxon king, King Ethelbert, and his people. Interestingly, Anglo-Saxon kings believed themselves to be descended from their god Woden - the god whose temple site I'd wanted to visit while in York. He was the best known of the many Anglo-Saxon gods and among other things was god of the dead which may explain why the Romans equated him with Mercury, guardian of the souls of the deceased.

When St. Augustine had successfully converted King Ethelbert, the king received a letter from Pope Gregory, addressing him as 'the glorious lord Aethelberht, king of the English', and saying complimentary things such as, 'Almighty God raises up certain good men to be rulers over nations in order that he may by their means bestow the gifts of his righteousness upon all those over whom they are set.' He sent the king many gifts, and assured him that he had been chosen by God because of his great qualities. What flattery!

"You know the Venerable Bede?" I asked Harry as we ate our sandwiches and drank from a bottle of water. We were, perhaps, letting down the tone of our hotel seated in its garden, but there was nobody else around to see us. It was an oasis of tranquillity with tables and chairs set out on grass with a few flowers, shrubs and a tall leafy tree for shade. The sound of wood pigeons cooing came to us from the depth of the foliage.

"Heard of him, but that's about all," Harry said.

"Well, he wrote The Ecclesiastical History of the English People in early seven hundred and something, and in it he describes how King Ethelbert was converted by Augustine."

"Good for him."

"I expect it helped that Ethelbert had a pious wife, Queen Bertha, who was already a Christian. She was French, and had only agreed to marry Ethelbert on the understanding she was allowed to continue practising her Christian faith."

A seagull sailed overhead reminding me that the English Channel was not far off. St. Augustine had arrived by sea and had first set foot in England on the nearby Isle of Thanet. He'd immediately sent word to the king announcing his arrival, and the fact that he'd come all the way from Rome to see him. I opened Bede's book where I had put a marker. "Augustine came," I said, and began to read aloud: "'bearing the best of news, namely the sure and certain promise of eternal joys in heaven and an endless kingdom with the living and true God to those who received it.'" I put the book down. "Do you really think you'll go to heaven when you die?" I asked incredulously.

"Well, clearly Augustine believed it."

"Anyway, King Ethelbert only agreed to meet Augustine in the open air, I think under an oak tree, believing, according to Bede, that if he was to meet Augustine in a building he might fall victim to some magic trickery. Shall I read you Bede's account?"

I read on from Bede's book: "'...they came endowed with divine not devilish power and bearing as their standard a silver cross and the image of our Lord and Saviour painted on a panel. They chanted litanies and uttered prayers to the Lord for their own eternal salvation and the salvation of those for whom and to whom they had come.' Can you imagine that?" I asked Harry. "What would you do if you were approached by a man with forty friends, chanting and praying for your salvation? You'd run a mile."

"Well - no. Yes. Perhaps."

"Anyway, King Ethelbert was very polite and - " I scoured the text and read on from the book. "'Then he (the king) said to them: "The words and the promises you bring are fair enough, but because they are new to us and doubtful, I cannot consent to accept them and forsake those beliefs which I and the whole English race have held so long. But as you have come on a long pilgrimage and are anxious, I perceive, to share with us things which you believe to be true and good, we do not wish to do you harm; on the contrary, we will receive you hospitably and provide what is necessary for your support; nor do we forbid you to win all you can to your faith and religion by your preaching.'"'" I closed the book. "So that's how it all started," I said.

"Are we off to see the cathedral?" Harry asked, picking up his stick from the grass. I gathered up our sandwich wrappings, and threw a crust to a solitary magpie who hopped along, took it in its beak and flew away into the tree with it. 'One for sorrow' flitted through my mind, but I quickly dismissed such foolish superstition. It was Easter, and there were more serious things to think about.

∾❦∾

My first impression of the interior of the cathedral was its immense lofty grandeur; its multiple archways, high vaulted ceilings, soaring columns, and steps leading to higher levels going eastwards towards the High Altar. It was a deliberate architectural feature designed to give the pilgrim a sense of mounting towards God. On this first visit, however, I led Harry downwards (a contrary pilgrim) because I'd been told to see the crypt which by chance that afternoon was open to the public.

The crypt was mysterious and ancient with a low vaulted ceiling supported by sturdy Romanesque columns and capitals. It had several ancient chapels with stained-glass windows. Centrally placed in the crypt was the stupendous Chapel of Our Lady Undercroft with a finely sculpted Gothic screen behind the altar, and wooden chairs placed before it.

A notice announced that the chapel was set aside for silent prayer. Its sombre lighting was relieved by a couple of tiered wrought-iron candle stands on which were numerous night-lights lit by those with prayers and petitions. I lit my own with a sort of plea for continued good health for Harry and myself. Harry sat down at once, whether to pray or rest his back, I wasn't sure, and I sat beside him.

In 1993 excavations had been undertaken before the re-laying of the floor above in the nave. At its east end wall-foundations had been found which were thought to have been part of St. Augustine's early church. Built with Roman stone and bricks, the foundations might well have been those of an even earlier church built before the Romans departed in 410 A.D., leaving Britain for the Anglo-Saxons to march in bringing their own gods with them.

The Romans had named the days of the week after their gods or the planets they represented, and the Anglo-Saxons followed on with the idea. For reasons best known to themselves, the Romans named Friday, the fifth day of the week, after Venus, their goddess of love, calling it 'Veneris dies', and the French followed their lead, calling it 'Vendredi'. The Anglo-Saxons called it after Woden's wife Freya, hence our English Friday. That day was Friday, Good Friday.

The fourth day of the week was named by the Anglo-Saxons after their god of thunder, Thor, hence our Thursday. Wednesday was known to the Romans as 'Mercurii dies', Mercury's day - 'Mercredi' to the French - and, since Mercury was equated with Woden, so the Anglo-Saxons called it Woden's day, our Wednesday. As for the second day of the week, that became Tuesday because the Anglo-Saxon god Tiw, their god of war, was the equivalent of Mars, the Roman god of war. The Romans called the second day of the week 'dies Martis', and the French called it 'Mardi'.

I left Harry resting or praying to do more exploring. I went up again to the nave and found myself in Trinity Chapel built as a shrine to Thomas Becket who, on being appointed Archbishop in 1164 by Henry II, had wanted to free the Church from the monarch's authority over it. 'Who will rid me of this turbulent priest?' had been said by Henry II in anger. His words were taken literally by four knights who hurried to Canterbury to do what the king clearly wanted done. On learning of the murder which had taken place here in the cathedral, the king had been full of remorse. As a penance, he'd come to Canterbury walking barefoot through the city, before submitting himself to a whipping.

The circular Trinity Chapel with its lofty vaulted ceiling, surrounded by stained-glass windows was superb. Thomas Becket's shrine had, apparently, first been in the crypt and had become the most popular place for pilgrims (hence Chaucer's Canterbury Tales written in the fourteenth century), bringing to it vast sums of money till Henry VIII did his worst, declaring it and all such places of pilgrimage to be focuses of undesirable superstition.

I went back down to the north side of the crypt. There I saw a door open to the Chapel of the Holy Innocents. In the far corner of it, seated silently and patiently was a woman priest in black. A notice outside invited anyone to enter who wanted to confess his or her sins.

If there be one among you that is willing
To have my absolution for a shilling
Devoutly given, come! and do not harden
Your hearts but kneel in humbleness for pardon;
Or else, receive my pardon as we go.
You can renew it every town or so
Always provided that you still renew
Each time, and in good money, what is due...
What a security it is to all
To have me here among you and at call
With pardon for the lowly and the great
When soul leaves body for the future state!...

Chaucer: The Pardoner's Tale

I didn't want to confess anything but I had a question regarding St. Martin's Church where Queen Bertha had worshipped and, because there was nobody else around to ask, I entered. As I tiptoed towards her a look of expectation came into her eyes. At last a penitent!

"I'm so sorry to bother you," I said in a hushed voice, "but can you tell me if you think St. Martin's church will be open if I walk there now?"

Her expression never faltered. Her serene and gentle eyes radiated goodwill. "I think you're too late," she replied. "It's quite a long walk."

"About how long would it take on foot?" I asked.

"About half an hour, perhaps?" she answered.

"Thank you so much," I said. And I crept away again leaving her to resume her quiet wait for penitents.

I had considered experimenting with a confession, something I had never done in my life, but as my chief sin was not really believing in God, I thought it best to stay silent on the matter. Besides, I reckoned that if God really wanted me to believe without doubt then he had only to make himself totally and absolutely real to me. So over to God.

I returned to Harry and we went up to the Quire for evensong where we were ushered into the carved oak stalls with the High Altar to the east.

The music that evening was glorious with men and boys singing an anthem which filled the cathedral with the grief of the dying Christ on the cross. The poignancy of the soprano and tenor voices in the minor key set the atmosphere for this Good Friday evening service. I heard the words 'was crucified... suffered and was buried under Pontius Pilate...'

That day at evensong I soaked up the atmosphere and, like a weak swimmer, submerged myself in the waters of Christianity and swam with the experts and, presumably, with those who floundered hopelessly like me in their beliefs. To be amongst those of Olympic Games standard was rather special. The next day I would be there again.

❧❦❧

The nine-thirty morning service was held in the Jesus Chapel at the eastern most extremity of the cathedral crypt. It had a painted ribbed ceiling and central boss in gold and maroon and the letters I and M (for Jesus and Mary) at spaced intervals between the ribs. The morning sun refracted the rich colours of the stained-glass window above the altar which depicted the Virgin Mary crowned and enthroned with the baby Jesus on her lap holding the Gospels in one hand while the other was held up in blessing.

There were about thirty people, with five clerics robed in black seated on the front row of chairs set in a semi-circle. Interestingly, there was no music, only the spoken word and, therefore, a concentration on the text with pauses whenever there was a red asterisk at the end of a sentence. The simplicity of the service, the sincerity of the clergy with no unnecessary piety, meant I was able to swim again in these Christian waters, admiring those who had reached the highest standards in the disciplines of the faith.

After the service Harry decided to get on with a who-done-it he was reading, so returned to the hotel garden. Before leaving the cathedral, I found myself beside the Dean steps near the cloisters from where I could hear boy choristers rehearsing. I imagined it was for the Vigil to be held that evening. The purity of their voices accompanied by a piano floated out through an open window.

Nearby stood a woman guide, identified by a yellow sash, who was also listening. I asked her about the Vigil. She told me that the Archbishop would light the Easter Candle outside the west door before leading the congregation into the cathedral. There would also be a baptism and seven confirmations that night.

"I am one of the confirmation candidates," she confided.

"You are?" I must have looked surprised. "How lovely to have such conviction," I said.

"It's been a long time coming," she said. "For many years I never went to church - that was when I was growing up in South Africa."

"So what brought you to England?" I asked.

It transpired that her husband was Viennese and a non-practising Catholic, and that they had come to England two years earlier so that their sons would get a good education. Since then she had come frequently to services, had joined fellowships, and become a Friend of the Cathedral. Her increasing interest and acceptance of the tenets of the Anglican Church made her want to be confirmed in the faith.

"And your husband?" I asked.

"Oh, he's still not ready to commit himself," she replied.

"What about your boys?"

"They're not interested at all. They're teenagers and have their own lives. You can't force anyone," she said. "Everyone is different. Belief comes in its own time when you are ready. Nobody can be pushed."

"I will see you tonight, then," I told her. "It's been nice talking to you."

We arrived early at the cathedral for the Vigil in order to get a good seat. The sombre lighting in the nave with its soaring columns and fan vaulted ceiling were deeply mysterious. Everyone was handed a long white candle with a ruff of paper around its base, together with an Easter Vigil service sheet. I began to read its introduction.

'From earliest times Christians have gathered through the night of Easter Eve to recall the story of God's saving work, from creation through to the death and resurrection of our Lord Jesus Christ. However, the Easter Liturgy is not merely a presentation of God's work. It is meant to be a real experience of new life for the worshipper, a passing from darkness to light which offers hope to all the faithful. Indeed, the themes of death to life, darkness to light, destruction to new creation occur over and over again in the various sections of the service: the Lighting of the Paschal Candle, the Readings, the Renewal of Baptism Vows, and the Eucharist in which all are united with Christ in his death and resurrection.'

Surely, from time immemorial there had been this human

yearning to see beyond death, to believe in an afterlife; to get beyond death to life, from darkness to light, from confusion to calmness? Mithraism had recognized the human need to overcome darkness with light. The ancient Babylonian god Tammuz had been killed but had been resurrected. Osiris, the great Egyptian god, had been killed, dismembered but had been reassembled. So too in ancient Greece, Persephone's abduction to the underworld and Hades, had been overcome by her annual resurrection in the spring. Dionysos, god of wine, also had been a dying and resurrected god.

Really Harry and I were participating in an eternal annual cycle. We were facing death but looking beyond complete obliteration to new life. It really didn't matter if it was true or not, it was a fact of life that death would ultimately come, and the terror, or rather the despair and despondency, had to be overcome so that life (of the living rather than the dead) could cast away darkness and move into a new light in life. Nature itself was a supreme example of death and rebirth.

Um.

I preferred not to think about dying, or to worry about which of us would die first, Harry or me? Probably anything I imagined would never take place. Much better to take any harrowing situation as it presented itself and cope with it when and if it happened. Meanwhile we were here in Canterbury Cathedral.

That morning I'd visited St. Martin's church where King Ethelbert's devout queen had practised her Christian faith. It was the oldest church in continuous use in the English-speaking world. It had a squat stone tower, and small tiled spire rising from its centre. At the time of Ethelbert it must already have been nearly two centuries old as it had been built as a church by the Romans before they'd left Britain in 410 A.D. St. Augustine had arrived in England in 597. Thanks to St. Augustine's successful mission the king had been baptized at Pentecost that same year, the day which celebrated the coming of the Holy Spirit fifty days after Easter, known in the Anglican Church as Whitsunday because it was customary to wear white for the occasion.

From St. Martin's church I had walked back via St. Augustine's Abbey. I'd spent the greater part of that afternoon wandering about its thirty acres with an audio strung around my neck. From it I learned that the Abbey had been founded by St. Augustine about 598 A.D. The voice of the present Archbishop informed the listener that it could be said Augustine, when he brought Christianity to England, had been the first to bring Britain into the European community - an interesting thought.

The Abbey had been founded to mark the success of St. Augustine's mission with the conversion of the king and many thousands of his subjects. The worship of the Anglo-Saxon gods had petered out as money and encouragement from Rome had poured in for the construction of impressive stone buildings, many replacing the wooden pagan temples. Pope Gregory had instructed Augustine to build on the old heathen sites, and advised that the pagan festivals should be replaced with the feasts of the martyrs.

While waiting in the cathedral for the Easter Vigil to begin, I toyed with the word Easter. I had read that the word for what is now our April was named after the Anglo-Saxon goddess Eostre. But really very little is known about her except that the Venerable Bede wrote that 'Eosturmonath has a name which is now translated "Paschal month", and which was once called after a goddess of theirs named Eostre, in whose honour feasts were celebrated in that month. Now they designate that Paschal season by her name, calling the joys of the new rite by the time-honoured name of the old observance.'

"So what?" said Harry, when I told him this interesting bit of information.

I wasn't deterred. "And the Anglo-Saxon for March was Hredmonath, or Hrethmonath, as Bede called it. Hretha, or Rheda, or Hrede was another goddess who was honoured at this time. But really nothing is known about any of these so-called goddesses. But it all goes to show there has always been a Spirit - an eternal something or another to which people turned."

"Keep your voice down," Harry whispered into my ear. He changed the subject, wanting me to ask my neighbour how long this service would last.

I enquired and was told it would continue till past midnight.

Harry hissed into my ear again. "After the Easter Candle lighting I'll probably go back to bed," he said, and put his hand to his back. "I could do with a pain-killer. Last night was agony."

I wanted to say something like from agony would come relief, that there could be no appreciation of good health without first experiencing ill health. From death comes life. But I merely nodded, and said to expect me back when the Vigil was over.

"Have you been to one of these Vigils before?" I asked the woman beside me. She was middle-aged, on the plump side with long curly blonde hair and a placid face. She was wearing a printed dress and jacket and had a woolly stole around her shoulders.

"Oh, yes. I come every year," she said.

"Do you live in Canterbury?"

"No, but I'm only four miles away. I'm looking forward to tomorrow when I can stop fasting."

"Oh, do you fast?"

"I've given up chocolate and wine for Lent," she said.

"Really? I'm afraid I haven't given up anything."

She quizzed me sideways, decided I wasn't totally despicable, and said: "It's a small discipline I like to keep up."

Forty days of fasting in Lent; forty days in the wilderness for Christ being tempted by the devil; forty years in the Sinai wilderness for the Israelites getting out of Egypt; forty companions who came with St. Augustine to help convert the heathen. Forty seemed to be another of those mystical numbers.

We are hurrying to the great West Door of the cathedral where the Vigil is about to begin. There are faint glimmers of stars tonight, but my eye is drawn to a lighted brazier with flames leaping upwards from it. I'm hemmed in by people but get glimpses of the Archbishop's cream and gold mitre above the heads in front of me, and occasionally his bespectacled face with its ragged grey beard, and his dark fly-away Rumpole of the Old Bailey eyebrows.

Ah! I have wormed my way forwards and I can see the Archbishop's upper half. He is robed in a gold cope and has a cream and gold embroidered stole. There is an energy about him, and there is nothing pious in his bearing, no look-at-me-the-archbishop-who-has-reached-the-pinnacle-of-godliness. He is refreshingly unpompous.

Other heads jostle for a place to witness what is going on. The Archbishop makes symbolic signs over the large Easter Candle - I learn later they are the Greek letters Alpha and Omega, the sign of the cross and the date of the year. A taper is lit from the brazier and brought to the Archbishop to light the Paschal Candle. The Archbishop proclaims: 'May the light of Christ, rising in glory, banish all darkness from our hearts and minds.'

From this candle others are lit and the Easter Candle held by whoever holds it, leads the Archbishop and other church dignitaries into the cathedral. This is the cue for Harry to limp away back to the hotel. I light my candle from someone else's nearby and slowly follow after the throng into the dark interior of the cathedral nave whose vastness and soaring columns and fanned ceiling are mysterious with the myriad shadows cast by the myriad candles. The service continues with readings, prayers and psalms sung by the choir - of men only this evening - with intermittent moments of silence. There is a smell of candle smoke.

I'm enjoying the music, the organ and choir, and the carefully choreographed celebration - yes, it is theatrical. The main characters move and speak with conviction. Words spoken with conviction are believable only while in the presence of the speaker. It is in the chamber of ones inner self when one is alone again that questions arise and doubts set in.

Here in the cathedral my candle appears to be burning down quicker than anybody else's. I wonder how long it will be before it expires. To be the only one whose candle goes out I feel has to be an ill omen, or a deliberate public humiliation cast on me from on high for my lack of faith.

I can just see the Easter Candle being carried around before the altar with a man censing it. Now the choir (tonight wearing white surplices) process eastwards and follow the Archbishop who is mounting the steps towards the intricately carved stone screen surrounding the arched entranceway to the Quire. Everyone is on the move in this darkly shadowed nave of the cathedral, their candles flickering as they follow the Archbishop. One of the statues in this carved Gothic stone screen is of King Ethelbert.

Once in the semi-lit Quire I seize my opportunity and take a front seat on the right. Others ahead of me have already filed into the pew and I am at the end of it with the male choristers on my left; there is a handsome young chorister at the end of his pew beside me.

The Litany continues to be sung and the congregation responds. I follow the words in the service sheet:

> *Give us true repentance;*
> *forgive us our sins of negligence and ignorance*
> *and our deliberate sins;*
> *and grant us the grace of your Holy Spirit*

to amend our lives according to your holy word.
Holy God,
holy and strong,
holy and immortal,
have mercy upon us.

With the Litany over there is a moment of silence before we all stand and the organ thunders, bells ring out and the Archbishop proclaims: 'Alleluia! Christ is risen.' And all those around me respond: 'He is risen indeed. Alleluia!' The cathedral lights go up and mercifully, because by now I am seriously worried about my candle, all hand-held candles are blown out.

The Archbishop stands before the High Altar flanked by two clerics wearing gold and red as the choir sings Gloria in Excelsis, which I have since learned existed in the fourth century A.D. I am being positively deafened by the male choristers on my left and the equivalent number opposite. Although I have next to no faith, I am enjoying the faith of others who are carrying me along with them; I am enjoying the beauty of the moment; enjoying the perfection of those who have reached the pinnacle of their careers: the Archbishop, the organist, the choristers, all performing together at Canterbury Cathedral, the cradle from which Christianity in England grew and developed.

Now the organ thunders and the choristers sing at full throttle a hymn which we all join in. To my amazement I find myself singing, and my voice seems to have rejuvenated itself; I am hitting the high notes which normally elude me.

The Archbishop is standing on the steps before the High Altar. And there behind the High Altar is St. Augustine's marble chair placed on a higher level for all to see. It is on that chair that all new Archbishops are enthroned.

St. Augustine had taken the baptismal name of Augustine because of his admiration for St. Augustine of Hippo who lived 354-430 A.D. For long the latter had been an ardent follower of Manichaeus, who'd taught a form of Zoroastrianism, which had originated in Persia (Mithraism was a Roman version of it). Zoroastrianism believed in the struggle between light and darkness, goodness and evil. Later Augustine of Hippo had become Christian due in part to his mother who'd been a devout Christian. In his Confessions St. Augustine of Hippo described his own inward struggle, and wrote regarding 'the eye of my soul' and about God as 'Light Unchangeable'. He was quite frank about his own immoral life as a young man, hence his famous words, 'Give me chastity and continency, only not yet.'

Until this moment I have given no thought to the woman guide I met this morning who told me she was going to be confirmed. I now watch as the Archbishop descends the steps from the High Altar followed by the seven candidates for confirmation and the one for the renewal of baptismal vows. I do not recognize the woman guide but she is one of the seven. There is a copper bowl of water on a table centrally placed beyond the choir stalls, and the candidates now stand in a semi-circle around the table while the Archbishop makes the sign of the cross on each forehead. Each is asked whether he or she wishes to be baptized, or confirmed: 'Are you ready with your own mouth and from your own heart to affirm your faith in Jesus Christ?' With their affirmation he now addresses us: 'Faith is the gift of God to his people,' he says. 'In baptism the Lord is adding to our number those whom he is calling. People of God, will you welcome these candidates and uphold them in their life in Christ?' All around me say: 'With the Help of God, we will.'

Further questions and answers to the candidates take place. The Archbishop swims with excessive ease in these deep spiritual waters. A youngish woman with long fair hair bends her head over the bowl of water and the Archbishop pours what looks like a white saucer of water over her head. The water trickles down her face and into her eyes and she hastily wipes herself dry with a handkerchief, or maybe it is a special sanctified cloth provided for the occasion.

The Archbishop now asks the congregation questions to which they answer with the words of the Creed. I remain silent because I cannot bring myself to say the words 'I believe...' when I know I don't.

With the Creed over and the baptism done the Archbishop unexpectedly strides down our side of the choir stalls dipping what looks like a bunch of rosemary in holy water and flicking it at us as he passes. I am liberally sprinkled and the Archbishop gives me what looks like a defiant glare as he goes by. "Take that!" he seems to be saying as he showers me with his holy water. His 'look' will stay with me for ever.

Now the confirmation candidates go up the steps to the High Altar and the Archbishop stands praying over them. They kneel as he anoints each one with chrism (a mixture of oil and balsam) and lays his hands on his or her head.

We all stand as the Deacon tells us to give each other the sign of peace, whereupon everyone turns and shakes hands with his neighbours. The good-looking young chorister who has been deafening me, grips my hand in a vice saying 'Christ is risen!' and I mumble back 'peace be with you' which is what the man on my other side said to me first. This goes on for a while and is followed by the celebration of the Eucharist. I find myself obediently going up to the High Altar steps and kneeling down. There should be a belief detector which rings a bell if an unrepentant sinner dares join the true believers at the altar. But if the all-knowing God exists, he doesn't leak the facts to the Archbishop who says the words 'The Body of our Lord Jesus Christ, which was given for thee, preserve thy body and soul unto everlasting life...' He is so unpretentious, and his gold vestments and sincerity are such a balm to my turbulent doubts and contrariness, that I do what everybody else is doing at the altar rails. The priest following behind with the wine presents me with a long stemmed chalice, and says the words 'The Blood of our Lord Jesus Christ, which was shed for thee, preserve thy body and soul unto everlasting life...' and I sip the wine which I think is of a rather superior quality.

I come down the altar steps and return to my place with the male-voiced choir singing an anthem. As has always been the case I am solemn and devout-looking, but I find I am no more a believer now than I was before which is a shame, because I have for long been waiting for that roll of drums which I imagine goes with enlightenment. But ever since my first communion when I expected something magical or mystical to happen, I've been disappointed. I can only suppose nothing comes because there's nothing to come, or if there is then I am being deliberately overlooked by whatever or whoever has the power to change things.

So I'm by-passed - out in the cold. That's what God (if he exists) wants for me. I'm playing in the playground while the great spiritual minds continue with their belief. They are happy. I am not unhappy.

I find myself singing, my voice drowned by the male choristers and the thundering of the organ.

> *Thine be the glory, risen, conquering Son,*
> *Endless is the victory thou o'er death hast won;*
> *Angels in bright raiment rolled the stone away,*
> *Kept the folded grave-clothes where the body lay.*

Thine be the glory, risen, conquering Son,
Endless is the vict'ry thou o'er death hast won.

The Archbishop says a final prayer, then candles are lit from the great Paschal Candle and are given to the newly baptized and those who have been confirmed. Everything is symbolic and as holy as anything can be. Like a rabbit in the headlights I am mesmerized. But I know that as soon as I am out of this sublime and sacred environment and am back in my natural habitat, I shall revert to my normal state, to the myriad questions that have no believable answers.

I shake hands with the Archbishop who is on the steps leading down to the nave, and expect to get another accusing glare, but he barely glances at me as he extends his hand to the next person.

❧❦❧

Easter Day and it is afternoon and the sun continues to shine. Harry and I are seated in a punt with the boatman rhythmically punting us out of Canterbury. This is Harry's treat, something I think he will enjoy as a sideline to all our church-going. I was hoping we would punt into Canterbury to see parts pedestrians fail to see, but it is Harry's choice today and he has chosen to punt out into the countryside.

The boatman tells us that the Romans used to bring their boats up this river which means it must once have been deeper. I peer at the long trailing weeds on the river bed. But what is above on the surface draws my attention too: the ducks floating peacefully, the fresh spring foliage of the weeping willows, the flower-beds of brilliant coloured tulips in the public park where people are enjoying the fine weather. Canterbury from the punt as it drifts along presents quite a different picture than from the road.

There are clouds of river insects hovering over the water and they divide as we pass through them. The boatman tells us that pilgrims used to walk along this river bank to Canterbury. Amidst birdsong - we have now left civilization and human chatter behind - the boatman informs us that once farmland came right up to the river bank, but now it is well back to allow for a cycle path; once you could see cattle and sheep grazing, but not now; now the river banks have nettles and cow parsley growing so high that no fields can be seen.

We pass beneath a concrete bridge over which the main road passes. Cars whizz, and the sound of traffic disturbs the tranquillity.

Soon it is a steel and brick-built railway bridge. The tail end of a train disappears from view. It is amazing this modern age with its speedy forms of transport. Once people went on foot, or trundled along in waggons, or went on horseback if speed was necessary.

Not only is transport faster now, but news is immediate. At the Easter Morning service which we attended in the cathedral (where else?) I was astonished to see a man beside me check his mobile phone for text messages, an incongruous act, even sacrilegious.

We had been seated on the north side of the nave behind a wide-girthed column so we could see little of what was going on. I had just been able to glimpse the Archbishop's cream and gold mitre and the gold crook of his crozier as he processed up the aisle followed by civic dignitaries dressed as though for a Gilbert and Sullivan show, with ostrich feathered headgear, full-bottomed judicial wigs accompanied by their wives in an assortment of hats. Their entry had been greeted by a fanfare together with the organ at its most fortissimo. When we'd arrived the cathedral bells had been peeling and there'd been a sense of excitement as people came hurrying from all directions for the service.

On our way from the hotel we'd passed a low mound on which the Garden of Gethsemane had been imaginatively created with a large hollow granite rock from which a great stone had been drawn to one side revealing the empty tomb of the risen Christ.

The choir had included the boy choristers today who sang Gloria in Excelsis in Latin, while we in the congregation sang our part in English. I have come to the conclusion that it really doesn't matter a hoot that I am totally bamboozled and perplexed by Christianity. So long as there are people like the Archbishop, priests and others who do believe, people like me can tag along or not which will make no difference to the Church at large. Those who are firmly convinced Christians who elaborate, explain and try to make others see the truth of their beliefs, can voice their beliefs as loud as they like, or write screeds of facts, but it is always from their standpoint of belief. Others like myself can read the screeds and listen for ever and a day, but there will always be the unanswered questions, the non-comprehension of the message which appears to be pure fantasy.

The Archbishop's message from the pulpit that morning was on happiness and how it can't be faked, or conjured up at will, and when the moment of happiness has passed it is then only a memory. Well, I am happy at this moment drifting along on this fine April afternoon in a punt with Harry by my side.

"What is that?" I enquire of our boatman, as we pass a short granite pillar of sorts. We have turned about and are being punted gently back.

"That," says our boatman, "is a mile stone. It is exactly one mile from here to the cathedral. It was put there so pilgrims would know they had nearly reached their goal."

Steeped in history.

It is said that when King Ethelbert was baptized, ten thousand of his subjects were suddenly converted and wanted to be baptized also. It is more than likely that those ten thousand were baptized in this river, the river Stour, together with their king.

On this return trip we go a slightly different way around an island. We come to an ancient stone arched drover's bridge, and our boatman bows low while we pass beneath it.

"You may like to know," our boatman says, "that mile stone is on the ancient Roman road of Watling Street. It comes from the Isle of Thanet, goes through Canterbury and on to London."

"I've seen Watling Street behind St. Paul's Cathedral," I reply.

"It was a track long before the Romans," says our boatman. "But the Romans made it permanent by paving it."

We have now come round the island. As I put my hand in the water and glance down at the trailing weeds below I see a shoal of tiddlers. There are trout in the river, we are told, but they are nocturnal and only rise at night. We come back again to the weeping willows and the beds of hostas and brilliant coloured tulips. A couple of teenage boys are paddling. A duck is followed by her ducklings, little balls of fluff with beaks; they leave a wake behind them. A black moorhen with beady eye and red beak disappears into the reeds along the bank.

It has been a gentle interlude, this our trip on the river Stour. The boatman deftly brings our punt around and with difficulty we get up from our recumbent positions. Harry grimaces as he feels back-pain. The boatman offers a steadying arm and with the help of his stick Harry manages to get himself onto the stone steps, and I follow after him.

I am sorry about his back, but it means we take another taxi to return to our hotel. We have to count our blessings, I tell Harry who merely grunts.

We were back idling in the hotel garden with mugs of tea. I had the Venerable Bede's book open before me and was reading aloud to Harry. It was a letter written by Pope Gregory to Ethelbert. This time he was making it quite clear that he wanted conversions: "'...Increase your righteous zeal for their conversion; suppress the worship of idols; overthrow their buildings and shrines; by exhorting them, terrifying, enticing, and correcting them, and by showing them an example of good works; so that you may be rewarded in heaven by the One whose name and knowledge you have spread on earth. For He whose honour you seek and maintain among the nations will also make your glorious name still more glorious even to posterity.' So what do you think of that?" I asked Harry putting the book down.

"He obviously felt strongly about it!"

"Well, he was Pope, I suppose. But then - " And I picked up the book again and read what I had marked: "'Besides, we would wish your Majesty to know that the end of the world is at hand, as we learn from the words of Almighty God in the holy scriptures; and the kingdom of the saints which knows no end is near. As the end of the world approaches, many things threaten which have never happened before...' And here we are fifteen hundred years on and the world hasn't come to an end at all. Explain that!" I said. "The Venerable Bede telling porkies to frighten us."

I was ready for a confrontation with Harry, but the sound of misery beyond the garden gate leading to the road and front entrance to the hotel encroached on our world; sobs were interspersed with high falsetto broken sentences. When we had come through this gate earlier we had seen a dark-haired youth standing with a mobile phone clamped to his ear, his face against the woven panel gate. At first I'd thought he was laughing, but it was soon apparent he was in the depths of despair. He was clearly foreign and I supposed he was speaking to his family back home. His Easter greeting. As we'd approached he'd sobbed and turned away continuing his grief-stricken conversation. He must have said goodbye because there'd been silence for some while, but now he was on his mobile again.

"Do you think I ought to go and comfort him?" I asked dubiously. I was no good at putting an arm around anybody, let alone a stranger. I was better at waiting patiently for the distress to pass and then trying to cheer the person up. I supposed a good Christian would have done something. But I did nothing, and mercifully the sobbing as suddenly stopped.

"There!" said Harry. "His money's probably run out - or his mobile needs recharging."

Everything comes to an end and is replaced by something else. Never mind how desolate life seems, there will be something that will relieve it, or at least change it. Life may stretch away before you like a desert, but in the endless apparent nothingness there is something. As the Archbishop said about happiness that morning: It sometimes needs profound suffering for a resurrection to be experienced. You can't have a permanently happy society in an unpredictable world - or words to that effect.

The cathedral bell began to ring. I could see the long shadows cast by the late afternoon sun and realized I might as well end the day with Compline, the last service I would attend in the cathedral. I had only to cross the road.

I am having one last exploration of the cathedral, both around it and inside again. I never cease to be amazed, not only by the beauty of the building itself, but by the welcoming smiles of all who serve there. Maybe they get their cue from the Archbishop who has no airs and graces, is not sanctimonious, but dons his mitre and his cope and stole and strides forward to do the task in hand.

I walk around outside, passing the infirmary ruins to the east of the cathedral, then pleasant houses with wisteria and lilac in full bloom, the King's School, then back under Norman arches where I find a door open to stone steps at the east end of the cathedral. I walk up them into the Quire, around St. Augustine's chair which is in shadow, then around to the south side where I see the memorial to the Black Prince who won great victories for the English against the French in the fourteenth century. His wife was known as 'the Fair Maid of Kent'; she it was who lost her garter at a public ball and, to save her embarrassment the Black Prince's father, Edward III, with whom she was dancing, picked it up and put it on his own leg saying, 'Honi soit qui mal y pense' (Evil to him who evil thinks). That incident is the origin of the Most Noble Order of the Garter, the highest order of chivalry in England. Its membership is limited to twenty-six people who wear below the left knee a garter of dark blue velvet with the 'Honi soit' motto on it.

I pass through Trinity Chapel again, and pause to look at a paved area at the centre of which is a single lighted candle burning in honour of Thomas Becket. I don't remember seeing the candle there before and wonder if it was symbolically extinguished on Good Friday to be relit on Easter Day. I go down some steps on the north side where I find myself in the Martyrdom where Thomas Becket was murdered. Replicas of the weapons which killed him hang on a wall. On the north side of the Martyrdom I see a plaque announcing that Pope John Paul II and Robert Runcie, Archbishop of Canterbury, knelt there together in prayer on the twenty-ninth of May, 1982. Their prayers were for Church unity. Several decades later and it is as divided as ever. The Emperor Constantine would be disappointed after all the effort he made to end disputes in the Church.

I find myself walking the length of the flagged cloisters under its multiple-fanned ceiling curving down to the triple-arched open Gothic stone work beyond which is a quadrangle of grass. When I return I go up some steps and find myself in the Chapter House which has an amazing ceiling like gilded intricately woven cobwebs, with a large arched stained-glass window at the far end.

Perhaps all this beauty is an expression of what men imagine God to be?

But it is time to leave, and I take one last look around then turn away because all things must come to an end.

"Well, there you are, you've now done Canterbury," Harry said as the train carried us back past the apple orchards in blossom, and the acres of hops that grace the Kentish countryside. "So where to next in your great search for enlightenment?"

I looked out of the train window. I had to admit I'd reached the end of the road with my quest for gods, either past or present. "That's it," I said. "If God exists then I'll just have to wait till he chooses to make himself evident to me."

Recently I'd picked up the book To be a Pilgrim written by Cardinal Basil Hume. At the time it flitted through my mind that the book was being brought to my attention by a divine hand placing it before my eyes; that by reading it Christianity would be made clear to me before my pilgrimage to Canterbury. The book was written with devout faith and was almost persuasive until, as with so many scholarly and pious writers, the Cardinal, writing from his standpoint of firm conviction and faith, went over the top beyond all reason and wrote about 'God's will' and 'God's plan', which immediately prompted me to think that if God had a will and a plan, then why didn't he will and plan for us all to believe the same thing without doubt so there were no divisions in the Church? Why, if God was all powerful and had a will and a plan had he not by now willed and fulfilled his plan, and made it quite clear for us poor mortals what his plan exactly was? Harry's response when I grumbled these complaints was that God had given men free will to make choices right or wrong, which to me was just another red herring, as men had free will whether God existed or not.

The one thing I was certain of was that human beings had wills, and human beings had plans. Humans knew what they wanted and worked towards getting whatever it was. In order to help them in their endeavours humans drew on the world's energies and harnessed water-power, wind-power and solar-power. For matters beyond their control such as natural disasters, they called on invisible energies to help, and it seemed to me to matter little that men down the ages had called such invisible powers by the name of Zeus, Athena, Jupiter, Apollo, Minerva, Mercury, Cernunnos, Woden, Thor or just God as we do today.

Oh, well. I had been to Canterbury, had given it my all by joining in with what was worshipped and believed in this day and age, and was leaving as totally bemused and uncomprehending of the invisible God as ever.

"Well, I can't help you then," said Harry when I told him. "Nobody can help you. Bad luck!" He turned to a dog-eared page and began to read, leaving me to mull over my misfortune and incredulity that so many others truly did believe.

> 'So, in our search after the Deity
> That Heaven in her secrecies may hide,
> We shall be burnt on earth, most certainly.'
> To which Cecilia valiantly replied:
> 'Men might fear death and would be justified
> In seeking to preserve their lives, dear brother,
> If there were only this life and no other...'

'But there's a better in another place
That never shall be lost. Be not afraid;
God's Son has told us of it, by His grace,
The Father's Son, by whom all things were made;
Those creatures in whom reason is displayed
The Holy Ghost proceeding from the Father
Dowers with a living soul, believe it rather.

'By word and miracle the Son of God,
When in this world, declared and we have learned
There was an after-life for all who trod
The path He chose.' 'Dear sister,' he returned,
'Did you not say just now, in what concerned
The being of God, there was but One, and He
Was Lord in truth? Yet now you speak of three.'

'That too I shall explain,' she said.........................

....

                    Chaucer: The Second Nun's Tale

GLOSSARY

AHURA MAZDA - The great creator God of Persia, god of all goodness and light.

ALATOR - A Celtic deity meaning 'huntsman'. The Romans honoured him as Mars Alator.

ALAUNA - The goddess of the river Alun at St. Davids.

ANDRASTE - A warrior goddess, patron goddess of the Iceni tribe in Britain. Boadicea was queen of the Icenis.

ANNWFN - The Welsh for Annwn, the underworld.

ANNWN - The underworld in Celtic myth, ruled over by Arawn.

APHRODITE - Greek goddess of love who was known as Venus by the Romans.

APOLLO - Son of Zeus and twin sister of Artemis. He is god of light with the epithet Phoebus, and is also god of music, archery and prophecy.

ARAWN - King of Annwn (the underworld).

ARES - Greek god of war, known to the Romans as Mars.

ARTEMIS - Twin sister of Apollo and Greek goddess of wild animals, fertility and childbirth.

ARTHUR, King - Semi-divine hero believed to have existed between the post Roman period and early Saxon invasion.

ASCLEPIUS - Son of Apollo and god of healing and medicine.

ATHENA - Greek goddess of wisdom, arts and handicraft.

BACCHUS - God of wine, equated with the Greek god Dionysos.

BALDER - The beautiful son of Frigga and Odin in Nordic mythology.

BELTANE - The Celtic festival of fire and fertility held at the beginning of May.

BENDIGEIDFRAN - See Bran.

BLADUD, King - Discoverer of the healing waters of the hot springs at Bath and founder of the city.

BOADICEA - Queen of the Iceni tribe in Essex. She led a revolt against Roman rule in 60 A.D.

BOIA - A Welsh Druid chieftain.

BRAN - Son of Llyr. He is a semi-divine giant, and was once king of Britain.

BRANWEN - Sister of the giant Bran whose marriage to the King of Ireland who ill-treated her caused Bran to invade Ireland where he was fatally wounded.

BRIGANTIA - Patron goddess of the Brigantes, a Celtic tribe who controlled the greater part of northern Britain. She guarded all aspects of life from agriculture, fertility, healing and victory.

BRIGHID - Daughter of Dagda, and Celtic goddess of fire, the hearth and poetry. With Christianity she became St. Brigit or Brigid.

BRITANNIA - The embodiment of Britain, and protective goddess of the land. The Romans equated her with Minerva.

BRUTUS - First king of Britain, descended from the Trojans whose forbears founded Rome. He was believed to be the great grandson of the Trojan prince Aeneas whose mother was Aphrodite, goddess of love.

CAUTES - Torch bearer to Mithras. His torch was symbolic of light, and he held his torch upwards towards the sky.

CAUTOPATES - Torch bearer to Mithras. His torch was symbolic of darkness and he held his pointing downwards.

CERNUNNOS - The great horned god and Celtic deity, possibly connected to the Irish Finn McCool who was associated with deer.

CERIDWEN - Early British fertility goddess, possesor of the Celtic cauldron of poetry, wisdom and rebirth.

COCIDIUS - A Celtic hunting god of the woodlands. The Romans honoured him as Mars Cocidius.

CONDATIS - The Celtic god of the confluence of rivers, of water and healing, who became equated with Mars under the Romans and known as Mars Condatis.

CORINEUS - Another Trojan who joined Brutus when he sailed for Britain.

CORMELIAN - A giantess, wife of Cormoran.

CORMORAN - The Cornish giant who built St. Michael's Mount.

COVENTINA - A Celtic water goddess.

CYBELE - The Great Mother, Asiatic goddess of the powers of nature.

DAEDALUS - A skilled craftsman in antiquity who, in order to escape from the maze at Knossos where King Minos incarcerated him to keep him from leaving the island, made wings for himself and flew from Crete to Sicily.

DAGDA - King of the Tuatha de Danann.

DEMETER - Goddess of corn in ancient Greece.

DIANA - Roman Goddess of the hunt, as well as fertility and childbirth, the Greek Artemis.

DIONYSOS - Greek god of wine and drama who died annually and was resurrected in the spring.

DIOSCURI, The - Twin sons of Zeus and Leda, described as mortals in epic poetry but worshipped as deities, protectors of seamen.

EOSTRE - A Teutonic goddess who gave her name to Easter.

EPONA - A prominent Celtic goddess of the horse in Gaul, known in Wales as Rhiannon.

EXCALIBUR - King Arthur's magic sword.

FINGAL - A legendary Scottish giant who had his cave on the Isle of Staffa known as Fingal's Cave.

FINN McCOOL - A legendary Irish giant who was said to live on the Giant's Causeway in Northern Ireland. He later became identified as a hero warrior with a brave band of followers. He was said to have been an incarnation of the Celtic antlered god Cernunnos.

FREYA - In Nordic mythology the goddess of love, beauty, fertility, war and death, and wife of Odin. Her place was usurped by Frigga who by Odin became the mother of Balder.

FRIGGA - See Freya.

GOGMAGOG - A giant in Britain who later became two giants Gog and Magog.

GREEN MAN - Often to be found as carvings in churches, his face surrounded by foliage sprouting from his nose, mouth or ears. He represents ancient natural vegetative deities and rebirth throughout the world.

GWION - Servant to Ceridwen. He stirs her cauldron containing a magic potion the first three drops of which if swallowed will give inspiration and knowledge, but any more will be poison. Three drops splash onto his fingers which he sucks, and he is instantly inspired with knowledge.

GWYNN AP NUDD - He represents the dark forces of the underworld and guards its gates. His Hounds of Hell seek out the souls of the dead or dying on the night of Samhain.

GWYTHYR AP GREIDYAWL - Spirit of the light half of the year.

HERCULES - Noted for his strength, courage and endurance, and famous for his twelve labours.

HERMES - Greek god who guided the souls of the dead to Hades. In Roman times he became Mercury.

HORNED GOD - A universal and common Celtic deity who could be linked to Cernunnos who was depicted wearing antlers.

IMBOLC - A Celtic fire festival held on the 1st February marking the start of the farming season.

INCUBI - Small winged creatures who could magically turn themselves into men.

ISIS - Egyptian goddess, wife of Osiris and mother of Horus, who encapsulated the virtues of the archtypal Egyptian wife and mother.

JANUS - A Roman two-faced god who looked in opposite directions.

JUPITER - Supreme god of the Romans, equated with the Greek Olympian Zeus, god of the heavens and of justice.

KELPIE - A Highland mythical water-sprite in the shape of a horse.

LOKI - A sometimes malicious, sometimes mischievous god in Nordic mythology.

LLEU - The Welsh Celtic god of light.

LLYR - A Celtic sea god, and father of Bran, Branwen and Manannan.

LUDD, King - A humanised deity-king of Britain.

LUGH - The Irish Celtic god of light.

LUGNASADH - Celtic harvest festival.

LUGOS - The continental Celtic god of light.

LUNA - The moon goddess.

MANANNAN - A sea god, son of Llyr and brother of Bran and Branwen.

MANAWYDAN - The Welsh name for Manannan.

MAPONUS - A Celtic god meaning 'divine son'. Under the Romans he became equated with Apollo.

MARS - Roman god of war, equated with the Greek god Ares.

MEDUSA - One of the Gorgons. They had hideous faces with glaring eyes and serpents for hair.

MERCURY - Roman god, equated with the Greek god Hermes, guardian of the souls of the dead.

MERLIN - The magician linked with King Arthur. In Welsh Celtic myth he was a culture hero and bard.

MINERVA - Roman goddess of wisdom and the arts, equated with Athena of ancient Greece.

MITHRAS - Persian god of light.

MOGUNS/MOGONS - Little is known about this god who was worshipped by the Romans in Britain as a god of might. He is believed to be Celtic in origin.

MORGAN LE FAY - A lake or river goddess, guardian of the mysteries of Avalon, concerned with death and rebirth. She took Arthur away to be healed when wounded and was possibly his sister.

NEPTUNE - Roman equivalent to the Greek Poseidon, god of the sea.

NEREUS - A Greek sea-god who had the ability to change himself into different shapes when pursued.

NODENS - The Celtic god of the river Severn, associated with healing.

OSIRIS - An important deity in ancient Egypt associated with death, resurrection and fertility.

OSSIAN - Or Oisin, which meant 'small deer'. He was Finn McCool's son. His mother was Sadbh, a beautiful red doe who became human when she met Finn.

OSTARA - Pagan lunar goddess of fertility.

PANDORA - First woman fashioned out of clay whose box when opened released sins into the world, keeping hope alone inside the box.

PERSEPHONE - Demeter's daughter who was abducted by Hades, god of the underworld, and was only released on the understanding that she returned to Hades for the winter months.

POSEIDON - Greek god of the sea, earthquakes and horses. In Roman times he was known as Neptune.

PWYLL - Prince of Dyfed (today's county of Pembrokeshire). He was married to the goddess Rhiannon and features in stories told in the medieval Welsh tales put together in The Mabinogion.

REMUS - Son of Mars and a Vestal Virgin, twin brother of Romulus.

RHIANNON - The Welsh equivalent of Epona, goddess of the horse in Gaul. Her name came from the Celtic goddess Rigantona, the Great or Divine Queen, hence Roman worship of her as Regina. She married Pwyll then, on his death, married the god Manawydan.

ROMULUS - Son of Mars and a Vestal Virgin, twin brother of Remus. It was Romulus who founded Rome.

SADBH - A beautiful girl who refused the advances of a Druid and had a curse put on her so she turned into a red deer. The curse was lifted when she met Finn McCool and they had a son named Ossian.

SAMHAIN - The Celtic festival held at the beginning of November which was Christianized and became All Saints' Day.

SERAPIS - An Egyptian god. He was a fusion of the Egyptian god Osiris and the Apis bull with Hellenistic gods such as Zeus, Hades, Asclepius and Dionysos.

SILVANUS - A Roman woodland god.

SOL - The sun god.

SULIS - An early goddess of hot springs.

SULIS MINERVA - The fusing of the Celtic Sulis and Roman Minerva.

TAMESIS - Goddess of the river Thames.

THOR - Son of Woden. He wields a hammer and is god of thunder and strength.

TIW - The Anglo-Saxon god of war.

TRITON - A merman, son of Poseidon.

TUATHA DE DANANN - The fifth wave of migrants to Ireland according to Celtic myth.

VENUS - The Roman equivalent of the Greek goddess of love, Aphrodite.

WODEN - An important Anglo-Saxon god who carried off the dead.

ZEUS - Supreme Greek Olympian god.

ZOROASTRIANISM - A religion which originated in Persia. It believed in the struggle between light and darkness, goodness and evil.

JILL DUDLEY'S
NEXT BOOK

MORTALS & IMMORTALS
A SATIRICAL FANTASY
& TRUE-IN-PARTS MEMOIR

Jill Dudley was born in Baghdad and educated in England. Her first play was performed by the Leatherhead Repertory Company, since when she has written plays and short stories for radio. She returned to Iraq in 1956 when her husband was working out there, and after the Iraqi revolution they came back to England where they bought a dairy farm. When they retired from farming in 1990 they travelled extensively in Greece and she began a new and successful career in travel writing.